THE CONSTITUTION OF VIETNAM

This new book examines constitutional debate and development in one of the most dynamic and rapidly changing societies in Asia, and will be of use to scholars and students of comparative law, comparative constitutional law and Asian law, and practitioners interested in Asia or in Vietnam. The book discusses and analyses the historical development, principles, doctrines and debates which comprise and shape Vietnamese constitutional law today, during a time of reform and debate. The chapters are written in sufficient detail for anyone coming to the subject for the first time to develop a clear and informed view of how the constitution is arranged, how it works, and the main points of debate on it in Vietnamese society. It is written in an accessible style, with an emphasis on clarity and concision.

The book discusses and analyses the origins of Vietnamese constitutional thought; the first (1946) Constitution of independent Vietnam; Constitutional dialogue and debate in the late 1940s and 1950s, including the work of dissidents in the 1950s; the 1959 Vietnamese Constitution; constitutional dialogue and debate in the 1960s and 1970s; the 1980 Constitution; the rise of *doi moi* (renovation) and debates over constitutionalism in the 1980s; the 1992 Constitution, including the role of legislative, executive and judicial sectors, constitutional power and enforcement, constitutional rights and obligations, and other issues; constitutional dialogue and debate in the 1990s; the constitutional debate and revision process of 2001 and the current Vietnamese Constitution; the rise of debate over judicial independence and constitutional enforcement and review in Vietnam; comparison to constitutional developments and debates in China; constitutions and constitutional issues in the former South Vietnam; the links and tensions between state and party constitutions; and concluding analysis of 60 years of the development of Vietnam's Constitution and constitutionalism.

Constitutional Systems of the World
General Editors: Peter Leyland and Andrew Harding
Associate Editors: Benjamin L Berger and Alexander Fischer

In the era of globalisation, issues of constitutional law and good governance are being seen increasingly as vital issues in all types of society. Since the end of the Cold War, there have been dramatic developments in democratic and legal reform, and post-conflict societies are also in the throes of reconstructing their governance systems. Even societies already firmly based on constitutional governance and the rule of law have undergone constitutional change and experimentation with new forms of governance; and their constitutional systems are increasingly subjected to comparative analysis and transplantation. Constitutional texts for practically every country in the world are now easily available on the internet. However, texts which enable one to understand the true context, purposes, interpretation and incidents of a constitutional system are much harder to locate, and are often extremely detailed and descriptive. This series seeks to provide scholars and students with accessible introductions to the constitutional systems of the world, supplying both a road map for the novice and, at the same time, a deeper understanding of the key historical, political and legal events which have shaped the constitutional landscape of each country. Each book in this series deals with a single country, and each author is an expert in their field.

Published volumes

The Constitution of the United Kingdom
The Constitution of the United States

Forthcoming titles in this series

The Constitution of South Africa
Heinz Klug

The Constitution of Japan
Shigenori Matsui

The Constitution of France
Sophie Boyron

The Constitution of Australia
Cheryl Saunders

The Constitution of Ireland
Colm O'Cinneide

Link to series website

http://www.hartpub.co.uk/series/csw

The Constitution of Vietnam

A Contextual Analysis

Mark Sidel

•HART•
PUBLISHING
OXFORD AND PORTLAND, OREGON
2009

Published in North America (US and Canada) by
Hart Publishing
c/o International Specialized Book Services
920 NE 58th Avenue, Suite 300
Portland, OR 97213-3786
USA
Tel: +1 503 287 3093 or toll-free: (1) 800 944 6190
Fax: +1 503 280 8832
E-mail: orders@isbs.com
Website: www.isbs.com

Hart Publishing Ltd, 16C Worcester Place, Oxford, OX1 2JW
Telephone: +44 (0)1865 517530 Fax: +44 (0)1865 510710
E-mail: mail@hartpub.co.uk
Website: http://www.hartpub.co.uk

British Library Cataloguing in Publication Data
Data Available

ISBN: 978-1-84113-739-1

Typeset by Compuscript Ltd, Shannon
Printed and bound in Great Britain by
TJ International Ltd, Padstow, Cornwall

In memory of Lê Mai (1940–96)

Distinguished Vietnamese patriot and diplomat

Acknowledgements

I am grateful to my family for their tolerance of my long interest and many trips to Vietnam, and to a large number of friends and colleagues for discussions of Vietnam's constitutions, debates over constitutional questions in Vietnam, and related issues of Vietnamese law and legal reform over a number of years. My deep thanks to Stephanie Balme, John Bentley, Ngo Nhu Binh, Nicholas Booth, Luu Tien Dung, Trinh Tien Dung, John Gillespie, Andrew Harding, Peter Leyland, Bui Thi Bich Lien, Do Dinh Luong, Pham Duy Nghia, Pip Nicholson, Dang Hoang Oanh, Hong Nhung Pham, Nguyen Minh Phuong, Nguyen Hung Quang, Matthieu Salomon, Bui Ngoc Son, Ta Van Tai, Phan Nguyen Toan and others.

I have learned much from the writings of several generations of distinguished constitutional scholars and commentators in Vietnam, including Ngo Huy Cuong, Nguyen Dang Dung, Nguyen Huu Dang, To Van Hoa, Vu Dinh Hoe, Bui Ngoc Son, Ngo Ba Thanh, Nguyen Van Thao, Nguyen Manh Tuong and Dao Tri Uc. Some of these writers and teachers I have met and some I have not, but I consider all of them to be my teachers and I am grateful for their work. An earlier generation of scholars and judges sought to develop constitutional law in South Vietnam, and they too deserve to be recognised: Le Van Binh, Nguyen Van Bong, Nguyen Dinh Chan, Truong Tien Dat, Tran Thuc Linh, Vu Van Mau, Nguyen Quang Quynh and others.

Andrew Harding and Peter Leyland are exemplary editors of Hart's *Constitutional Systems of the World* series and it is my pleasure and honour to work with them. Putachad Leyland painted the striking artwork that graces the cover of this volume, and I am grateful to her. Richard Hart and his colleagues at Hart Publishing are models of publishers and editors on important issues.

Some of the themes of this volume have been discussed in presentations, lectures and papers presented at Harvard Law School, the Institut d'Etudes Politiques de Paris (Sciences Po), the University of Iowa, Melbourne Law School, the University of Victoria School of Law, the United Nations Development Programme Office for Vietnam (Hanoi), the Association for Asian Studies, the workshop on the protection of constitutional rights held in Pescara (December 2007) and other venues. I am grateful to those who invited me to speak and to those who listened and commented.

Time and research for writing this volume were supported by many sources. The precious gifts of time for research and travel funds were provided by the Faculty Scholar award at the University of Iowa, funded by the College of Law and the Office of the Provost. I am grateful to the University of Iowa College of Law and Dean Carolyn Jones; the Obermann Center for Advanced Studies at the University of Iowa and Director Jay Semel; and the university's International Programs and Center for Asian and Pacific Studies.

Other institutions that supported this research in various ways include the United Nations Development Programme (Hanoi), Harvard Law School, Vermont Law School and other institutions. My thanks to Tom Frusciano and his colleagues at the Rutgers University Library for facilitating access to the papers of Professor Albert Blaustein, who advised southern Vietnamese law schools and legal institutions in the late 1960s and early 1970s.

I am particularly grateful to John Bergstrom at the University of Iowa Law Library, who obtained many obscure volumes on Vietnamese law and constitutional issues from a myriad of library sources. The entire staff of the University of Iowa Law Library is a pleasure to work with and I am grateful to them.

Portions of chapters six, seven and nine are adapted and updated from materials originally published by Cambridge University Press and the *Singapore Journal of International and Comparative Law*.

Contents

Introduction

T HIS VOLUME HAS several purposes. One is to provide
detailed information on the evolving Vietnamese Constitution
of the earlier Democratic Republic of Vietnam (DRV, 1945–76)
and current Socialist Republic of Vietnam (SRV, 1976 to the present), tracing Vietnam's modern constitutional history from the 1946
Constitution through the Constitutions of 1959, 1980, 1992 and the
important revision of the 1992 Constitution completed in 2001. The
first six chapters cover that ground. However, they also introduce a
second major aim of this book, which is to provide some sense of the
constitutional dialogues and debates that have occurred in the DRV
and SRV at various points in their existence and that are of particular
importance today. So each of the initial six chronological chapters also
indicates particular areas of constitutional conflict, and how debates and
dialogues—as well as ongoing political, economic, foreign policy, and
other challenges—influenced the changing Vietnamese Constitution.

The final three chapters discuss several of the key debates roiling
Vietnamese constitutional law today. Chapter 7 analyses a case study
in the very difficult—and highly politicised—problem of implementing constitutional guarantees. There are many formal constitutional
guarantees in Vietnam's current Constitution (1992, as amended), and
a number could be chosen to illustrate the problems that arise when
party and government seek to draft laws and policies that fulfil party
and state goals in an environment where a broad constitutional freedom
has also been promised. I have chosen one on which there has been
extensive debate, controversy and drafting in Vietnam—the guarantee
of freedom of association in article 69 of the 1992 Constitution, which
has been carried through each successive Vietnamese Constitution
since 1946, and the long history of attempts to rule and legislate on
associational life in Vietnam.

Chapters 8 and 9 examine important current controversies in
Vietnamese constitutionalism. One is the problem of judicial independence, which was always a muted discussion in Hanoi, particularly given the long history of dominated courts in the DRV and

the SRV. However, in recent years, and particularly in the wake of an important case of interference with the judiciary by high-ranking party and state officials in the major port city of Hai Phong, the question of judicial independence has come to academic, political and popular attention in Vietnam. Chapter 8 traces and analyses the new discussions on judicial independence and their roots in the recent Hai Phong case.

Chapter 9 deals with the key issue of constitutional review, and the question of who and which institutions determine whether laws and the acts of official institutions—party and state institutions—are constitutional or unconstitutional, and what to do if they do not pass constitutional muster. This is a difficult problem in any society and societies have come to different methods for determining constitution- ality and its implications. Vietnam's political leaders, constitutional and legal drafters, legal scholars, officials, dissidents and others have been engaged in a discussion of the problem of constitutional review (often called 'constitutional protection' in Vietnam) for some years now, quite publicly, and more quietly as far back as the late 1980s and 1990s. There are a number of options available for consideration as Vietnam debates constitutional review, including the possibility of forming a constitu- tional court, a constitutional commission under the National Assembly (the national legislature) or other models, and Chapter 8 outlines those important and continuing debates.

Throughout this volume and any discussion of Vietnamese consti- tutional debate, certain key issues continue to arise. They include the role of the Vietnamese Communist Party in Vietnam's constitutional system; the roles of the National Assembly and the government in Vietnam's institutional and governmental life; the status and role of the judicial system, and the prospects for strengthening judicial power and judicial capacity; the gradually narrowing role of the Vietnamese procuracy, an institution built on Soviet and Chinese models that was originally responsible not only for state prosecutions, but also as a kind of inspector-general over the entire legal and judicial system; and the crucial roles that legal officials, scholars and, at different points in Vietnam's modern history, dissidents have played in Vietnamese con- stitutional dialogue.

As in any other country, constitutional law in Vietnam is a process of constant dialogue and debate. In Vietnam (as in China and several other originally socialist countries), much of that debate occurred in ear- lier decades behind closed doors of party, state, legislative and drafting meetings. But in recent years, particularly since 1992, the dialogue and debate over constitutional issues in Vietnam has begun to come out into the open, more visible and accessible to domestic and foreign observers alike. This volume seeks to give some sense for how that dialogue and debate over the future of Vietnam's constitutionalism has occurred and the ways in which such national conversations are becoming more prominent today.

The 'Further Reading' sections at the end of each chapter guide the reader to other treatment of issues on that timeframe or theme, primarily in English. The bibliography at the end of the volume provides a more comprehensive listing of Vietnamese and English sources available on constitutional law and constitutionalism in Vietnam.

1

Key Themes in Vietnam's Constitutions and Constitutional Debates

INTRODUCTION

THIS BOOK SEEKS to outline and analyse some of the key aspects of Vietnamese constitutional development since the first modern Constitution of 1946 in the Democratic Republic of Vietnam (1945–76) and the Socialist Republic of Vietnam (1976 to the present). In doing so, I recognise and particularly highlight one key aspect of Vietnam's constitutional development here: the rights guaranteed by Vietnam's constitutions since 1946—particularly rights to speech, opinion, religion, the press, protection against arbitrary action by government and political authorities, assembly, forming associations, holding demonstrations and other fundamental rights—have never been consistently and energetically enforced, and at many points in modern Vietnamese history have been regularly and significantly violated. The discussions and debates over Vietnam's constitutions since 1946, and in particular over the past decade or so, have in part focused on strengthening the implementation and enforcement of those rights so that their utility in practice begins to come close to matching the strength of the constitutional terms.

However, Vietnam's debates on constitutional issues since 1946 have also implicated a wide array of other important themes, and they are also discussed throughout this volume. These key ongoing constitutional subjects include the relationship between the Communist Party, the Vietnamese state, and other institutions and social forces; the economic system of Vietnam and the role of state, private and collective economic forces in shaping Vietnam's development; the changing roles, powers and structure of the national legislature (the National Assembly) and the government apparatus; the role of the President of the nation; the roles and powers of local governments and legislatures; the authority, autonomy and structure of Vietnam's courts and prosecutorial institutions; ways of enforcing the constitution and the problem of constitutional review; the rights and work of associations and social organisations; the government's responsibilities for providing education, health and other social services; and other key problems.

Crucial to many of these questions is the role of the Communist Party and its relationship to the state and the Vietnamese Constitution. This has been an important issue since the 1946 Constitution, and readers will find it reflected in each chapter of this volume. In recent constitutions, the pre-eminent role of the party has been made abundantly clear. This has always been a matter of great contention among Vietnamese people overseas, some of whom have long called for the elimination of any constitutional provision on the leadership of the party, but it has recently come under discussion in Vietnam as well.

The role of the party is also important in the continuing discussions of the roles, powers and structure of the national legislature (the National Assembly), the national government, local governments and legislatures, the role of the courts and prosecutors, and recent debates over methods for enforcing the constitution and constitutional review. At each juncture, whether voiced formally or not, a key problem has been that the party is predominant in all of these institutions, but that the constitution does not spell out the party's full or detailed role, making structural change through constitutional revision an even more complicated matter than it otherwise naturally is. These themes recur throughout the volume.

A related theme is the growing but still limited power of legislative and government institutions and associations and social organisations outside the government and legislative structures. The somewhat more open Constitution of 1946 indicated that such institutions might have a degree of authority and autonomy that was belied by the more inflexible Constitutions of 1959 and 1980, when the formal roles of the legislature and government were broad, but their effective authority was relatively narrow, and associations and social organisations had little significant role in northern Vietnam or, after 1975, in reunified Vietnam.

Beginning with the 1992 Constitution, attempts were made to differentiate the role of the party from the role of these other institutions and to strengthen the work of national and local legislatures and governments, and of associations and social organisations. These attempts to restructure the workings of Vietnamese institutions have been slow and occasionally fitful. However, partly as a result of the institutional strengthening written into the 1992 Constitution, and partly as a result of decisions taken by the party and demands from below, legislative, governmental and associational actors in Vietnam have a broader role to play now than at any time since the 1940s in the Democratic Republic or Socialist Republic of Vietnam.

The consideration of these key themes in the context of changing constitutions and constitutional development in Vietnam flows through this entire volume and informs the discussion of each constitution and each major issue treated here. The constitution has both reflected and played a role in important decisions on each of these topics—the retention of the leading political role for the Communist Party in Vietnam; the gradually increasing role of the government, the National Assembly, and local governments and legislatures; the shift from a highly statist economic system to a much more diversified economy in which private business now plays a highly significant role; the attempts to build capacity without independence or autonomy into Vietnam's courts and the chafing at that system that is now beginning to be felt in Vietnamese legal and judicial circles; the narrowing of the roles of the procuracy (the state prosecutor's office) and the attempts to transform the procuracy into a state prosecutor's office rather than an overall inspectorate for the government and the legal system; the recent debates about constitutional enforcement and whether constitutional issues should be decided by the party, National Assembly, a special constitutional court or the regular judiciary; the rapid growth of associations and social organisations in practice, but continuing restriction in the legal provisions applicable to them; and other key developments.

In addition to these important topics, which are addressed throughout this volume, two other major themes are important to address in modern Vietnamese constitutional development. The first such area is the role of party constitutions and the relationship between these and national constitutions in the Democratic Republic of Vietnam and the Socialist Republic of Vietnam since the 1940s. The special problem of party constitutions (or charters, as they are sometimes called), in Vietnam and other party-dominated states is rarely raised in discussions of constitution-making in the party-run states and cannot be covered fully here, but demands at least initial treatment in part because of the complex relationship between the party itself, its constitutions and Vietnam's 1946, 1959, 1980 and 1992 Constitutions.

The second theme is the role of constitutions and constitutionalism in the former Republic of Vietnam (South Vietnam)—constitutions long since abrogated after the reunification of Vietnam in 1976, but which have a distinct role in Vietnamese constitutional development that is now being explored by constitutional drafters and scholars throughout Vietnam. Two constitutions were drafted in South Vietnam in the 1950s and 1960s and an energetic constitutional dialogue went on during part of that era. Today, the South Vietnamese constitutional experience is being put to use once again, this time as scholars and policymakers in Hanoi and Ho Chi Minh City debate issues of 'constitutional protection', the viability of a constitutional court, constitutional review and future revision or redrafting of the 1992 Constitution.

THE SPECIAL PROBLEM OF PARTY CONSTITUTIONS

The constitutions we discuss in this volume—the DRV and SRV state Constitutions of 1946, 1959, 1980 and 1992, revised in 2001—have not been the only constitutions in the Democratic Republic and Socialist Republic of Vietnam. The Vietnamese Communist Party has also promulgated a number of 'Party constitutions' (*Dieu le Dang*) in its nearly eight-decade history, and they demand at least some preliminary discussion of how they—and the party itself—relate to the state constitutions.

Party constitutions (sometimes translated as charters) have a long history in Vietnam. They go back to the first congress of the Indochinese Communist Party in 1935, and were promulgated at the second Party congress in 1951, the third Party congress in 1960, the fourth Party congress in 1976 and the fifth Party congress in 1982. Beginning with the sixth Party congress in 1986, and continuing at the seventh Party Congress in 1991, the eighth congress in 1996, the ninth congress in 2001 and the tenth congress in 2006, the existing party constitution of 1982 was revised, amended and then re-approved. Therefore, the existing Vietnamese party constitution is based on that formulated in 1982 and maintained since with amendments and revisions in the subsequent five party congresses.[1] The same general pattern holds in China: for each country, therefore, the current party constitution is based on a template first adopted in the early 1980s.

What do party constitutions do, and why should we be concerned with them? In general terms, the Vietnamese party constitutions have sought to delineate the structure of the party, define the party's activities, and specify the responsibilities of party members. To take the most

---

[1] The full text of the current Vietnamese party constitution is at <http://222.255.31.1 79:8080/tiengviet/tulieuvankien/vankiendang/?topic=191&subtopic=2>.

recently approved Vietnamese Communist Party constitution as an example, the party constitution adopted in 2006 includes an introduction on the political role of the party and chapters on the responsibilities, rights and admission of party members; organisational principles and structures of the party; the central leadership of the party; local party organisational structure and leadership; local party units; party organisations in the Vietnamese military and in the public security apparatus; the party's internal inspection functions and the delineation of the responsibilities of party inspection units; awards and discipline; the party's leadership of the state and of political and social organisations, and the Communist Youth League—the party's the youth wing; party finances; and implementation of the party constitution.

From that brief outline of the 2006 Party Constitution, it is clear that much of the document and of earlier party constitutions focuses on the party's internal issues. A good deal of the daily work involving the party constitution means that it, along with implementing documents issued by the party, serves as a kind of organisational charter for the party's activities. As party structures and other issues have evolved, the party constitution has evolved as well. The most recent revisions adopted at Vietnam's ninth party congress in 2001 and at the tenth party congress in 2006 provide a sense for how the document evolves over time to suit the party's needs and govern its activities.

Vietnam's ninth party congress in 2001 revised the party constitution 'to be consistent with the needs of work in party building in the new situation'. The changes included enabling party institutions to be restructured as the state administrative structure changed in the reform era; enabling party organisations to approve personnel transfers more efficiently; establishing and delineating the functions of higher party institutions such as the Party Secretariat and doing away with other central party institutions (such as the Standing Committee of the Political Bureau); adding a provision that the General Secretary of the party may hold his or her office for no more than two terms; dealing with amendments to facilitate party congresses at lower levels; and facilitating party inspection and financial work at the local levels.

The tenth party congress in 2006 revised the party constitution to re-emphasise the party's leading role under conditions of increasing social and economic diversity in Vietnam. It also amended the party constitution to provide for admission of party members from institutions and enterprises where no party youth organisations existed—a recognition that in many foreign-invested enterprises, for example, there are no party youth organisations from which to draw new party members, and that a means had to be determined to bring people into the party from such organisations.

Other amendments in 2006 re-emphasised the party's leading role in a changing state and society by strengthening the functions of party inspection units to investigate whether party members and officials are violating the 'programme, line, and policies of the party, the resolutions of party committees, and the ethics and way of living based on decisions of the Party Central Committee', expanding the range for disciplinary action against party members and officials at the local, party branch levels, and re-emphasising the party's leading role in managing officials in state, political and social organisations when the number and diversity of such institutions is expanding very quickly. At times, discussions of the party constitution and party policy have sparked controversy at party congresses, as well as within and without the party. Some of these conflicts came to light before and during the tenth party congress in 2006. Among the more controversial issues at the 2006 party congress was a proposal formally to permit party members to engage in private economic activities in the Political Report of the Congress and perhaps in the party constitution itself, a reform already approved in earlier decisions of the Vietnamese Communist Party's Central Committee and by the Chinese party. The debate over party members' economic activity brought together a number of issues, including the scope of the party constitution, the overlap between party and state constitutions and party authority and state law, and the role of party members.

Some party members and congress delegates agreed that party members should be allowed to engage in private economic activities, but asserted that they 'must implement the Party's line in an exemplary fashion'. Others took a different view of the role of party authority, asserting that party members engaged in private economic activity 'need only obey the law (like other citizens)'. Still others called for a special inspection system for party members engaged in business, so as to:

> supervise, in a detailed way, to avert the danger that Party members will degenerate or fall into engagement in exploitation (in the relationship of master and employee) and lose the spirit of comradeship. There must be provisions providing detailed restrictions on Party members engaged in private economic activities and supervision by Party organizations.

Still others disagreed altogether with allowing party members to engage in private economic activities as a violation of political principles and 'an encouragement to party members to "exploit"; when that happens these party members will depart from the ideals of the party ideals'.

Eventually, the presiding group drafting the Congress's Political Report recommended that the report contain the following formulation:

> Party members who engage in private economic activity must obey state law and policies in an exemplary way, and strictly obey the Party Constitution and the decisions of the Central Committee.[2]

This joint formulation, reconfirming that party members remain subject to both state law and party constitution and regulations, was adopted by the Party Central Committee with 88.35 per cent voting in favour and indeed appeared in the Political Report. It can reasonably be assumed that at least some of those who failed to raise their hands in support of this provision did so because they thought it was too weak in its provisions for enforcement against party members, or that they did not support party members engaging in private business activities.

Questions of the contents and enforceability of the party constitution, 'party law' and the relationship to the 'state' constitution and state law and regulation have also arisen in other contexts. In May 2005, for example, a group of senior retired party officials in Ho Chi Minh City (Saigon) sent a strongly worded petition to the party, alleging that the party leadership and Central Committee had 'violated Article 3' of the party constitution, which guarantees party members the right to petition and make suggestions to the party leadership, by failing to respond to the petitions and suggestions made by party members. 'The Party Constitution is the basic law with regard to Party members,' they argued. 'If the [Party] Constitution is made light of, then there is no other means for us' to petition the leadership. They lamented that no time limit for responding to party members' petitions and suggestions had been added to article 3 and asked the Congress to address the matter.[3]

These senior party members were also angered that the provisions of the party constitution on the Central Inspection Commission—which investigates wrongdoing and corruption by party members, an increasing problem in the *doi moi* (renovation) years—were very brief and general, and that the Commission's summary of its work said that 'everything

---

[2] This and the previous quotations are from the 'Report of the Presidium on the views expressed in discussion by delegates at the 10th Party Congress' (*'Ban trinh bay cua doan Chu tich ve y kien thao luan cua cac dai bieu doi voi cac van kien Dai hoi X cua Dang'*), <http://www.cpv.org.vn> accessed 25 February 2009.

[3] 'Letter of suggestions to the 12th Session of the Central Committee' (*'Thu kien nghi voi Hoi nghi Trung uong 12 Ban chap hanh Trung uong Dang'*) (31 May 2005) <http://www.doi-thoai.com/baimoi/0605_35.html>.

was achievements … that they had not found any violations of the [Party] Constitution'. The older cadres asked the Party Congress to address these violations by the Central Inspection Commission and not to avoid these cases of party wrongdoing or sweep them under the rug. Finally, the senior officials claimed that the:

> political system specified in the 2001 Party Constitution is not a dictatorship of the proletariat, but has become absolutist, severely lacking in democracy toward the people.

Decrying corruption, failure of party members, cadres and leaders to obey either state law or party rules, the petitioners called on the party to replace earlier and ineffective party resolutions that barred corrupt and other behaviour by party members with stricter regulations and enforcement through a strengthened inspection system that would supervise 'leaders of the Party and the state from the Center down to the base'.

Barely five weeks later, in early July of 2005, the former Prime Minister and very senior party official Vo Van Kiet wrote to the party leadership endorsing the views of the old party members expressed in their May letter. The former Prime Minister also asked for multiple amendments to the party constitution at the upcoming party congress. Furthermore, he also stated a broad view of the party constitution as far more than a party organisational document. That view reflected the opinions of many in Vietnam concerned with malfeasance by party members, but it also re-raised questions of the relationship between national and party constitutions and the overlapping responsibilities of party members to state and party law. The former Prime Minister and Political Bureau member wrote:

> We can say that the *Dieu le Dang* is the "law code" *(Bo luat)* of the Party, the "Constitution" *(Hien phap)* of the Party. Citizens and Party members must display exemplary behavior and pioneer in obeying the Constitution and laws of the state. At the same time, Party members … must obey the Party Constitution because it is the "law code" of the Party, the "constitution" of the Party. Every thought and action of a Party member must be based on that "law code". … In addition, because our Party is the Party in power, the Party constitution is the fulcrum for the people to inspect and supervise Party members, cadres and Party institutions and to contribute their views to building the Party.[4]

---

[4] 'Vo Van Kiet comments on the revision of the Party Constitution' (*'Vo Van Kiet doi hoi sua doi Dieu le Dang'*) (2 July 2005) <http://www.vnn-news.com/spip.php?article1524> accessed 25 February 2009.

Kiet proposed revisions to the party constitution to emphasise the role of democracy in party decision making; force the party to answer party members' petitions and views and distribute those petitions and opinions more widely; strengthen the role of national party congresses in determining rather than merely ratifying policy; move toward direct elections of the highest party leaders from the party congress, rather than elections of those leaders from the Party Central Committee; strengthen the role of Central Committee members in party affairs between party congresses, rather than the current situation in which the Party Political Bureau and Secretariat exercise almost all authority and the Central Committee is relatively uninvolved; and strengthen internal inspectorate functions within the party, when the party inspection commission now functions as an arm of the Central Committee, itself under the Political Bureau. 'Otherwise,' he wrote:

> who can inspect the Central Committee, the Political Bureau, and the Secretariat when the national congress of the Party convenes only once a term [five years]?

Inevitably, these issues are much more complicated than revisions to only a party internal organisational charter. The parallel existence of state and party constitutions in Vietnam, as in China and other single-party-dominated states, has long raised broader and larger questions about the roles of these constitutions that sit, at least in the view of some, somewhat uncomfortably side by side. Those issues include:

Since the state constitution continues to specify the leading role of the party in Vietnamese state and society (under article 4), does that mean that the party constitution trumps the state constitution? Or do they work in tandem, or in separate spheres? The current official view in Vietnam appears to be that they work in tandem, in separate if sometimes overlapping spheres (particularly when dealing with party members or officials who have committed criminal acts).

Is the party obligated to obey the state constitution under the article 4 requirement that party organisations 'operate within the framework of the [state] constitution', or merely the party constitution?

Are all state institutions—recognising that all Vietnamese state institutions have party branches or other organisations—subject to both constitutions?

Who enforces a party constitution—only the party itself, or do state institutions have any role in that enforcement, particularly with regard to the criminal or unconstitutional acts of party members or party organisations?

How can party members enforce their rights under a party constitution?
Is there any way for citizens to enforce a party constitution against the
party and party members? The party constitution does not currently
clearly provide for this.

These issues have been discussed quietly in Vietnam, usually well
outside the public eye, as they have also been in China. And they may
sometimes appear more important in the Vietnamese diaspora than
within the country. One reason for that is because the term for these
documents—the state constitution and the party constitution—are
different in Vietnamese and hold somewhat different meanings. The
state constitution is the *Hien phap*, or 'constitution', and holds the traditional meaning that we generally attach to a constitution. However,
the party constitution in Vietnamese is referred to by a different
term—*Dieu le*, which may be translated as 'a constitution', 'a charter'
or 'articles'.

In English, we use the same term for these party and state documents, but the difference in the Vietnamese terms implies a difference
in meaning. The term *Dieu le* implies an organisational document, a
document that governs the internal workings of an organisation (here,
the Communist Party). That does not resolve the difficulties or implicit
conflicts, but it does help to explain why many Vietnamese, including
many Vietnamese legal specialists, regard these two 'constitutions' as
governing separate spheres and arenas.

Despite that difference in terminology and meaning, the issues of
coverage, conflict, enforcement and assertion of rights raised above
continue to arise in Vietnam in connection with the party constitution.
Enforcement of the Vietnamese party constitution and other party
documents against corrupt or other wrongdoing party members, for
example, has proven difficult at the same time as party members and
institutions are often not subject to national law due to the party's
'leading role in state and society'. The unfortunate result can be two
constitutions, but little enforcement of either one against errant party
members. To cite but one example, at the Ninth Party Congress in
2001, the Party Central Committee reported that:

> the implementation of the resolutions, programmes, and policies of the
> Party is not good; discipline and rules are not yet strict ... Many cadres,
> Party members, and officials violate the laws and the Party Constitution
> but are not dealt with resolutely ... In the struggle against corruption
> and bribery ... we must strictly handle situations in which cadres, Party
> members and officials at any level and in any sphere of work use their

powers to engage in corruption in accordance with law and the Party Constitution.[5]

The relationship between the state and party constitutions is likely to continue to be discussed, at least quietly, as an issue in Vietnam. Furthermore, it will be affected by a wider debate about whether, and how, to amend article 4 of the 1992 Constitution on the supremacy of the party when that constitution is revised yet again, perhaps in 2011 or 2012. That key issue—as important in Vietnam as it is to the Vietnamese diaspora, some of whom call for its removal—is crucial in recalibrating the relationship between party and state, and between state and party constitutions.

THE DEATH OF SOUTH VIETNAM'S CONSTITUTIONS—AND THE BEGINNINGS OF RE-READING IN VIETNAM TODAY

Coverage and space permit only a brief discussion of constitution-making in South Vietnam (the Republic of Vietnam) before the south was reunified with the north in 1975. The leadership of South Vietnam promulgated two constitutions, in 1956 and 1963, but of course neither of them is now in force. However, their history remains of interest for two important reasons. First, the South Vietnamese constitutions are a partial window into constitutional thought—primarily elite, ruling constitutional thought—in the south in the 1950s and 1960s. Secondly, and of more relevance today, in recent years scholars and policymakers in Hanoi, Ho Chi Minh City and other parts of Vietnam have begun to re-examine some features of South Vietnamese constitution-making in the 1950s and 1960s as Vietnam re-explores concepts and models of constitutional review, the possible formation of a constitutional court, 'constitutional protection' and other difficult issues.

The Constitution of 1956

The South Vietnamese Constitution of 1956 reflected the desire of the then-leader of south Vietnam, Ngo Dinh Diem, for exceptionally strong executive powers. It was drafted quickly by a National Constitutional Assembly under Diem's direction and promulgated on

---

[5] Political Report of the Central Committee at the Ninth Party Congress (2001).

26 October 1956. Its 'central theme,' wrote a contemporary American observer, was:

> executive leadership and control. The legislative branch is given important powers and duties, but these are overshadowed, at times even in the field of law making, by those of the President.

In addition, the drafters 'found considerable difficulty' in providing for the independence of the judiciary, so that:

> in the end the organization of the courts and the selection and control of the judges was left to be determined by law.[6]

Article 3 set the tone for the entire constitution, with the key passage on executive authority in the last sentence of the paragraph:

> The Nation vests the executive functions in a President elected by the people, and the legislative functions in a National Assembly also elected by the people. The separation of powers between the executive and the legislative agencies must be clear. The activities of the executive and the legislative agencies must be brought into harmony. The President is vested with the leadership of the Nation.[7]

The American JAC Grant explained that:

> [t]he first [part] of this Article is essentially as it was written by the Assembly, save that at the President's request the order of the two halves of the first sentence was reversed. The [last sentence—'The President is vested with the leadership of the Nation.'] was added in the final revision requested by the President. It gives the key to all that follows.[8]

Another commentator agreed on the importance of the President as defined in the 1956 Constitution, adding a view as to its provenance:

> Like the presidential office in contemporary France, the President of Viet-Nam holds a position of strength so that he is unquestionably the dominant figure in political life, holding a position of *arbitrage*, above both government and legislature, as chief of state; yet he *is* the government, as sole executive.[9]

Beyond the power of the President, what follows in the 1956 Constitution are sections that provide for a legislature and a judiciary and other matters of state, but that still leave much to be decided by the executive and

---

[6] JAC Grant, 'The Viet Nam Constitution of 1956' (1958) 52:2 *American Political Science Review* 437.

[7] 1956 Constitution of the Republic of Vietnam (South Vietnam), art 3, re-punctuated.

[8] Grant, n 6 above.

[9] FJ Corley, 'The President in the Constitution of the Republic of Viet-Nam' (1961) 34:2 *Pacific Affairs* 165.

an executive-driven law-making process. The Constitutional Assembly had proposed a chapter on the National Assembly followed by the chapter on the Presidency, 'follow[ing] the American practice of putting the legislative branch first'. The two chapters were reversed in the final draft, with the Presidency coming first, 'at the President's request'. The size of the National Assembly itself would be established by law, not in the constitution. Its term of office is:

> set at three years, a reduction, at the request of the President, from the four-year term provided in the Assembly draft.

Executive and legislative were kept separate and there was no mention of ministerial service as legislators:

> the President had his eye upon the American system of an independent executive, and did not wish to see any semblance of French parliamentary responsibility creeping in.[10]

Very broad Presidential emergency powers were adopted by the Assembly and became part of the constitution. In addition, the President was given full foreign relations powers, the power to declare war and make treaties, serve as commander of the military and 'make all military and civil appointments'.[11]

Under such a system, it is not surprising that the judicial independence could not be secured, despite a broad constitutional provision that '[t]he judiciary shall have a status which guarantees its independent character'.[12]

> When it came to implementing this ambition neither the drafting committee nor the Assembly, nor after them the President, was too successful, if indeed they were successful at all. We secure our judicial independence by giving judges security of tenure and guaranteed salaries. Viet Nam was not willing to do this, although there seems to be no other way.[13]

Yet at the same time, a constitutional court was established to 'decide the constitutionality of laws, decrees, and administrative regulations',[14] as President Diem had recommended in his pre-draft message to the Constitutional Assembly. This was clearly noted in Hanoi, decades later, as Vietnam once again began to debate mechanisms for enforcing the

---

[10] Grant, n 6 above.
[11] Corley, n 9 above.
[12] 1956 Constitution of the Republic of Vietnam (South Vietnam), art 4.
[13] Grant, n 6 above.
[14] 1956 Constitution of the Republic of Vietnam (South Vietnam), art 85.

constitution and deciding upon constitutionality. In the history of the period, there is little to indicate that the Constitutional Court had any real strength, authority or activity, a fact that may also not be lost on Hanoi today.

Fundamental rights such as freedom of expression and freedom of the press were guaranteed in the constitution, but they were significantly limited in their scope.

> Every citizen has the right to freedom of expression. This right may not be used for false accusations, slander, outrages against public morals, incitations to public disturbances or for the overthrow of the republican form of government.

Furthermore, any such freedoms were subject to the limitation that:

> All activities having as their object the direct or indirect propagation or establishment of Communism in whatever form shall be contrary to the principles embodied [in the Constitution],

and:

> Whoever abuses the rights recognized in the Constitution with the object of jeopardizing the republican form of government, the democratic regime, national freedom, independence, and unity shall be deprived of his right.

The President was allowed to suspend rights of travel, residence, speech, press, assembly, association, formation of labour unions and strikes 'to meet the legitimate demands of public security and order and of national defense' during the first term of the National Assembly, until October 1959.[15] In the wake of the promulgation of the constitution, the Diem government continued and accelerated a pattern of censoring and at times closing newspapers with which it disagreed, sometimes using or ignoring the work of thugs in doing so. Diem was pleased with the constitution he had so strongly influenced.

> The vital issue is to establish an effective state apparatus ... A weak and powerless Executive will bring about discontent and indignation ... This might pave the way for revolution ... A strong and efficient executive organization capable of rapidly solving the complex and urgent problems, is a guarantee for the democratic regime.[16]

The hope of some Vietnamese and foreign observers was that Diem would use the executive-focused constitution in the enlightened interests of his

---

[15] 1956 Constitution of the Republic of Vietnam (South Vietnam), art 16.

[16] Diem, quoted in Grant, n 6 above.

nation. Diem, of course, turned out not to be the 'accountable magistrate' many wanted. Instead, as a commentator wrote in *Foreign Affairs* in 1957:

> From the beginning Diem … ruled virtually as a dictator. South Viet Nam is today a quasi-police state characterized by arbitrary arrests and imprisonment, strict censorship of the press and the absence of an effective political opposition.

Even *Life* magazine, quoted by Grant, found that:

> Behind the façade of photographs, flags and slogans there is a grim structure of decrees, political prisons, concentration camps, milder 'reeducation centers', secret police.[17]

Another American observer summarised the constitutional scene in South Vietnam:

> Despite the constitutional trappings, the real constitution of South Vietnam was the personal family rule of the Ngo [Dinh Diem] family.[18]

Furthermore, an American legal adviser to the South Vietnamese Government, Albert Blaustein, wrote that:

> the Constitution, indeed, had left the door open to dictatorship. In fact, the Ngo Dinh Diem regime, in its last years in power, was engaged deeper and deeper into a regime of individual power and a dictatorial interior policy.[19]

The 1956 Constitution had significant American influences, what Bernard Fall called 'cultural transference' in a constitution that 'borrows largely from the American example, but which also contains some elements of the French Constitution of 1946'. Fall wrote dryly and with considerable understatement that 'more could have been done to give the system a more effective, if not more representative, character'. In addition, he was among the first foreign observers to point out that major portions of the constitution were not being implemented: 'Although the Constitution now has been operative for nearly two years', Fall wrote in 1958, the Constitutional Court:

> has never been appointed—thus depriving the country of any check on the constitutionality of government actions … One other defect which must be

---

[17] Grant, n 6 above.

[18] IM Sacks, 'Restructuring Government in South Vietnam' (1967) 7:8 *Asian Survey* 515; and USAID/Vietnam Program Office, 'A Summary of Vietnam's New Constitution' (Background Paper No 2-67, 1967).

[19] AP Blaustein, *Blaustein on 1967 GVN Constitution* (c. 1972) (manuscript by Professor Blaustein, on file at the Vietnam Archive, Texas Tech University, retrieved 24 February 2008).

remedied soon is the obvious powerlessness of the National Assembly ...
The most important issues of government business are simply never submitted to it for discussion but—like the land reform, for example—simply
promulgated by Presidential decree.[20]

These issues came to the fore in a particularly poignant way—and in
comparison to the situation in the north—at the late 1950s trial of *Thoi
Luan* (*Chronicle of the Times*), the most prominent southern opposition
newspaper. *Thoi Luan*'s publisher engaged in a notable colloquy with
the court, including one of the few open comparisons of southern and
northern constitutions in 1950s Vietnam:

> President [of the tribunal]: 'Why did you make pro-Communist propaganda,
> outrage the nation, and say that our Constitution was not as good as that of
> the Communists?'
>
> Whereupon Mr. Thien [the publisher] speaks of Article 98 of the Constitution
> which permits the President of the Republic [Diem] to suspend the exercise
> of civic freedoms, thus putting the Constitution of Viet-Nam in a state of
> inferiority.
>
> The President [of the tribunal] reproaches Mr. Thien with having written
> that persons had been arrested and their trace never found. He invites him
> to cite names. Mr. Thien seems embarrassed but as he is pressed by the
> President, he replies: 'The *doc-phu* [mandarin of governor's rank] has been
> arrested a few days ago, and there are other names which I would not like to
> cite, but here is a letter which may be illuminating.' Mr. Thien hands a letter
> to the President, who reads it and no longer insists.[21]

Southern Constitutional Politics in the 1960s

Perhaps not surprisingly, Diem's Constitution of 1956 fell into disuse
in the early 1960s. Diem was then overthrown in November 1963, and
unstable military and civilian governments ensued. One of the military
governments that followed, led by General Nguyen Khanh, promulgated a Charter in 1964 that in formal terms promised separation of
powers and respect for fundamental liberties. However, in the view of
the American adviser Albert Blaustein, it merely:

> provided for a militaristic dictatorship ... [T]he Armed Forces Council ...
> was the supreme body vested with national leadership. Elected by the Armed
> Forces Council, the Chairman of the Republic of Vietnam was the Chief of

---

[20] B Fall, 'South Viet-Nam's Internal Problems' (1958) 31:3 *Pacific Affairs* 241.
[21] Ngon-Luan, 14 March 1958, quoted in Fall, n 20 above.

State. The power of the RVN Chairman was even more extensive than that vested in the President [under the 1956 Constitution]. He held sway over the whole governmental structure.

What followed were 'waves of demonstrations against the Charter'.[22] The military government's Constitutional Act No 1 (4 November 1964):

> provided for a militaristic centralization of powers with both the Executive and Legislative powers in the hands of the military junta … Judicial power … was never recognized. In other words, under the military junta's ruling system, the Judicial power continued to be a staff arm of the Executive power … Commission of such extensive powers to the provisional government indeed aroused great astonishment among politicians and jurists.[23]

The 1964 Charter, the failed attempts to implement it and the widespread protests that ensued were, in the words of one foreign observer:

> General Nguyen Khanh's attempt to become the de Gaulle of South Vietnam through the promulgation of the Vung Tau Charter … General Khanh was forced to beat ignominious retreat when the students took to the streets in protest, and that marked the beginning of the end for him.[24]

After continuing disorder in 1964 and 1965, a committee of military figures headed by Nguyen Van Thieu took power in June 1965, quickly promulgating yet a new Constitutional Charter (19 June 1965, also known as a provisional constitution), which remained in force until the 1967 Constitution was promulgated. The 1965 Constitutional Charter institutionalised the military's National Leadership Council (earlier known as the National Directory) and named its Chairman as Chief of State. Professor Blaustein called this the establishment of:

> [a] centralized military government … [N]ational sovereignty resided in the Armed Forces Council and the National Directory was designated to exercise such powers. [It] grasped all the three powers: the legislative, the executive and the judicial power together.

There was no recognition of separate judicial power, and '[t]he provisional Constitution failed to deal with fundamental liberties of the Vietnamese citizens'. The provisional constitution was used, for example, to justify the establishment of special courts to:

> render sentences without possibility of appeal against speculation, black marketing, laying in of stock, illegal transfer of funds, bribery and embezzlement

---

[22] Blaustein, n 19 above.
[23] Ibid.
[24] Sacks, n 18 above.

of public funds…[This] added to strengthening the absolute power of the National Directory and deprived the Vietnamese citizens of minimum guarantees for individual liberties and the right to legal counsel and defense.[25]

In short, political disorder and military factions vying for power bred constitutional absolutism.

The 1967 Constitution

A Constituent Assembly was formed in September 1966 and spent six months drafting a new constitution, which was approved by the Assembly in March 1967 and promulgated the next month. Executive authority was once again at the core of this constitutional drafting effort. Professor Blaustein describes the goals of the drafters of the 1967 Constitution as:

> establish[ing] a strong and stable executive power so that it can be in a position to pacify the country and put into application a large program of national reconstruction and … to discard all possibilities of a return to dictatorship in any form whatsoever.[26]

The United States was considerably more involved in the preparation of the 1967 Constitution than it had been in 1956. To assist in the drafting of the 1967 Constitution, the US Government dispatched advisers and supported translation into Vietnamese of American constitutional texts and earlier commentaries such as the *Federalist Papers*. There was resistance to this constitutional process from at least 'a strong faction' in the South Vietnamese military, which did 'not favor the entire constitutional process because it strengthen[ed] the political position of the civilian element in decision-making'.[27]

In the constitutional drafting process that resulted, both military and civilian officials sought to legitimise their leadership. The Constituent Assembly elected to write the new constitution was:

> united in their determination … to hasten the process by which the military government would be replaced by an elected government, hopefully with civilian leadership … In all events, the new constitution was to restructure government in South Vietnam on a democratic basis and avoid a repetition of the descent into the authoritarian abyss that was the hallmark of the Diem experience.

---

[25] Blaustein, n 19 above.
[26] Ibid.
[27] Sacks, n 18 above.

The results were a compromise in which the Constituent Assembly 'did take into consideration the wishes of the military leadership but clearly showed its independence'. The 1967 Constitution sought to ameliorate presidential power by dividing executive authority between a president and a prime minister, and to increase the authority of the national legislature as well as the courts, and to decentralise village administration. The national legislature was changed from unicameral in 1956 to bicameral in the 1967 Constitution, and its powers were strengthened 'to afford more control over the executive'.[28] The military was also intended to play less of a role under the new constitution; for example, the Armed Forces Council now advised the President rather than, as in the 1956 Constitution, serving as highest legislative authority.

However, as Sacks and others point out:

> despite all the efforts to circumscribe the position of the President in the new system, he still remains a dominant and centrally strong figure.

The 'ingredients that produced a Ngo Dinh Diem' found their way into the new constitution.

> The members of the Constituent Assembly [were] caught between their desire for stability, which they know is not likely on the basis of improvised coalitions, and the need to ensure the rights of opposition which failed to survive the onslaught of the autocratic President Ngo Dinh Diem ... It is this same underlying need for stability that led the Assembly to create in the institution of the Presidency a force for unity, yet try to safeguard the rights of the people by institutionalising the right of opposition.[29]

The 1956 Constitution's promise of an independent judiciary had turned out to be hollow, and the civilian drafters of the 1967 document sought to strengthen the judiciary's role and autonomy. One way in which they did so was not to continue the role of a separate constitutional court in deciding on the constitutionality of laws and regulations, as in the 1956 Constitution, but to give that role to the Supreme Court itself. The constitution also sought to shield Supreme Court appointments from some of the politicisation of executive and legislative appointments by giving the judges', prosecutors', and lawyers' associations a direct role in listing judges from which the National Assembly would choose and the President appoint. However, the terms remained limited to six years.

For US officials, the shifts in constitutional treatment of the judiciary were a point of pride in the new constitution. 'The Constitution

---

[28] Ibid. See also Blaustein, n 19 above.
[29] Sacks, n 18 above.

of April 1, 1967 effected radical changes in the organization and administration of justice', the American legal adviser (funded by the US Agency for International Development (USAID)) to the Vietnamese Supreme Court's Chief Justice told the Vietnam Council on Foreign Relations two years after the constitution was promulgated.

> Prior to that date, the Judiciary lacked independent status and functioned under the administrative control of the Executive branch of government through the Ministry of Justice. The new Constitution provides that the Judiciary shall be organized as a separate branch of government, with an autonomous budget. In this respect, it follows the US concept in contrast to France where the constitution merely guarantees the independence of the Judiciary but leaves its administration to the Executive ... Supreme Court justices in Viet Nam are nominated by their associates, the Prosecutors and the Lawyers, elected by the National Assembly and appointed by the President ... Thus the role of the Executive in Viet Nam in composing the Supreme Court is very nominal compared to the US.

Despite these improvements, he did not point out that the Vietnamese judges had a six-year tenure versus lifetime tenure in the United States, an important contributor to judicial independence.[30]

At the local government level, and over the objections of the military accustomed to determining local appointments, elections were mandated for villages, provinces, autonomous cities and Saigon, both for local councils and, except for the village level, local executive officers. In a compromise with the military, the constitution provided for government appointment of civil servants to work on security and local administration, to allow local council members and officials to be dismissed by the President and, specially, to allow the President to appoint province chiefs during the first presidential term under the new constitution.[31] This compromise—more local autonomy, local elections, but also continuing powerful central and military roles—helped to provoke continuing conflict involving the Constituent Assembly and the military.

> [T]he military leaders strongly disliked the idea that these officials, who wield extensive powers in their respective areas, should be elected rather than appointed.[32]

---

[30] FG O'Neill, 'The Legal System of Viet Nam' (Vietnam Council on Foreign Relations, address delivered on 22 September 1969).

[31] See, eg United States Military Assistance Command, Vietnam Office of the Judge Advocate, *The Constitution of Vietnam: Analysis and Comparison* (Saigon, 1967).

[32] R Devereux, 'South Vietnam's New Constitutional Structure' (1968) 8:8 *Asian Survey* 627 (originally published by American-Asian Educational Exchange, Inc, 1968).

This complex history of southern constitution making, the uses of constitutions by strong civilian and military leaders, the difficulty in achieving autonomy for the courts, the hollow promise of citizens' rights and other issues ended in May 1975 when north Vietnamese and Viet Cong forces took Saigon. However, while the southern constitutions of 1956 and 1967 and the efforts in between may have had little legalising effect on southern society, they did spark significant academic work by southern Vietnamese legal scholars and officials. From the mid-1950s to the early 1970s, the scholars and officials Le Van Binh, Nguyen Van Bong, Nguyen Dinh Chan, Truong Tien Dat, Tran Thuc Linh, Vu Van Mau, Nguyen Quang Quynh and others produced sophisticated constitutional commentaries, constitutional law texts and other volumes seeking to describe, explain and analyse these ultimately unsuccessful but still important processes in the south.[33]

One might think that South Vietnam's constitutions and the rich commentaries and texts on what is now dead constitutional law would be themselves consigned to the dustbin of history. However, in recent years, northern scholars and officials—including such important commentators as Professors Nguyen Dang Dung, Nguyen Van Thao and Bui Ngoc Son—have disinterred this important body of constitutional scholarship that was produced under difficult political and work conditions in the south. They have employed and extended the concepts of judicial review, constitutional protection, individual rights and other ideals discussed there, giving the life's work of that small band of southern scholars and officials a new use in assisting wide-ranging explorations of constitutional reform in the Socialist Republic of Vietnam.

These northern scholars and commentators have not only relied on southern work from an earlier era: they have also explored theory and constitutional developments in Europe, North America, Asia and elsewhere. However, they have not ignored the initial, if often failed,

---

[33] See, eg Le Van Binh, *Luat Hien-Phap* (*Constitutional Law*) (Saigon, 1961); Nguyen Van Bong, *Luat Hien-phap va Chinh-tri-hoc* (*Constitutional Law and Political Science*) (Saigon, 1971); Le Dinh Chan, *Luat Hien-phap va cac linh-che chinh-tri Viet-Nam* (*Constitutional Law and Political Institutions in Vietnam*) (Saigon, 1971); Truong Tien Dat, *Hien-phap chu-thich* (*Comments on the Constitution*) (Saigon, 1967); Vu Van Hien, *Nen biet qua ve phap-luat Viet-Nam* (*Outline of Vietnamese Law*) (Ha-Noi, 1949); Vu Van Mau, *Co-luat Viet-Nam* (*The Vietnamese Legal System*) (Saigon, 1971, 2 vols); and Quoc Thong Vu (Government Office), *Mot vai nhan xet ve vien Bao Hien* (*Observations on the Constitutional Court*) (Saigon, 1956). Other Western materials on constitutional developments in South Vietnam (in addition to those cited in the text) include C Frederick, *The South Vietnamese Constitution of April 1, 1967: The Institutionalization of Politics in the Second Republic* (PhD thesis, University of London, 1969).

explorations of these core concepts in their own country in a different era and under very different political circumstances. At a time when the reception of constitutional concepts such as individual rights and constitutional review from American or French sources may remain somewhat fraught in Hanoi—and may be regarded as attempts to export the 'separation of powers' to Vietnam—the fact that southern intellectuals, judges and officials were discussing many of these same concepts in the same country merely two decades ago can have a useful legitimising and explanatory power.

FURTHER READING

South Vietnamese Constitutional Development

Blaustein, AP (c 1972) *Blaustein on 1967 GVN Constitution* (manuscript by Professor Blaustein, on file at the Vietnam Archive, Texas Tech University, retrieved 24 February 2008).

Constitution of the Republic of Viet Nam (1956).

Constitution of the Republic of Viet Nam (1967).

Devereux, R (1968) 'South Vietnam's New Constitutional Structure' 8:8 *Asian Survey* 627 (New York, originally published by American-Asian Educational Exchange, Inc, 1963).

Fall, B (1958) 'South Viet-Nam's Internal Problems' 31:3 *Pacific Affairs* 241.

Grant, JAC (1958) 'The Viet Nam Constitution of 1956' 52:2 *American Political Science Review* 437.

Sacks, IM (1967) 'Restructuring Government in South Vietnam' 7:8 *Asian Survey* 515.

USAID/Vietnam Program Office (1967) *A Summary of Vietnam's New Constitution* (Background Paper No 2-67).

United States Military Assistance Command, Vietnam Office of the Judge Advocate (1967) *The Constitution of Vietnam: Analysis and Comparison* (Saigon).

2

The 1946 Constitution: A Charter for Independence and Unity

T ODAY IN VIETNAM there is a sense of nostalgia for the 1946 Constitution, adopted by the National Assembly on 9 November 1946. Vietnamese scholars and many informed citizens look back on the 1946 Constitution as an example of the inclusion of at least some democratic principles, an ethos of participation, and accountability of government leaders and legislators, rather than a harsh political line. The contexts of the Vietnamese constitutions that were to follow, particularly those of a Vietnam at war and pursuing a hardened socialist line in 1959, and the constitution promulgated after the defeat of South Vietnam and during a period of strong socialist ideology again, in 1980, were very different from the attempt to build a broad national consensus by a new and fragile regime in 1946.

Bernard Fall, the renowned journalist and analyst of Vietnam, noted that the 1946 Constitution:

> was adopted at a time when the regime of Ho Chi Minh still operated on a coalition basis, with French troops and American observers still in Viet-Nam and the nearest major communist armed forces almost three thousand miles away.[1]

In his groundbreaking study of the Viet Minh regime, published in 1956, he provides a sense for the 1946 document that reads as true today as it did then:

> The [1946] Constitution gives a generally 'Western democratic' impression to the reader in that it does not deal in economic theories and does not

---

[1] B Fall, 'North Viet-Nam's New Draft Constitution' (1959) 32:2 *Pacific Affairs* 178.

make use of stereotyped communist phrases, such as the 'working people' or the 'victory of the dictatorship of the proletariat.' As a matter of fact, neither does it resemble the French Constitution of 1946, with its detailed provisions ... Like the Democratic Republic's declaration of independence, it appears designed to provide 'reader appeal' in the Anglo-Saxon countries, and particularly the United States.[2]

The constitution was brief, consisting of a preamble of six paragraphs and 70 relatively brief articles—a programme for national integrity and at least the rhetoric of democratic principles, although of course there were many in the party who honoured these principles in the breach rather than in the norm. The preamble emphasises that role of the August 1945 Revolution in winning back 'sovereignty for the country, freedom for the people and [founding] the republican democratic regime', as well as ending colonialism and feudalism. Furthermore, as with other post-colonial constitutions, the duties set forth for the nation in the 1946 Vietnamese Constitution were 'to defend the integrity of our territory, win back total independence and rebuild the country on a democratic foundation'.[3]

The preamble, intending to establish an inclusionary tone for a regime that had not yet consolidated its authority, established the principles of the constitution as 'the union of all the people, irrespective of race, sex, class and religion' and 'the guarantee of the rights of democratic freedom'.[4] Socialism was not mentioned, although it was certainly the long-term goal of the Vietnamese Party. Nor was the party formally mentioned in the text.

The constitution defined Vietnam as 'a democratic republic [where] [a]ll state powers belong to the people, irrespective of race, sex, property, class and religion' and, although Ho Chi Minh's government was new and fragile, as 'an indivisible and monolithic bloc'.[5]

RIGHTS AND DUTIES IN THE 1946 CONSTITUTION

The key section on duties and rights—which appears in most socialist constitutions and in each Vietnamese constitution since 1946—was

---

[2] B Fall, *The Viet-Minh Regime: Government and Administration in the Democratic Republic of Vietnam* (New York, Institute of Pacific Relations, 1954) 13–14. See also B Fall, 'North Viet-Nam's Constitution and Government' (1960) 33:3 *Pacific Affairs* 282; B Fall, 'Notes and Comment: The President in the Constitution of the Republic of North Vietnam' (1960) 34 *Pacific Affairs* 165; and B Fall, 'Constitution-Writing in a Communist State— The New Constitution of North Vietnam' (1960) 6 *Howard Law Journal* 157.

[3] 1946 Constitution, Preamble, para 4.

[4] 1946 Constitution, Preamble, para 5.

[5] 1946 Constitution, arts 1 and 2.

particularly brief in the duties it imposed on citizens. These were duties much briefer and more general than would appear in later constitutional drafting efforts. In two short articles, the new Vietnamese state required of its citizens only that they 'must defend the Country, respect the Constitution, obey the Law' and that they have 'the duty to perform military service'.[6]

The rights section was considerably more detailed, although implementation would become a major issue. However, at least in rhetorical terms, it guaranteed:

equal rights in political, economic and cultural terms;
equality before the law and the right to participate in government, 'depending on their own abilities and virtues';
equal rights and special assistance for national minorities;
gender equality;
'rights to freedoms of speech, of the press, of association and meeting, of belief, [and] of residence and travel in the country and abroad';
the right not to be arrested or detained 'without a judicial decision' and rights against violation of residence and correspondence 'contrary to law';
the right to own property;
rights for 'intellectual and manual workers'; and
assistance to the elderly and handicapped, and for children for education.

The rights provisions also guaranteed free primary schools, with existing private schools (of which there were still quite a few in 1946) 'free to operate', which 'must teach in accordance with the State programme' and a right of refuge in Vietnam for people 'struggling for democracy and freedom'.[7] Many of the rights enumerated were intended to indicate the democratic nature of the new government and to reach out to other forces in Vietnamese society.

The 1946 Constitution is celebrated in Vietnam today as a potential model for democratic participation under party rule, most notably in the area of recall of officials and referenda on government policies. The section of the constitution on election, recall and referenda first provided for universal suffrage and 'free, direct and secret' elections, freedom to vote; it then provided the people with 'the right to recall

---

[6] 1946 Constitution, arts 4 (re-punctuated) and 5.
[7] 1946 Constitution, arts 6–16.

their representative whom they elected' and 'the right to referendum on the Constitution and on important issues concerning the destiny of the country'.[8] Both of these provisions are detailed further in the constitution, as well as a further provision for votes of confidence and recall of the Standing Committee of the National Assembly discussed further below.

These provisions for recall and referenda would not be carried over into the 1959, 1980 and 1992 Constitutions, and would become one of the calls for constitutional reform in the 2001 revision of the constitution (which revised the 1992 Constitution) and beyond. They are also hailed today as the best evidence of the more democratic and participatory nature of the 1946 Constitution.

THE ECONOMIC SYSTEM

In keeping with the new government's attempt to reach out to as many forces in society as possible during a time when its own survival was by no means assured, the 1946 Constitution said nothing about socialist transformation, central planning, the dominant role of state enterprises or any of the themes that would come to dominate the Constitutions of 1959 and 1980. Other than guaranteeing the right to ownership of property in article 12, the 1946 Constitution had virtually nothing to say about the economic system that the new government sought to build.

THE ROLE OF THE LEGISLATURE AND ITS STANDING COMMITTEE

The 1946 Constitution, like all of the subsequent constitutions, established the National Assembly as the national legislature to 'decide on all national issues, promulgate laws, vote on the budget, and approve treaties'. Proportional representation was constitutionally determined at one deputy per 50,000 population, a provision not repeated in later constitutional efforts, and, given the divided and regional nature of Vietnam, deputies were required to 'represent not only their own locations but the whole nation', a provision also eliminated in the later constitutions. The

---

[8] 1946 Constitution, arts 17–18 and 20–21.

constitution provided that the National Assembly would meet twice a year, in May and November, and specially when called by deputies or the government.[9]

The 1946 document took the lead of the Soviet Union and other countries in establishing a small group, a Standing Committee, within the larger National Assembly to vote on decrees and laws, call the National Assembly into session and 'control and criticize the Government'.[10] As in the Soviet Union and China, this smaller, internal group would come to dominate the work of the national legislature, carrying out most of its work and liaising closely with an overlapping group of party and government leaders. Only in the 1980s, in China, and in the 1990s, in Vietnam, would there be further real discussion of the appropriate relationship between an executive body and a broader and supposedly representative legislature.

The Standing Committee was given a broad role in the 1946 Constitution and this role would only continue to expand in future constitutional drafting efforts. Subtle or direct restraints on Standing Committee authority would disappear in later constitutions; for example, the requirement that decrees and laws adopted by the Standing Committee need to be re-submitted to the full National Assembly would be weakened or not included in the 1959, 1980 and 1992 Constitutions.

The Standing Committee was also given responsibility for calling Assembly elections, calling the Assembly into session, prolonging the term of the National Assembly in times of war, declaring or ending war 'when the National Assembly cannot meet', consenting to the arrest or prosecution of National Assembly deputies when the Assembly is not in session and other tasks.

An interesting control or checking mechanism on the power of the Standing Committee was also included in the 1946 Constitution—and would disappear from later efforts. The 1946 document provided that:

> At the beginning of every session, after the work report by the Standing Committee, the question of confidence towards the Standing Committee may be put forward at the request of one-fourth of the total number of deputies. The entire Standing Committee shall have to resign in case of non-confidence,

although they may also be re-elected.

---

[9] 1946 Constitution, arts 23, 25 and 28.
[10] 1946 Constitution, art 36.

Given Ho Chi Minh's special status in north Vietnam and his role as President of the DRV, the constitution made special provision for his role and relationship with the National Assembly. Article 31 stipulated that the President shall promulgate laws adopted by the National Assembly within 10 days after notification, but that within that time period 'the President shall be entitled to request the National Assembly to proceed to a new discussion', in effect allowing Ho Chi Minh to reopen completed issues given his personal status. If, after further discussion, the National Assembly reconfirms their decisions, the President shall promulgate such laws.[11]

REFERENDA AND RECALL PROCESSES IN THE 1946 CONSTITUTION

Referenda

In one of its most famous provisions, the 1946 Constitution guaranteed that 'the people have the right to referendum on the constitution and on important issues concerning the destiny of the country'. The National Assembly was given an important intermediary and controlling role in the implementation of the 'referendum' power guaranteed to citizens in article 21. Article 32 provided that:

> Important questions concerning the destiny of the nation shall be submitted to a popular referendum if so agreed by two-thirds of the total number of [National Assembly] deputies.

The method of referendum would be 'defined by law'. Constitutional amendments also required adoption through a national referendum.[12]

Recall

Recall of National Assembly deputies and members of the Standing Committee was an important feature of the 1946 Constitution that would largely disappear from later constitutions, before making something of a comeback by popular demand 55 years later, in 2001. Article 20 provided that 'the people have the right to recall their representatives

---

[11] These provisions are contained in arts 31, 35 and 37–40 of the 1946 Constitution.
[12] 1946 Constitution, arts 21, 30 and 70.

whom they elected', although such recall procedures focused largely on action by the National Assembly. The procedures stipulated in the constitution required that one-quarter of the electors (voters) of the province or city that elected that deputy request such a recall vote. If that threshold was reached, the National Assembly would vote on the recall of the deputy, with a two-thirds vote of the deputies requiring the official in question to resign under article 41. This recall provision did not survive into later constitutions, and today is recalled fondly by intellectuals and legal reformers as a democratic feature of the 1946 Constitution.

Recall also applied to the members of the National Assembly's Standing Committee. Article 39 of the 1946 Constitution provided that:

> At the beginning of every session, after the work report by the Standing Committee, the question of confidence towards the Standing Committee may be put forward at the request of one-fourth of the total number of deputies. The entire Standing Committee shall have to resign in case of non-confidence,

although they could also be re-elected. Finally, recall was also available against the members of local people's councils and administrative committees under article 61 of the 1946 charter.

There is no evidence of substantial usage of either the referenda or recall provisions of the 1946 Constitution, particularly in the confused and conflicted politics of the time. However, today, these multiple processes for the recall of elected deputies and other officials are spoken of with respect in Vietnam as Vietnamese scholars, and some citizens, seek to reach back to principles enshrined in the 1946 Constitution, with referenda and recall provisions particularly important in that debate on democratic processes in Vietnam.

THE ROLE OF THE PRESIDENT

The 1946 Constitution gave special deference to the role of the President of the Democratic Republic of Vietnam—not surprising given that the President was Ho Chi Minh. The 1946 Constitution provided that the President was to be chosen by the National Assembly, although of course in reality that decision came from party political leadership, and with a renewable term of five years.

As discussed above, article 31 gave the President the authority to request that the National Assembly re-visit and re-discuss decisions on laws already taken. The President also chose the Prime Minister, with a requirement that the Prime Minister sit in the National Assembly.

The 'authority' of the President was defined in article 49 to include:

representing the country;

'assum[ing] the function of Commander-in-Chief of the National Army, nominat[ing] or dismiss[ing] generals and high-ranking officers of the Infantry, the Navy and the Air Force';

nominating the Prime Minister, Council of Ministers and senior government officials;

chairing the Government Council;

promulgating laws;

awarding medals and other honours;

promulgating amnesties;

signing treaties;

accrediting Vietnamese diplomats and receiving foreign diplomatic representatives; and

declaring war or the end of war.[13]

THE GOVERNMENT

The 1946 Constitution defined the government of Vietnam as consisting of the President, the Vice President and the Council of Ministers, itself consisting of the Prime Minister, any vice premiers, ministers and vice ministers. Under article 52, the government was given authority to:

execute (implement) laws and decisions passed by the National Assembly;

submit drafts of decrees to the Standing Committee of the National Assembly 'in special cases and when the National Assembly is not in session';

revoke orders and decisions of lower governmental agencies;

appoint and dismiss government personnel;

implement military mobilisation laws and undertake 'all means necessary for the defence of the country'; and

draft annual budgets.

---

[13] 1946 Constitution, arts 31, 45, 47 and 49.

Upon confirmation by the National Assembly, the Prime Minister then chose ministers from among deputies, also subject to Assembly voting, in a system also viewed with approval today by those seeking to bring more democratic processes into the constitution. Vice ministers were chosen by the Prime Minister subject to approval from the Government Council and could come from within or outside the National Assembly, a gesture toward political opponents of the regime and other forces at a politically fractured time. Furthermore, as an accountability provision, the constitution required that decrees issued by the government must be signed by the President, but also 'countersigned by one or more Ministers who shall be responsible before the National Assembly'.[14]

The 1946 Constitution also provided that the National Assembly may vote no confidence in any minister or in the Council of Ministers, a provision deleted in the 1959, 1980 and 1992 Constitutions, and then re-inserted in a somewhat different form in 2001 when the 1992 Constitution was revised after heated debate in the National Assembly and the party. Article 54 of the 1946 Constitution provided that:

> Any Minister who does not obtain the confidence of the National Assembly shall have to resign. The whole Council of Ministers shall not be jointly responsible for the acts of a Minister.

However, this right to vote no confidence was itself curtailed and controlled:

> [T]he National Assembly only must vote on the issue of confidence when it is put forward by the Prime Minister, the Standing Committee [of the National Assembly] or one-fourth of the deputies.

This provision does not seem to eliminate the possibility that the Assembly could vote on no-confidence motions that came from other quarters or a lower proportion of deputies.

In the event that the National Assembly voted no confidence in the Council of Ministers, the President was given the right to re-submit the issue to the Assembly for re-discussion. If the Council of Ministers lost a no-confidence vote a second time, it 'must resign'.

Ministers were required under article 55 to:

> give verbal or written answers to question[s] by the National Assembly or its Standing Committee … within 10 days after the receipt of questions,

---

[14] 1946 Constitution, arts 45, 47 and 53.

another accountability provision that would be revived in the 1990s. The intense and sometimes harsh questioning of government ministers, first authorised in the 1946 Constitution, would become one of the most popular features of the National Assembly in the era of *doi moi* (renovation).

LOCAL GOVERNMENT

The 1946 Constitution established three broad administrative sub-divisions (*bo*) in north, central and south Vietnam, with each such *bo* further divided into provinces. Below provinces were districts, and below districts were communes. At the level of provinces, cities, provincial towns and communes, People's Councils were to be elected by universal and direct suffrage 'to decide on problems belonging to its own locality', although such decisions could not contravene higher decisions. Members of People's Councils were made subject to recall.[15]

Administrative Committees were to be elected at all levels—at the level of the *bo*, the three large national sub-divisions above the provincial level, provinces, the district just below the provincial level, cities, provincial towns and communes. The Administrative Committees at the *bo* level and at the district level below provincial level were to be elected by the People's Councils of their constituent provinces and cities. The Administrative Committee at the district level was to be elected by its constituent commune People's Council. All the other Administrative Committees—at the provincial, city, provincial town and commune levels—were to be elected by their parallel People's Council at the same level.

Administrative Committees were given responsibility for:

> executing orders from higher authorities, executing decisions of the People's Council of its locality, after approbation by higher authorities, and controlling administrative affairs of its locality.

They were to 'be responsible to higher authorities and to the People's Council of its locality'. Members of Administrative Committees were also made subject to recall, although we have no record of actual recalls of members of administrative committees or people's councils.[16]

---

[15] 1946 Constitution, arts 57, 59 and 61.
[16] 1946 Constitution, arts 58–61.

In the years of war and, after 1954, political consolidation that followed the 1946 Constitution, administrative committees and people's councils would be accused of rump trials and extra-judicial punishment, including killings, of citizens who opposed the DRV Government. Such local entities also played a significant role in the harsh land reform of the 1950s, and the 1946 Constitution was unable to play any role in ameliorating those mistakes and that harsh treatment.

THE JUDICIARY

Although Vietnam had traditionally had weak courts, the seeds for a largely powerless court system under the DRV were reconfirmed in the 1946 Constitution. The 1946 Constitution defined the Vietnamese judicial system as comprising the Supreme Court, Courts of Appeal, and courts of second and first instance (article 63)—a four-level court system, although virtually no cases would make it through all four levels. Judges were appointed by the government (article 64), but a form of judicial autonomy was also stipulated. Article 69 provided that: 'In judgment, judges shall obey only the law. Other agencies shall not interfere with the judgment.' This provision has been honoured in the breach rather than the norm for much of recent Vietnamese history, especially for high profile and political cases; the problem of judicial autonomy or independence is dealt with at greater length in Chapter 8.[17]

The constitution included some democratising features in the judicial process, including importing a Russian and Chinese provision for 'people's assessors' in criminal cases 'to express their views in minor cases, or to jointly take decisions with judges in criminal cases' (article 65). The constitution prohibited 'acts of torturing, violence and persecution against accused and condemned persons' (article 68), although these would emerge as problems in the war years and the consolidation of the party's power in the 1950s.

A provision was made for the National Assembly to 'organize a special court' in situations where the President, Vice President or a member of the National Assembly is prosecuted (article 51). No provision was made for prosecutorial or police authorities in the 1946 Constitution, and thus no checks on their power were provided.[18]

---

[17] See also To Van-Hoa, *Judicial Independence* (Lund, Jurisförlaget i Lund, 2006) (particularly Pt V, chs XVI–XIX).

[18] 1946 Constitution, arts 51 and 63–69.

INTERPRETATION, ENFORCEMENT AND AMENDMENT
OF THE CONSTITUTION

No provision—whether in the National Assembly, as in later constitutions, or in other bodies—was made for interpretation or enforcement of the constitution in 1946. Certainly, judicial review was not provided. Nor was interpretation and enforcement given over to the National Assembly or its Standing Committee, even in rhetorical terms, as would occur in later constitutional efforts. This subject is discussed in considerably more detail in Chapter 9.

The 1946 Constitution stipulated in article 70 that constitutional amendments could be requested by two-thirds of National Assembly deputies; the National Assembly shall elect a committee to draft constitutional amendments when such a request has been made and constitutional amendments approved by the National Assembly 'must be submitted to a national referendum'.

THE 1946 CONSTITUTION IN THE LIGHT OF HISTORY

Today in Vietnam the democratic features of the 1946 Constitution are harkened back to as a goal for current and future Vietnamese constitution-making. In particular, there is frequent reference to the procedures for recall of senior government officials, National Assembly and Standing Committee members, and local officials, and the provisions for referenda on the constitution, important national questions and constitutional amendments. These are important features in their own right, but they are also cited as nostalgic examples of a spirit of coalition building and tolerant politics that is said to have imbued the 1946 Constitution and to have been marginalised or eliminated in the 1959 and 1980 documents.[19] The context of the times is important here: Ho Chi Minh's government was highly fragile, buffeted by domestic and foreign forces, and was forced to retreat from Hanoi soon after the 1946 Constitution was adopted. The constitution was

---

[19] See, eg Bui Ngoc Son, *Tu tuong lap Hien cua Ho Chi Minh* (*The Constitutional Thought of Ho Chi Minh*) (Hanoi, Political Theory Publishing House, 2004); Do Ngoc Hai, *Hien phap 1946 ban Hien phap dat nen mong cho nen lap hien Nha nuoc Viet Nam* (*The 1946 Constitution: Setting a Foundation for Constitution Making in Viet Nam*) (Hanoi, National Political Publishing House, 2006); and Nguyen Van Thao, *Xay dung Nha nuoc phap quyen duoi su lanh dao cua Dang* (*Building a State Ruled by Law under the Leadership of the Party*) (Hanoi, Judicial Publishing House, 2006). For a superb sense of the times, see D Marr, *Vietnam 1945: The Quest for Power* (Berkeley, University of California Press, 1997).

as much a programme for national unity under party leadership as it was a structure of government, and it was intended to be as broadly based and inclusive as possible to attract support for the new government.

THE AFTERMATH OF THE 1946 CONSTITUTION

Many of the detailed provisions of the 1946 Constitution remained in abeyance for the next eight years, as Ho Chi Minh's forces fought the French and other enemies from their bases outside Hanoi. In these years, constitutional 'norms', if such a term can even be used, were often obeyed in the breach rather than on a consistent basis. The land reform movement of the 1950s and its implementation conflicted sharply with the inclusionary words and provisions of the 1946 Constitution and would spark open opposition from a few intellectuals based in Hanoi. In the mid- and late 1950s, that opposition coalesced around a group of intellectuals, journalists and other writers who had joined with the Viet Minh in the 1940s and early 1950s. Their protests against extra-judicial arrests, trials, killings, seizure of land and other violations, and their proposals for enforcement of the democratising principles of the 1946 Constitution would, in turn, earn them harsh treatment from the party in the late 1950s and beyond.

Two prominent intellectuals took the lead in the mid- and late 1950s in criticising the party's departure from the principles of the 1946 Constitution. Nguyen Huu Dang, a prominent Hanoi intellectual, had joined with Ho and the Viet Minh forces many years earlier. Nguyen Manh Tuong, a famous scholar with dual doctoral degrees in law and literature from the University of Montpelier in France, had returned to Vietnam to teach and write and had initially adapted to party control. Nguyen Huu Dang joined Ho Chi Minh's first government in 1945, and played a major role in planning the 2 September 1945 ceremony in Ba Dinh Square where Vietnam's independence was declared. They and others were important participants in criticising party excesses in the 1950s, both through new periodicals that daringly opened broad discussion in Hanoi and through dialogue with the government and statements at some official meetings.[20]

---

[20] For further discussion of this period, see G Boudarel, 'Intellectual Dissidence in the 1950s: The Nhan Van-Giai Pham Affair' (1990) 13.

These figures expressed their approach to the role of law in the mid-1950s in two strands of thought. First, they emphasised the need for sharply strengthened, considerably more independent legal pro-cesses under considerably less day-to-day party control, with more vigorous protection of individual liberties and autonomy for the legal system.[21] As Nguyen Huu Dang noted:

> [W]e are used to looking down upon bourgeois legal principles, so that among a large number of people this state of affairs has turned into con-tempt for the law in general. It is also because, during our long and hard resistance, we were used to solving all questions within our groups, at our convenience. We were accustomed to resorting to a 'rule of thumb' to move things along every time our work ran into a regulation. We have been used to replacing law with 'viewpoint'.

The solution, according to Dang, was not a firmer political 'viewpoint', but embracing legal norms as a standard for conduct.

> To have a firm point of view is very valuable, but this is not sufficient in itself ... A complete legal code would be a guarantee for the democratic nature of our regime. It will be the main track for the train smoothly speed-ing our people toward socialism. It is due to the lack of a legal code that our agrarian reform has bitterly failed ... It is due to the lack of a legal code that a police agent can ask for a marriage certificate from a couple sitting on the bank of the 'little lake' waiting for the moonrise, that a census cadre can watch at the door of a house, making its tenants so uneasy that they cannot eat or sleep ... It is due to the lack of a complete legal code that shameless political slanders and threats can be made.

The measures proposed by Dang and others were spirited and dar-ing. They included a new constitution that would replace the 1946 Constitution and further enshrine the rights embodied in that docu-ment; more authority for and more frequent meetings of the National Assembly:

> because in peacetime there is no reason why the National Assembly should entrust all its work to its standing committee, which, so far, has been practi-cally inactive

and 'reorganization of the judiciary, and giving it real power'.[22]

Vietnam Forum 154–174; and Kim Ninh, *A World Transformed: The Politics of Culture in Revolutionary Vietnam, 1945–1965* (Ann Arbor, University of Michigan Press, 2002).

[21] See also the discussions of state and party constitutions in ch 1.

[22] Nguyen Huu Dang, 'It is Necessary to Have a More Regularized Society' *Nhan van* no 4 (5 November 1956).

Nguyen Huu Dang discussed the core problem of constitutionalism in the next, and as it turned out, last issue of *Nhan Van*. Dang continues to argue that law and its enforcement are necessary for consolidation of socialism in the north, not an inconvenience or a luxury that can be deferred until reunification is completed. In addition, consolidation of law requires promulgation of a new or amended constitution adequate to current needs. At another level, however, Dang seems to be aware that he is fighting different forces: not only those who regard law as an inconvenience, but some who seek to roll back even the very limited protections provided in the 1946 Constitution and the laws and regulations promulgated under it. By late November 1956, that view is also of deep concern:

> I only want to assert one thing, that no matter what the content of a future Constitution may be, the parts of the 1946 Constitution relating to guarantees of democratic freedoms cannot be changed, because this is the basis of a democratic regime.
>
> Today ... some say about the 1946 Constitution, the 1946 Constitution is a blanket, strategic concession to the gang of the Vietnamese Nationalist Party aided by the Chinese Nationalists, and to those who did not follow the revolution at the time ... It is all the more inadequate in the present situation, when the people's government has made great progress. Since the forces of the workers and the peasants are now greatly developed, of course one should be stricter, instead of falling back to the level of bourgeois democracy of 1946.
>
> Actually, there is no opinion that is more anti-democratic than the one stated above.[23]

Thus, even in late 1956, the democratic dissidents were drawing distinctions between some in the party leadership who favoured the perhaps somewhat gentler instrumentalism of the early DRV years, and those who favoured even less autonomy than already existed for an already highly controlled, instrumentalised legal system, and more repression.

Nguyen Manh Tuong made similar criticisms in his far-reaching and famous attack on the land reform campaign delivered before a meeting of the Fatherland Front in 1956. The backdrop for his comments was the implementation of the Land Reform Law of 1953, which assumed far more importance in villages under party control than did the 1946 Constitution. Indeed, the 1953 Land Reform Law has been called a

---

[23] Nguyen Huu Dang, 'How are Democratic Freedoms Guaranteed by the Vietnamese Constitution of 1946?' *Nhan van* no 5 (20 November 1956).

kind of second DRV Constitution, supplementing the 1946 document, by at least one prominent Vietnamese legal scholar. The excesses of land reform and class struggle in north Vietnam, particularly from 1953 to 1956 before the party began correcting some of those errors, and particularly through the extra-legal measures carried out in the name of land reform law by 'special courts' and administrative committees, animated Tuong's criticisms:

> Administrative measures, and particularly legal measures, when correctly used, can ensure the success of the revolution. What did we want then? We wanted to discover the enemies of the peasants, of the revolution, in order to suppress them. But if we were prudent, if we wanted to safeguard the prestige and the success of the revolution, we should not forget that revolutionary justice must not miss its target: the enemy. A slogan has been put out: Better kill ten innocent people than let one enemy escape. This slogan is not only leftist to a ridiculous degree but it is also harmful to the revolution ...
>
> We have the means of discovering our enemies ... we must avoid mass repression and ... we must not kill innocent people.[24]

Professor Tuong then outlined the safeguards that he believed would better serve the revolution. At the time these procedural steps were proposed (and proposed carefully, as is clear in Tuong's careful reticence from calling directly for judicial independence), they constituted perhaps the single most clear-cut call for legal reform in the Democratic Republic of Vietnam of the 1950s:

> The first principle is: Those who committed crimes many years ago should not be punished for those crimes now ... The second principle is: The responsibility falls on the guilty person only, not on wives, children or relatives ... None of the Western countries has proceeded in such a manner for four hundred years. Responsibility before the law is always individual ...
>
> The third principle is: We cannot condemn a man without valid evidence ...
>
> The fourth principle is: The interest of the defendant must be taken into consideration in the process of investigation and accusation. The prisoner at the bar has the right to be represented by counsel ...
>
> How can these principles be applied to our Land Reform? The reform could certainly continue, but the punishment of reactionaries should not be settled

---

[24] Nguyen Manh Tuong, 'Qua nhung sai lam trong Cai cach Ruong dat' ('Concerning Mistakes Committed in Land Reform'), delivered in 1958, <http://www.talawas.org> accessed 25 February 2009; an English translation is in Hoang Van Chi, *The New Class in North Vietnam* (Saigon, Cong dan, 1958). For more information on Vietnamese land reform, see E Moise, *Land Reform in China and Vietnam: Consolidating the Revolution at the Village Level* (Chapel Hill, University of North Carolina, 1983).

by the Special People's Court[s], obviously so full of shortcomings ... On the contrary, having mobilized the spirit of the people and listened to their denunciation, we should charge the ordinary People's Court to investigate, to examine, to interrogate, to judge, while the defendants should have the right to defend themselves and to be represented by counsel. We only hate the crime they might have committed; their human dignity we respect. We ought to have confidence in the court and to provide all necessary guarantees for the judge to enable him to perform his duty free from any administrative pressure and quite separate from the executive. I say separate but not independent.[25]

Tuong, however, went further. He sought to 'analyze the causes of our errors', and among those causes one was stated in the strongest possible terms.

We despise legality. A Polish professor, Mr. Mannell, when lecturing at the Ministry of Justice, reported that in Poland, immediately after the revolution, the politicians completely despised legality. They thought that they were talented enough to take upon themselves the direction of justice; to compel justice to serve political interests without paying any attention to fundamental principles of law ... All this does not surprise us. At the beginning the politicians were crazy with their successes, naturally, for those successes were imposing ... Our politicians are biased by their prejudice against legality, thinking that justice is only a spoke to be put into the wheel. They do not understand that, on the contrary, legality serves to prevent the car from being overturned ... A great danger lies in the fact that the politicians think that they are above the law ...

Politics still considers justice a poor relative ... Although there exists in our country a Ministry of Justice as well as many tribunals, laws and regulations; a politics of legality seems to be totally non-existent ... Politics is leading justice—that is perfectly right—but politics is impinging on justice, replacing justice.[26]

For these views, Nguyen Huu Dang, Nguyen Manh Tuong and others were severely criticised, and their professional and personal lives crushed. The criticism of *Nhan van Giai pham* took into account the views of Dang, Tuong and others on problems in the role of law, and directly criticised those views.

There are few other episodes of direct expression of conflicting views on the development of the role of law and the legal system before 1975. The more closed political atmosphere after *Nhan van Giai pham* and

---

[25] Ibid.
[26] Ibid.

the unifying mobilisation that came with the onset of the US war are among the reasons for that. Among the very few other episodes in this period available to us that may be interpretable as involving contending approaches to the role of law is the 1967 trial of the philosopher Hoang Minh Chinh and a number of others charged with 'revisionist' and 'counter-revolutionary' activities. But that episode—the last major flare-up of political dissent in northern Vietnam before the late 1970s—remains murky and insufficiently documented. It is discussed briefly in Chapter 3.[27]

FURTHER READING

The 1946 Constitution of the Socialist Republic of Vietnam (adopted by the National Assembly of the Socialist Republic of Vietnam, 9 November 1946).

Fall, B (1954) *The Viet-Minh Regime: Government and Administration in the Democratic Republic of Vietnam* (New York, Institute of Pacific Relations).

—— (1966) *Viet-Nam Witness, 1953–66* (New York, Praeger).

Kerkvliet, B (2005) *The Power of Everyday Politics: How Vietnamese Peasants Transformed National Policy* (Ithaca, Cornell University Press).

Moise, E (1983) *Land Reform in China and Vietnam: Consolidating the Revolution at the Village Level* (Chapel Hill, University of North Carolina).

Ninh, K (2002) *A World Transformed: The Politics of Culture in Revolutionary Vietnam, 1945–1965* (Ann Arbor, University of Michigan Press).

Pham Van Bach and Vu Dinh Hoe (1984) 'The Three Successive Constitutions of Vietnam' 1 *International Review of Contemporary Law* 105.

[27] S Quinn-Judge, 'The Ideological Debate in the DRV and the Significance of the Anti-Party Affair, 1967–68' (2005) 5:4 *Cold War History* 479.

3

The 1959 Constitution: A Charter for Socialism in the North

HE SITUATION IN 1959 was very different from that in
1946. After years of consolidating victory in the north, and
after the suppression of intellectual flowering in the late 1950s,
Vietnam's first explicitly socialist constitution was adopted by the
National Assembly on the last day of December 1959. Ho Chi Minh
outlined the key transition between the old and the new constitution
when he told the National Assembly in 1959 that:

> the 1946 Constitution, the first democratic constitution in our history, was
> well-suited to the situation and the revolutionary tasks of that era. It has ful-
> filled its mission. However, it is no longer suitable for today's new situation
> and new revolutionary tasks. So we must revise that Constitution.

Ho's words to a group of children as he left the National Assembly
in Hanoi in December 1959 after the voting on the new constitution,
reported by Bernard Fall, made the new direction clear. 'When you
grow up', he told the children, 'you will have a Communist constitution'.[1] The 1959 document was regarded as a first step in that
direction.

The 1959 Constitution of the Democratic Republic of Vietnam
was promulgated at a time when the north was pursuing heavily state-
oriented and centralised economic policies and becoming involved in a
conflict of gradually increasing intensity in the south. This constitution
clearly reflected the turn toward socialist economic development in
the north, as well as the north's hardened politics. It was considerably

---

[1] B Fall, 'North Viet-Nam's Constitution and Government' (1960) 33:3 *Pacific
Affairs* 282.

less cordial to the broad united front of political parties, intellectuals, business people and others that the new regime had tried to reach, at least in rhetorical terms, in the 1946 Constitution. It was much more directly focused on building a socialist economic state, and with 'fill[ing] in some of the obvious gaps in the 1946 document', as Bernard Fall put it, especially in outlining the structure of local administration, the National Assembly and the judiciary.

Fall put the contrast between the 1946 and 1959 Constitutions particularly clearly:

> The [1946] Constitution gives a generally 'Western democratic' impression to the reader in that it does not deal in economic theories and does not make use of stereotyped communist phrases, such as the 'working people' or the 'victory of the dictatorship of the proletariat.' … Like the Democratic Republic's declaration of independence, it appears designed to provide 'reader appeal' in the Anglo-Saxon countries, and particularly the United States … [T]he regime no longer seeks to attract popular sympathies in the South simply by posing mainly as an anti-colonialist and nationalist state [as in the 1946 Constitution].

The new constitution was, Fall put it, 'a radical departure from the 1946 constitution'.[2]

The 1959 Constitution was:

> an almost complete antithesis of the earlier document. It deals in extreme detail with economic theories and makes abundant use of stereotyped communist phrases and ideas. The regime appears to have wanted to make it clear to everyone that it was 'advancing step by step from people's democracy to socialism.' In fact, compared with similar documents from other Soviet bloc countries, its revolutionary virulence and preaching tone make it stand out as remarkably doctrinaire.[3]

The 1959 Constitution was drafted over several years, beginning in 1957, with drafts released to party cadres and officials in July 1958, and to the public in April 1959. It began with a preamble that was significantly longer and more politically doctrinaire than its 1959 version. The preamble reviewed the previous 85 years as an era in which 'the Vietnamese people consistently united and struggled against

---

[2] B Fall, 'North Viet-Nam's New Draft Constitution' (1959) 32:2 *Pacific Affairs* 178.

[3] Ibid. For more of Bernard Fall's superb work on the 1959 Constitution, see B Fall, 'Notes and Comment: The President in the Constitution of the Republic of North Vietnam' (1960) 34 *Pacific Affairs* 165; and B Fall, 'Constitution-Writing in a Communist State—The New Constitution of North Vietnam' (1960) 6 *Howard Law Journal* 157.

domination by the foreign aggressors in order to liberate their country'. It lauded the 1946 Constitution:

> which clearly endorsed the great successes of our people and highlighted the determination of the entire nation to safeguard the independence and unity of the Fatherland and to defend the freedom and democratic rights of the people.[4]

And, it reviewed the history of war after 1946 against the French, ending with Dien Bien Phu and the 1954 Geneva Agreements.

The preamble summarised the political history of the north and south since 1954:

> Since the restoration of peace, in completely liberated North Vietnam, our people have carried through the national people's democratic revolution. But the South is still under the rule of the imperialists and feudalists, our country is still temporarily divided into two zones.[5]

In this area it clearly set out the political and military struggle within and between northern and southern Vietnam that was to dominate the politics of the country.

The tasks laid out for the Vietnamese people in this 1959 preamble were different from those mentioned in 1946, and were focused on building socialism as well as national unification:

> The Vietnamese revolution has moved into a new position. Our people must endeavour to consolidate the North, taking it towards socialism; and to carry on the struggle for peaceful reunification of the country and completion of the tasks of the national people's democratic revolution throughout the country.

In addition, as with each successive Vietnamese constitution, the primary reason for revising and amending the 1946 Constitution and releasing a new constitution at the end of 1959 was 'to adapt [the 1946 Constitution] to the new situation and tasks'.[6]

In Fall's words, this was:

> not [only] a basic statement of political aims, but a campaign document, a political pamphlet to be used in the immediate struggle ahead against 'French and American imperialists working hand in glove with the feudal forces.'[7]

It thus had multiple audiences, far beyond committed revolutionaries in the north.

---

[4] 1959 Constitution, Preamble, paras 3 and 5.
[5] 1959 Constitution, Preamble, para 8.
[6] 1959 Constitution, Preamble, paras 9 and 12.
[7] B Fall, *Viet-Nam Witness, 1953–66* (New York, Praeger, 1966).

DEFINING THE NATION IN THE 1959 CONSTITUTION

In many respects, the 1959 Constitution was considerably more detailed and specific than its 1946 counterpart. While the description and definition of Vietnam in the 1946 Constitution included the key descriptions of Vietnam as a 'democratic republic' and 'an indivisible and monolithic bloc comprised of Bac Bo, Trung Bo, and Nam Bo' (1946 Constitution, arts 1 and 2), the 1959 Constitution described the Democratic Republic of Vietnam, 'established and consolidated as a result of victories won by the Vietnamese people in the glorious August Revolution and the heroic resistance', as a 'people's democratic state', a step on the road toward socialism in socialist theory. It also provided somewhat more details on rights and assistance for national minorities, at least in rhetorical form, and it mentioned the Marxist concept of 'democratic centralism' for the first time in northern constitution-making.[8] Party leadership was clearly stipulated in the preamble.

THE ECONOMIC AND SOCIAL SYSTEM OF EARLY SOCIALISM

The 1959 Constitution defined both the current economic and social systems in north Vietnam and the types of economic and social systems that Vietnam's leaders aspired to achieve. The 1946 Constitution had been notable in the absence of such definitions, most likely to attract a broad base of support in an unsettled environment. However, the directions for the economy were clear from the opening article of the chapter on the economic and social system in the 1959 document:

> The Democratic Republic of Vietnam is advancing step by step from people's democracy to socialism by developing and transforming the national economy along socialist lines, transforming its backward economy into a socialist economy with modern industry and agriculture, and an advanced science and technology.[9]

The central role of the state was now crystal clear throughout this new constitution: 'The State leads all economic activities according to a unified plan' and:

> relies on the organs of State, trade union organizations, co-operatives and other organizations of the working people, to elaborate and carry out its economic plans.

---

[8] 1959 Constitution, arts 2–4.
[9] 1959 Constitution, art 9.

While the 1946 Constitution guaranteed the right to individual ownership of property, a politically solidified party in the north provided a clear and inflexible hierarchy of property ownership in the 1959 Constitution:

> In the Democratic Republic of Vietnam, during the present period of transition to socialism, the main forms of ownership of means of production are: State ownership, that is, ownership by the whole people; co-operative ownership, that is, collective ownership by the working masses; ownership by individual working people; and ownership by the national capitalists.

Of those, 'the State sector of the economy … plays the leading role in the national economy'.[10]

The state-run economy was not yet exclusive. The 1959 Constitution also provided that the state 'encourages, guides and helps the development of the co-operative sector', 'protects the rights of peasants to own land and other means of production' (although a widespread collectivisation movement was underway in the north), 'protects the right of handicraftsmen and other individual working people to own means of production' (although many small businesses had already been taken over by the state) and 'protects the right of national capitalists to own means of production and other capital'. Here, again, much nationalisation had already taken place, and the 1959 Constitution recognised this with the provision that the state:

> encourages and guides the national capitalists in following the path of socialist transformation through the form of joint State-private enterprises, and other forms of transformation.[11]

An overall restriction on private property was included, as well as statements of protection for 'private means of life'—somewhat contradictory provisions that might well have caused justifiable confusion for Vietnamese citizens in the north:

> The State strictly prohibits the use of private property to disrupt the economic life of society, or to undermine the economic plan of the State

and: 'The State protects the right of citizens to possess lawfully-earned incomes, savings, houses, and other private means of live.' Rights to inherit property were also constitutionally protected. Furthermore, requisition or nationalisation of private property was to be carried out:

> only when such action is necessary in the public interest … with appropriate compensation … within the limits and in the conditions defined by law.[12]

---

[10] 1959 Constitution, arts 10–12.
[11] 1959 Constitution, arts 13–16.
[12] 1959 Constitution, arts 17–20.

RIGHTS AND DUTIES OF CITIZENS

The 1959 Constitution promised:

equality before the law;
the right to vote and to stand for election;
gender equality 'in all spheres of political, economic, cultural, social and
    domestic life';
protection of mothers and children;
protection of marriage and the family; and
freedom of speech, the press, assembly, association and demonstration,

with the additional provision that '[t]he State guarantees all necessary
material conditions for citizens to enjoy these freedoms'. The 1959
Constitution also promised:

freedom of the person, including freedom from arrest except by decision
    of a court or prosecutor;
inviolability of citizens' homes and of mail, and freedom of residence
    and movement;
'the right to complain of and denounce to any organ of State any servant
    of the State for transgression of law', with provisions for rapid
    handling and for compensation for infringement of rights;
the right to work;
the right to rest;
the right to support for those who are old, sick or not strong enough
    to work;
the right to education; and
'freedom to engage in scientific research, literary and artistic creation
    and other cultural pursuits'.[13]

The constitution also noted that 'the State protects the proper rights
and interests of Vietnamese workers abroad'; and guaranteed asylum:

> to any foreign national persecuted for demanding freedom, for supporting
> a just cause, for taking part in the peace movement, or for engaging in sci-
> entific activity.[14]

---

[13] 1959 Constitution, arts 22–34.
[14] 1959 Constitution, arts 36–7.

In article 38, however, the constitution provided a significant burden on this otherwise rhetorically impressive listing of protected rights. Article 38 provided that:

> The State forbids any person to use democratic freedoms to the detriment of the interest of the State and of the people.

This limitation was listed at the end of the section defining citizens' rights (articles 22 to 38) and was clearly intended to apply to each of the rights enumerated.

Interestingly, the prohibition against 'us[ing] democratic freedoms to the detriment of the interest of the State and of the people' in the 1959 Constitution found its way into the 1980 Constitution, but only as a limitation on the article providing for freedom of speech, the press, assembly, association and demonstration, rather than a limitation on the other rights mentioned. In that sense, the 1959 prohibition can be regarded as a more significant limitation than its use in 1980, for in 1959 it applied to the exercise of any and all rights guaranteed in the constitution.

In the 1946 Constitution, a very brief duties section came before the rights section and listed only four fundamental duties for citizens: to defend the country, respect the constitution, obey the law and perform military service (1946 Constitution, articles 4 and 5). The 1959 Constitution expanded somewhat on those duties. It required that citizens of the Democratic Republic of Vietnam 'abide by the Constitution and the law, uphold discipline at work, keep public order and respect social ethics', 'respect and protect public property', 'pay taxes according to law' and 'perform military service in order to defend the Fatherland' because 'defend[ing] [Vietnam] is the most sacred and noble duty of citizens'.[15]

THE ROLE OF THE NATIONAL ASSEMBLY
IN A SOCIALIST STATE

In basic terms, the role and status specified for the National Assembly in the 1959 Constitution was similar to the provisions stipulated in 1946. The National Assembly was defined as 'the highest organ of State authority' and 'the only legislative authority of the Democratic Republic of Vietnam'. National Assembly terms were slightly lengthened from three to four years.[16]

---

[15] 1959 Constitution, arts 39–42.
[16] 1959 Constitution, arts 43–5.

However, beyond the basic, defined role of the National Assembly, the functions of the legislature were specified in considerably more detail in 1959 from the functions delineated for the National Assembly in 1946. Article 50 of the new constitution gave the National Assembly responsibilities to:

'enact and amend the Constitution', 'enact laws', 'supervise the enforcement of the Constitution';

elect the President and Vice President and choose the Prime Minister after recommendation by the President;

select other senior government officials;

select the members of the National Defence Council;

elect the heads of the Supreme People's Court and the Supreme People's Procuracy (state prosecutor's office);

remove the President and Vice President and other senior officials;

determine and approve national economic plans and examine and approve the state budget;

fix taxes;

make administrative changes to ministries and other agencies;

deal with provincial and other internal boundaries; and

decide on amnesties and 'questions of war and peace'.

Most of these were standard tasks under socialist systems and socialist constitutions. However, the duty of 'supervis[ing] the enforcement of the Constitution' in article 50(3) is worth noting. This was the first time in northern constitution-making that constitutional provision had been made for any form of constitutional interpretation and review. That supervision was, at root, a hollow duty and promise, for Vietnamese scholars have now clearly noted that the National Assembly in fact handled no constitutional cases nor supervised the enforcement of the constitution in the years after 1959. But this provision, and similar but more complicated provisions inserted in later constitutions, presaged what would become a major debate in the late 1990s and later on constitutional interpretation and enforcement in Vietnam, and would lead to calls for the establishment of a constitutional court or commission, or some form of judicial review, in Vietnam. These issues are discussed in greater detail in Chapter 9.

Since the National Assembly was still defined as meeting only twice a year and did so in largely formal sessions, the Assembly's Standing Committee continued to assume a powerful role in legislative affairs.

The Standing Committee was charged with a wide range of duties as the 'executive body of the National Assembly', including:

conducting election of deputies;
convening the Assembly;
'interpret[ing] the laws';
enacting decrees;
deciding on referenda;
supervising the work of the Council of Ministers, the Supreme People's Court and the Procuracy;
'revis[ing] or annul[ling] decisions, orders, and directives of the Council of Ministers which contravene the Constitution, laws, and decrees';
revising or annulling inappropriate local decisions or dissolving People's Councils in serious circumstances;
appointing senior government officials when the Assembly is not in session;
appointing and removing senior judges and prosecutors, and ambassadors;
ratifying and abrogating treaties;
deciding on military and diplomatic grades and ranks;
granting pardons, state orders, medals and titles of honour;
proclaiming war in the event of armed attack when the Assembly is not in session; and
deciding on military mobilisation and martial law.

Reflecting the increasing complexity of legislative work, more subordinate agencies were established under the National Assembly, including a law committee, planning board and budget commission, and other committees as the Assembly might establish.[17]

In a move that would prove important in debates on constitutional review, the Standing Committee was also given the task of constitutional review by the 1959 Constitution in article 53, in addition to the review power provided to the National Assembly. This change was made in light of the increasingly important role of the Standing Committee. Many years later, in the first years of the twenty-first century, debate would swell on constitutional review and the role of the Standing Committee—especially when there was no exercise of

---

[17] 1959 Constitution, arts 51, 53 and 57.

the right to review constitutional issues by the Standing Committee during the term of this constitution or, in fact, under later constitutions as well.

The formal right of Assembly deputies to question senior government officials and ministries, first provided for in the 1946 Constitution, was maintained in the 1959 Constitution. In a minor departure from the 1946 Constitution, which mandated replies in 10 days, the 1959 Constitution required replies to deputies within five days unless investigations were required, and in such cases one month was allowed for replies to deputies' queries.

In a broad but rhetorical and toothless continuation of one of the most well-known features of the 1946 Constitution, article 5 of the 1959 Constitution continued to permit recall of National Assembly and People's Council deputies 'by their constituent[s] … if they show themselves to be unworthy of the confidence of the people'. However, this was a considerably more general provision than the 1946 Constitution's two-step recall provision that mandated a deputy's resignation if one-fourth of his or her provincial or municipal electors request his or her recall, and if revocation of his or her status is approved by two-thirds of the National Assembly's deputies (1946 Constitution, article 41). The 1959 provision was very general, provided for no process and appears to have been largely unenforceable in practice. Vietnamese scholars have indicated clearly that virtually no recalls took place after 1959 that were unrelated to legislators' criminal or moral issues.

In addition, a number of other referenda and recall provisions in the 1946 Constitution were not included in 1959. These included the 1946 provision for votes of no confidence against government ministers, and even against the entire Council of Ministers (Cabinet) (1946 Constitution, article 54). This was a provision much debated in the 2001 revision of the 1992 Constitution, when a form of no-confidence vote against ministers or other government leaders was reinstated in a move that harkened back to the 1946 Constitution.

Other recall measures also failed to find their way into the 1959 Constitution, including a 1946 provision allowing for votes of no confidence in the Standing Committee of the National Assembly (1946 Constitution, article 39), and a provision allowing for recall of members of People's Councils and Administrative Committees at the sub-national level (1946 Constitution, article 61). By 1959, although a general provision for recall of National Assembly and People's Council members was written into the new constitution, for all intents and purposes the right of recall and referendum was dead.

THE ROLE OF THE PRESIDENT

The President—still Ho Chi Minh—was given a similar range of duties in the 1959 Constitution as he had been given in 1946, including:

promulgating laws and decrees;
appointing and removing the Prime Minister and other senior officials;
conferring amnesties, pardons, medals and the like;
proclaiming war and ordering mobilisation;
proclaiming martial law;
appointing Vietnamese diplomats and receiving foreign diplomats; and
ratifying treaties pursuant to National Assembly decisions.

The President was also made 'supreme commander of the armed forces of the country and … president of the National Defense Council', empowered to attend and preside over meetings of the Council of Ministers (in place of the Prime Minister), and empowered to chair 'special political conferences' to deal with 'major problems of the country'.[18]

THE ROLE AND FUNCTIONS OF THE GOVERNMENT

Writing on the 1959 Constitution, Bernard Fall noted dryly that 'like the other Communist regimes, the DRVN seems to be intent upon developing a certain top-heaviness in state control organs'.[19] Like the 1946 Constitution, the 1959 Constitution established the Council of Ministers as:

> the executive organ of the highest organ of state authority … the highest administrative organ of the Democratic Republic of Vietnam

responsible to the National Assembly, and consisting of the Prime Minister, vice-premiers, ministers and other senior officials. The Council of Ministers was tasked with 'formulat[ing] administrative measures, issu[ing] decisions and orders, and verify[ing] their execution … basing itself on the Constitution, laws, and decrees'.[20]

---

[18] 1959 Constitution, arts 63–7.
[19] B Fall, 'North Viet-Nam's New Draft Constitution' (1959) 32:2 *Pacific Affairs* 178.
[20] 1959 Constitution, arts 71–3 (art 73 reordered).

The Council of Ministers was charged with the usual governmental executive functions in broad terms, including:

drafting laws and decrees for submission to the National Assembly;
'centraliz[ing] the leadership' of ministries, other state agencies and the 'administrative committees at all levels';
correcting decisions made by ministries and local governments;
implementing economic plans and budgets;
controlling internal and foreign trade;
implementing the national economic plans and the provisions of the state budget; 'safeguard[ing] the interests of the state, ... maintain[ing] public order, and ... protect[ing] the rights and interests of citizens';
directing the armed forces;
conducting foreign relations; and
carrying out mobilisation, martial law and other defence tasks.

In what may have been an echo of the individual responsibility ethos of the 1946 Constitution that was reflected in recall and other provisions, the 1959 Constitution provided that:

> In the discharge of their functions, members of the Council of Ministers bear responsibility before the law for such acts as contravene the Constitution and the law and do harm to the State or the people.

The 'top-heaviness in state control organs' of which Fall spoke was also evident in the constitutional provisions for the procuracy, the Standing Committee of the National Assembly and other government bodies.[21]

THE CHALLENGES OF LOCAL GOVERNMENT

The 1959 Constitution made some changes in administrative divisions and government organisations at the local level. Under the 1959 formulation, Vietnam was divided administratively into provinces, autonomous zones and municipalities directly under central authority, with provinces divided into districts, cities and towns, and districts divided into villages and townlets. Each administrative level was required to establish People's Councils and Administrative Committees. Local People's Councils were the analogue to legislatures at the

---

[21] 1959 Constitution, arts 74 and 77.

local level, and supposedly elected by local citizens. The Administrative Committees were defined in article 87 as:

> [the] executive organs of the local People's Councils at corresponding levels, and … the administrative organs of the State in their respective areas.[22]

The functions of the People's Councils were more specifically defined in the 1959 Constitution, including implementation of law, local economic and cultural development and public works, dealing with local budgets and financial reports, maintaining public order and security, protecting public property and protecting the rights of citizens; and safeguarding rights of nationalities. The Councils were also assigned to elect and supervise Administrative Committees and lower People's Councils, including the power to dissolve lower People's Councils, and to elect and remove presidents of local people's courts.[23]

If the People's Councils were legislative organs and more, the Administrative Committees were executive and administrative authorities at the local level:

> [They] direct the administrative work in their respective areas, carry out the decisions issued by people's councils at corresponding levels and the decisions and orders issued by organs of state at higher levels.

Like the People's Councils, the Administrative Committees were given wide-ranging powers, including authority to revise or annul 'inappropriate decisions' of their departments or lower-level Administrative Committees, to suspend implementation of inappropriate decisions and to propose to People's Councils at corresponding levels the revision or annulment of such decisions.[24]

However, controls were also needed, particularly after abuses by administrative committees earlier in the 1950s during the implementation of land reform.[25] And so under article 91 of the new constitution:

> The Administrative Committees at all levels are responsible to the People's Councils at corresponding levels and to the administrative organs of state at the next higher level, and shall report to these bodies.

---

[22] 1959 Constitution, arts 78–80 and 87.
[23] 1959 Constitution, arts 82 and 84–6.
[24] 1959 Constitution, arts 87 and 89–90.
[25] See, among other sources, B Fall, 'North Viet-Nam's New Draft Constitution' (1959) 32:2 *Pacific Affairs* 178; Hoang Van Chi, *The New Class in North Vietnam* (Saigon, Cong dan, 1958); and E Moise, *Land Reform in China and Vietnam: Consolidating the Revolution at the Village Level* (Chapel Hill, University of North Carolina, 1983).

The Administrative Committees were also placed under the control of the 'Administrative Committees at the next higher level, and under the unified leadership of the Council of Ministers'.

THE ROLE OF THE JUDICIARY AND PROCURACY

The pattern of somewhat greater specification and detail in the 1959 Constitution, when compared to the 1946 Constitution, continued in the areas of the judiciary, public prosecution and inspection. The constitution names the Supreme Court, local people's courts and military courts as judicial organs and notes that the National Assembly may establish special courts. Local People's Councils elect and recall the heads of the local people's courts. The system of people's assessors (citizen judges), in use in the Soviet Union and China and stipulated by the 1946 Constitution, was retained in the 1959 Constitution, and was indeed somewhat strengthened by a provision in article 99 that 'in administering justice, people's assessors enjoy the same powers as judges'.[26]

The 1959 Constitution provided that '[i]n administering justice, the people's courts are independent (*co quyen doc lap*) and subject only to law'.[27] This was a formulation somewhat similar to that in the 1946 Constitution, which had provided that '[i]n administering justice, judges shall obey only the law. Other agencies shall not interfere with the judgment'. The 1959 constitutional provision did not explicitly forbid other agencies from interfering in the work of the courts, and so may be viewed as a weakening of judicial autonomy. It also had other limitations: both in 1946 and again in 1959, the autonomy provided to courts appeared to be limited to the trial stage (*xet xu*), although it has never been fully clear how broadly that term should be applied. On the slightly more positive side, the 1959 Constitution used the term 'courts' in defining the scope of non-interference, while the 1946 Constitution and later constitutions narrowed that to individual autonomy ('judges and people's assessors') rather than providing for any form of institutional autonomy. Accused persons were also given a 'right to defense', without specification under article 102.

Some of this may seem less than entirely relevant to modern readers, for we know that, during this period (and extending up until the present),

---

[26] 1959 Constitution, arts 84, 97 and 99.

[27] 1959 Constitution, art 100. The problem of judicial independence is discussed in more detail in ch 8.

Vietnamese courts have been dominated by party organisations at both national and local levels, and that any serious guarantee of judicial autonomy or independence has been a myth during Vietnam's recent constitutional history. However, even the rhetorical provisions are important, and their changes over time, for they now serve as a basis on which judges, lawyers, litigants and judicial reformers can raise the problem of judicial independence and argue for more rapid progress. These matters are discussed in more detail in Chapters 8 and 9.[28]

The 1959 Constitution also stipulated that '[t]he Supreme People's Court supervises the judicial work of local people's courts, military courts, and special courts'. The reporting relationships of the Supreme Court and the lower courts were detailed somewhat further than in 1946:

> The Supreme People's Court is responsible to the National Assembly and reports to it or, when the National Assembly is not in session, to its Standing Committee. The local people's courts are responsible to the local people's councils at corresponding levels and report to them.[29]

The continuing reporting relationship—and political and financial dependence on—local People's Councils and governments became a long-term problem of the courts, leading to a highly subordinate status, rampant interference in judgments, and tight political control. Not until the 1990s was this system openly debated. However, even in the 1959 Constitution it was abundantly clear that the courts were, in Bernard Fall's accurate words, 'the poor relation of the two other branches of the government', dominated by local People's Councils and by the party. That local courts were dependent on local People's Councils for their judicial staffing under article 82 and for other matters under article 104, for example, gave local administrators 'a whiphand over the local courts', which 'augur[ed] ill for [their] independence or immunity from local pressures'.[30]

The 1946 Constitution had made no provision at all for state prosecutors. The 1959 Constitution recognised the role that had developed since the 1946 Constitution of the *kiem sat nhan dan*, variously called state prosecutors, procuracy or 'people's organ of control [or supervision]'. The procuracy (as I will generally call it here after Soviet and Chinese practice) is a creation of the Soviet Union, an attempt to marry

---

[28] See also To Van-Hoa, *Judicial Independence* (Lund, Jurisförlaget i Lund, 2006) (particularly Pt V, chs XVI–XIX); and P Nicholson, *Borrowing Court Systems: The Experience of Socialist Vietnam* (Leiden, Martinus Nijhoff, 2007).

[29] 1959 Constitution, arts 103 and 104.

[30] B Fall, 'North Viet-Nam's New Draft Constitution' (1959) 32:2 *Pacific Affairs* 178.

public prosecution functions with the need for inspection and control of government actions.

Therefore, in accordance with Soviet and Chinese practice at the time, the 1959 Constitution stipulated that the procuracy:

> controls the observance of the law by all departments of the Council of Ministers, all local organs of State, persons working in organs of State, and all citizens.

The control was made clear: The procuracy 'at all levels work[s] only under the leadership of their higher control organs and the unified leadership of the [procuracy]'.[31] The much weaker courts reported to their local People's Councils rather than to a vertical professional network. The procuracy, on the other hand, had a broader role: as broad as, in Fall's words, 'controlling the rest of the government machinery'. The procuracy, he went on dryly, 'is unlikely to exercise a liberalizing influence on the structure of the regime'.[32] This structure was based on a theory of party dominance over the structures of law, in which the judiciary was highly subordinated and controlled, but the procuracy played a significantly stronger role in carrying out the party's will within the legal system.

AMENDMENT AND REVISION OF THE CONSTITUTION

Similar to the 1946 formulation, the 1959 Constitution gave the National Assembly the power to revise the constitution by a two-thirds vote. However, the power of the people to vote on constitutional changes through a referendum, a feature of the 1946 Constitution (article 70(c)), was removed.

THE PROBLEMS OF REFERENDA AND RECALL— AND DEMOCRATIC DECLINE IN THE 1959 CONSTITUTION

Two key features of the 1946 Constitution regarded as promoting people's participation and a spirit of democracy were the provisions for recall of executive and legislative officials, and the stipulations allowing popular referenda. Each virtually disappeared in the 1959 Constitution, another indication of the changed focus of the 1959 document—toward building socialism—and that, as Bernard Fall put it, the 'last rebellious

---

[31] 1959 Constitution, arts 105 and 107.
[32] B Fall, 'North Viet-Nam's New Draft Constitution' (1959) 32:2 *Pacific Affairs* 178.

intellectuals who had taken the "Hundred Flowers" of free discussion and criticism seriously [had] been brought to heel'.[33]

Reviewing an earlier discussion briefly, the referenda provisions of 1946 allowed popular votes on 'important issues concerning the destiny of the country' and on amendments to the constitution (1946 Constitution, articles 21, 32 and 70). The recall provisions were even broader, and they applied to both executive officials and legislative deputies: Article 41 of the 1946 Constitution mandated a National Assembly deputy's resignation if one-fourth of his or her provincial or municipal electors requested his or her recall, and if revocation of his or her status were approved by two-thirds of the National Assembly's deputies. Article 54 provided for votes of no confidence against government ministers, and even against the entire Council of Ministers (Cabinet). Still more recall provision allowed votes of no confidence in the Standing Committee of the National Assembly (1946 Constitution, article 39) and recall of members of People's Councils and Administrative Committees at the sub-national level (1946 Constitution, article 61).

There has long been debate on these provisions within and outside Vietnam. To some, the availability of referenda and its inclusion in a constitution establishing a system led by Ho Chi Minh and his forces were an indication of a democratic spirit in constitution-making that infused the Viet Minh in the mid-1940s and were later excised from constitutional drafting, but could be disinterred in a new era. To others, the provisions for referenda were but a kind of political trick intended to project an open and democratic air for the Viet Minh, who were, in their view, single party dictators at their core.

Referenda disappeared from the 1959 Constitution as well as from the constitutions of 1980 and 1992, strengthening the harder view within and outside Vietnam and at times leading to an over-emphasis on referenda (and recall) that may have been far out of proportion to its actual importance in the 1946 Constitution or its usage. However, as Vietnamese scholars increasingly call for a return to the 'democratic spirit' of the 1946 Constitution, the provisions on popular referenda and on recall of government officials and legislators are two of the most important longings for a constitutional past focused specifically on the 1946 Constitution.[34]

---

[33] Fall, ibid.

[34] See, eg Bui Ngoc Son, *Tu tuong lap Hien cua Ho Chi Minh* (*The Constitutional Thought of Ho Chi Minh*) (Hanoi, Political Theory Publishing House, 2004); Do Ngoc Hai, *Hien phap 1946 Ban Hien phap dat nen mong cho nen lap hien Nha nuoc Viet Nam* (*The 1946*

Although contemporary Vietnamese scholars focus on the referenda and recall provisions of the 1946 Constitution and their elimination in 1959, they are not the only indications of democratic decline in the 1959 document. The loftily stated but vague and weak protections for individual rights, combined with the weakness of the judiciary and its subordination to the party, local administration and the National Assembly resulted in a document that was 'extremely weak in its guarantees of justice and fair treatment to the individual citizen', as Bernard Fall pointed out in 1959.[35]

THE 1959 CONSTITUTION AND THE YEARS AFTER

Vietnam would not adopt another constitution after 1959 until 1980, after the war ended, Vietnam was reunified and the Communist Party had solidified power throughout the country. In those intervening years from 1959 to 1980—Vietnam's longest period with a single constitution since 1946—there were only occasionally alternative voices heard in the north on issues of constitutionalism.

Among the very few other episodes in this period was the 1967 trial of the philosopher Hoang Minh Chinh and a number of others charged with 'revisionist' and 'counter-revolutionary' activities. Those arrested in mid- to late 1967 included Chinh and a former secretary to Ho Chi Minh. The 'anti-party affair', as it is officially called in Vietnam, appears to have involved discussions on political change and perhaps constitutionalism, as well as important theoretical aspects of the Sino-Soviet conflict of the 1960s (in which Chinh and his colleagues were accused of standing on the Soviet side). The Hoang Minh Chinh affair appears to have been the last major flare-up of political dissent in northern Vietnam before the late 1970s.

The details of the 'anti-party affair' of the late 1960s remain somewhat murky to this day and have been insufficiently documented. However, Chinh, who was a senior party member and Director of the Institute of Marxist-Leninist Philosophy in Hanoi until he was removed in 1967, appears to have authored a long political document that may

Constitution: Setting a Foundation for Constitution Making in Viet Nam) (Hanoi, National Political Publishing House, 2006); and Nguyen Van Thao, *Xay dung Nha nuoc phap quyen duoi su lanh dao cua Dang (Building a State Ruled by Law under the Leadership of the Party)* (Hanoi, Judicial Publishing House, 2006).

[35] Fall, n 32 above.

have advocated a more democratic approach to government and constitutional affairs.[36] Certainly, later, in the 1990s, Chinh was among the domestic voices calling for abolition or significant amendment of article 4 of the 1992 Constitution, which maintains the leading role of the Communist Party. After this episode, there appears to have been little open dissent—at least little we can identify in the north—on constitutional issues through the war and into the late 1970s.

In the context of the times, Ho Chi Minh had expressed a sympathetic view of the 1959 Constitution in his speech on the revision of the 1946 Constitution at the National Assembly in December 1959:

> This Constitution will more greatly foster our people's spirit of patriotism and socialism, will mobilize our people to unite more closely … in order to build a peaceful, unified, independent, and prosperous Vietnam.

However, the 1959 Constitution had other goals as well—the preamble was a political call to the Vietnamese people and a review of history from a northern party perspective, for example. Bernard Fall identified another purpose for the 1959 Constitution: an 'added element of legality' that was:

> in fact, more important than might be imagined in the context of the struggle between the northern and southern Vietnamese regimes for the allegiance of the majority of the population.

He continued:

> The South had acquired a legal base of government through elections in 1955 and the proclamation and legislative ratification of a constitution in 1956. North Viet-Nam, however, had never fully put into operation its own constitutional organs … [As the DRV itself explained] 'Due to war conditions, though it had been adopted, the [1946] constitution [had] not yet been [fully implemented].' … In other words, the DRVN now [had] lost the initial headstart of 'legality' which it had gained in 1946 over any possible non-communist rival regime, and the northern administration will now in all likelihood seek to remedy this defect by holding new legislative elections and fully promulgating a new constitution.[37]

In short, the north had fallen behind in constructing a fully formed state, and the 1959 Constitution was one way of catching up.

---

[36] For a more detailed discussion of Hoang Minh Chinh and the 1967 events, see S Quinn-Judge, 'The Ideological Debate in the DRV and the Significance of the Anti-Party Affair, 1967–68' (2005) 5:4 *Cold War History* 479.

[37] B Fall, 'North Viet-Nam's New Draft Constitution' (1959) 32:2 *Pacific Affairs* 178.

Such external reasons for constitutionalisation—showing 'legality' in the battle for loyalty and victory with the south—may have been a factor in the drafting and promulgation of the 1959 Constitution. The lack of legality was a factor in the north, and the 1959 Constitution enabled a significant number of 'legalising' activities to go forward, as Fall pointed out in his early writing on the 1959 Constitution. Some Vietnamese commentators have also called the 1959 Constitution:

> the first [Vietnamese] socialist constitution providing a legal foundation for the building of socialism and the struggle to reunify the nation.[38]

A related problem of legality was the absence of democratic rights. A Hanoi party newspaper stated in 1956

> We must admit that we have no satisfactory laws in our cities upon which we can build legislation which protects our democratic freedoms. Violations against the democratic freedoms of the people become inevitable when there are no clear-cut laws regulating relations between the people and the cadres.

The new constitution could have also been intended to help with the lack of such 'clear-cut laws regulating relations between the people and the cadres'.[39]

The new constitution enabled the north to proceed with legalisation in various fields at least in form, if not entirely in substance, and that too was important. As Fall put it:

> a constitutional erosion process apparently had begun and its effects upon the day-to-day relations between the State and the individual could not be stemmed merely by the issuance of *ad hoc* laws and decrees designed to alleviate one particularly flagrant injustice or one glaring case of administrative failure.

Writing in 1987, on the cusp of transition from centralised socialism to reform but still employing the rhetoric of the past to describe the legalising effects of the 1959 Constitution, a group of prominent legal scholars in Hanoi called the 1959 Constitution:

> our country's first socialist Constitution. [It] acknowledged the victories of the resistance against French colonial aggression and the victories of the people's democratic revolution in the North, established a legal foundation

---

[38] Nguyen Ngoc Hien and Le Minh Tam et al, *Giao trinh Luat Hien phap Viet Nam* (*Text on Vietnamese Constitutional Law*) (Hanoi, Hanoi Law University, 1994).

[39] Fall, n 32 above.

for building state proletarian dictatorship and step by step perfecting the
socialist legal system across half the country.[40]

As the decades have passed, some of these rationales for the 1959
Constitution have begun to fade. The 1959 charter is now largely
regarded as an expression of the political will of the party in its time, a
charter for building socialism and the state apparatus, an anachronism
of an era of harder socialist policies. Fall wrote in 1959 that the new
constitution 'should go far towards eliminating any doubts as to the
totalitarian character of the regime being built in North Viet-Nam'.[41]
To this day most Vietnamese scholars would not use such a characteri-
sation. But in terms politically acceptable in Vietnam, Professor Nguyen
Dang Dung, a leading Vietnamese constitutional law scholar, has noted
that 'the system of concentrated bureaucratic subsidy sprouted from the
1959 Constitution'. That now largely repudiated system was the basis
for the 1959 Constitution, and the one that would come next, in 1980,
and the tide against it would not be turned until the 1992 Constitution
was drafted, six years after the *doi moi* (renovation era) began.

FURTHER READING

The 1959 Constitution of the Socialist Republic of Vietnam (adopted by the
National Assembly of the Socialist Republic of Vietnam, 18 December 1980).

Fall, B (1959) 'North Viet-Nam's New Draft Constitution' 32:2 *Pacific Affairs* 178.

—— (1960) 'North Viet-Nam's Constitution and Government' 33:3 *Pacific
Affairs* 282.

—— (1960) 'Notes and Comment: The President in the Constitution of the
Republic of North Vietnam' 34 *Pacific Affairs* 165.

—— (1960) 'Constitution-Writing in a Communist State—The New Constitution
of North Vietnam' 6 *Howard Law Journal* 157.

Nicholson, P (2007) *Borrowing Court Systems: The Experience of Socialist Vietnam*
(Leiden, Martinus Nijhoff).

Pham Van Bach and Vu Dinh Hoe (1984) 'The Three Successive Constitutions of
Vietnam' 1 *International Review of Contemporary Law* 105.

Quinn-Judge, S (2005) 'The Ideological Debate in the DRV and the Significance
of the Anti-Party Affair, 1967–68' 5:4 *Cold War History* 479.

To Van-Hoa (2006) *Judicial Independence* (Lund, Jurisförlaget i Lund) (particularly
Pt V, chs XVI–XIX).

---

[40] Ha Mai Hien et al, *Cac nganh luat trong he thong phap luat Viet Nam* (*The Branches of Law
in the Vietnamese Legal System*) (Hanoi, Law Publishing House, 1987).

[41] Fall, n 32 above.

4

The 1980 Constitution: A Charter for Reunification under Socialism

⟶━◆━⟵

HE 1980 VIETNAMESE Constitution was intended to provide a basic programme and structure for political consolidation and economic development under centralised socialist
principles after the north's victory in 1975 and subsequent reunification
of the country. It generally updated the 1959 Constitution rather than
embarking in new directions. This was, as the preamble to the 1980
Constitution explained, 'the constitution of the period of transition to
socialism on a national scale', now that north and south had been reunified and the Socialist Republic of Vietnam had been proclaimed. As
Phuong-Khanh Nguyen put it in her analysis of the 1980 Constitution:

> The fact that the country is now unified at the state level has given added
> urgency to the problem of unifying existing laws and developing new laws
> to govern both regions. The most important accomplishment of the unified
> National Assembly has been the issuance of a new constitution in December
> 1980.[1]

Given its timing four years after the reintegration of Saigon and the
southern part of Vietnam, it is not surprising that the 1980 Constitution
dealt directly with unification of the country, providing a lengthy history of Vietnam in the preamble through reunification in 1976 as the
Socialist Republic of Vietnam. Reunification was paired with Vietnam's
regional and international roles, including a paragraph added to the
preamble that harshly criticised 'Chinese hegemonist aggressors and
their henchmen in Cambodia' and lauded military victories against
Cambodia and China. The preamble emphasised proudly that Vietnam

---

[1] Nguyen Phuong-Khanh, 'Introduction to the 1980 Constitution of the Socialist
Republic of Vietnam' (1981) 7(3) *Review of Socialist Law* 347.

'has become an independent, reunified socialist state, a member of the world socialist community'.[2]

In more detail than in earlier preambles, the preamble to the 1980 Constitution made explicit the goals in drafting and issuing this new constitution:

> The Socialist Republic of Vietnam needs a Constitution institutionalizing the current line of the Communist Party of Vietnam in the new stage, namely a Constitution for the period of transition to socialism on a national scale. Continuing and developing the Constitutions of 1946 and 1959, the present Constitution sums up and affirms the gains of the revolutionary struggle of the Vietnamese people over the past half century, expresses the will and aspirations of the Vietnamese people, and guarantees the successful development of Vietnamese society in the coming period.

It continues, again in somewhat more explicit terms than those used in earlier constitutions:

> Being the fundamental law of the State, the present Constitution determines our political, economic, cultural and social system, the basic rights and obligations of citizens, the organizational structures and principles guiding the activities of State bodies. It specifies the relationships between the Party's leadership, the people's mastery, and State management in Vietnamese society.

In reality, the new constitution did not accomplish all of these tasks, particularly the difficult tasks of detailing the 'relationships' between party leadership, state management and the role of the people. However, it provided more specifics on economic policy in the post-unification era, and began a long process—not yet complete as of 2008—in delineating political, legislature, executive and legal functions in a changing era for Vietnam.

In the political conjuncture of the times, it was important for the constitution to emphasise Vietnam's special relationship with the Soviet Union and its ideological alliance with supporters around the world. Thus, the constitution also emphasised:

> the militant solidarity and great and effective aid of the Soviet Union and other fraternal socialist countries to [the] Vietnamese revolution; and of the forces of national independence, democracy and peace throughout the world which have actively supported the just cause of the Vietnamese people.[3]

---

[2] 1980 Constitution, Preamble, paras 2 and 10.
[3] 1980 Constitution, Preamble, paras 13, 15 and 16.

THE RELATIONSHIP BETWEEN THE PARTY
AND THE CONSTITUTION

The 1980 Constitution introduced the key article that emphasises the leading role of the Communist Party. Article 4 of the new Constiution stipulated that:

> The Communist Party of Vietnam ... is the only force leading the State and society, and the main factor determining all successes of the Vietnamese revolution. ... Its organizations operate within the framework of the Constitution.

This formulation, a strong and clear statement of the primacy of the party, would be repeated with some amendment in the 1992 Constitution and has remained the lynchpin for controversy over party control of the constitution and the applicability of the constitution to the Communist Party ever since. Those issues have been introduced in Chapter 1 (particularly the dual existence of state and party constitutions) and are discussed in more detail in Chapter 5. In addition, underlining once again the core role of the party and the supremacy of the party over the constitution, the preamble to the 1980 Constitution quoted extensively from the Fourth Party Congress to provide guiding principles for the constitution, and restates explicitly that the constitution 'institutionaliz[es] the current line of the Communist Party'.[4]

The only limitation on the Party's role is also stated in article 4: that '[the Party's] organizations operate within the framework of the constitution'.[5] Elsewhere, Chapter 1 on the political system also requires that:

> All State organs and social organizations, all State employees, all members of social organizations and all citizens must strictly abide by the Constitution

---

[4] 1980 Constitution, Preamble, para 15. See also ch 1 on the role and dual existence of state and party constitutions.

[5] The penultimate draft of the 1980 Constitution, dated 9 December 1980 (nine days before the National Assembly adopted the constitution), words this limiting phrase as follows: 'The Party's organizations operate within the framework of the State Constitution' (*Hien phap cua Nha nuoc*). The word "state" was deleted in the final draft adopted by the National Assembly. Officially there is no other constitution—the party constitution is called *Dieu le* (which may be variously translated as constitution, charter or articles), rather than a *Hien phap* (the formal term for constitution), and using the term 'state' could have been taken as over-emphasising the distinction between party and state for purposes of obeying the constitution. Constitution of the Socialist Republic of Vietnam (Draft) (Constitutional Drafting Commission of the National Assembly, 9 December 1980). See also ch 1.

and the law, and must struggle resolutely to prevent and oppose crimes and violations of the Constitution and the law

a stronger formulation than in the 1959 Constitution.[6]

THE ROLE OF THE NATIONAL ASSEMBLY, LOCAL PEOPLE'S COUNCILS AND MASS ORGANISATIONS

The chapter on the political system in the 1980 Constitution was similar in many ways to the definition of political institutions in the 1959 Constitution. It defines the role of the National Assembly, People's Councils and several important social organisations, with relatively minor changes from the 1959 Constitution. Formal legislative and supervisory power continued to rest with the National Assembly, although it remained a weak and subservient institution to the party and government. Political organisations under the Communist Party, such as the Vietnam Fatherland Front, Vietnam Confederation of Trade Unions, the Peasants Association, Women's Union, Communist Youth Union and other groups were explicitly recognised in the constitution, together with their mobilisational role in society.[7]

Despite the top-down concepts employed to describe these organisations in the 1980 Constitution, and the almost entirely mobilisational role they played, the 1980 document was important in recognising their role in society and naming them as constitutional and political actors in addition to the party itself. The 1992 Constitution and its revision in 2001 would begin a longer and difficult process of detailing these changing roles in a rapidly changing Vietnam.

The 1980 Constitution provides the National Assembly with powers similar to that granted by the 1960 Constitution. The 1980 text also included two important stipulations intended to emphasise the National Assembly's role in policy and in supervising state activities. In new sections, the constitution provided that the Assembly:

> decides on fundamental domestic and foreign policies, objectives for economic and cultural development, the main principles governing the organization and functioning of the State apparatus and the social relations and activities of citizens.

---

[6] 1980 Constitution, art 12.
[7] 1980 Constitution, arts 9 and 10.

It went on to note that the Assembly 'exercises the right of supreme supervision of all activities of the State'.[8]

Virtually all of this was rhetorical rather than real. For most of the 1980s, the National Assembly would play a similarly weak role in policy making and state supervision as it had in most periods since 1946. However, the 1980 Constitution was more clearly defining the importance of the Assembly's role through these provisions even if they could not be immediately implemented, including the important concept that the legislature supervises the activities of the executive. Reformers would seek to put these concepts into practice in later years, and they would be grateful that even the centralising party and drafters of 1980 saw fit to include them in the constitution at a relatively early stage.

Formal duties and power for the National Assembly and its Standing Committee were provided, largely similar to the 1959 Constitution. There had been no substantial increase in the actual strength of the legislature in the ensuing 20 years, making these provisions more rhetorical than real.[9] As in the 1959 Constitution, the National Assembly was given primary responsibility for supervising enforcement of the constitution, a rhetorical and formal provision in 1980 that would come under sustained discussion over the next several decades as Vietnam began to debate concepts of constitutional and judicial review.

THE ROLE OF GOVERNMENT AND EXECUTIVE AGENCIES

If the legislative bodies remained largely unchanged, continued attempts to improve the functioning of executive agencies were clearly reflected in the 1980 Constitution. A significant change that affected both legislative and executive structure was the formation of a new 'Council of State' as the 'highest continuously functioning body of the National Assembly and ... the collective presidency' of Vietnam.[10] As Phuong-Khanh Nguyen notes:

> the Council [of State] ... combined the functions previously assigned to the president of the Republic and the National Assembly's Standing Committee as provided in the 1960 Constitution.[11]

---

[8] 1980 Constitution, art 82.
[9] 1980 Constitution, arts 82–7.
[10] 1980 Constitution, art 98.
[11] Nguyen Phuong-Khanh, 'Introduction to the 1980 Constitution of the Socialist Republic of Vietnam' (1981) 7(3) *Review of Socialist Law* 347.

Vietnam had sought to formulate a useful role for the presidency of the state in the years after Ho Chi Minh died in 1969. The 1980 solution to this problem was to combine the Standing Committee of the National Assembly with the state presidency in a new Council of State that would exercise at least some leadership over both legislative and executive functions. In formal terms, the Council of State was tasked with:

> decid[ing] on important matters concerning the building of socialism and national defence; supervis[ing] the implementation of the laws, decrees and resolutions of the National Assembly and the Council of State; and supervis[ing] activities of the State apparatus

as well as 'act[ing] on behalf of the Socialist Republic of Vietnam in domestic and foreign affairs' through the Chair of the Council. Its specific duties as outlined in the 1980 Constitution generally combined the duties of the Standing Committee of the National Assembly and the President as they had been defined in the 1959 Constitution.[12]

Most governmental tasks were expected to be carried out by the Council of Ministers, a structure that remained in large part from the 1959 Constitution and was termed 'the Government of the Socialist Republic of Vietnam, the highest executive and administrative State body'.[13] In formal terms, the Council of Ministers, headed by a Chair who functioned as Prime Minister, reported to the National Assembly and the Council of State when the Assembly was not in session. The party went unmentioned here, as in much of the 1980 Constitution, but it is clear that the Council of Ministers reported primarily to the party and that senior members of the Council were also senior members of the party.

The arrangement for local political authorities is generally similar in the 1980 Constitution to that formulated in 1959. Like the 1959 Constitution, the 1980 Constitution provided for elected People's Councils that would:

> decide on, and take measures to build their localities in all fields, ensure the development of the economy and culture, the improvement of living standards of the local people and the fulfillment of the tasks assigned by the higher authorities.[14]

If the People's Councils had a quasi-legislative role, the People's Committees had an executive function, what the constitution called (perhaps somewhat confusingly) 'the executive bodies of People's Councils,

---

[12] 1980 Constitution, arts 98 and 100.
[13] 1980 Constitution, art 104.
[14] 1980 Constitution, arts 114–20 (quoted portion from art 114).

and … local administrative bodies of the State'. That terminological confusion actually reflected the multiple reporting responsibilities of People's Committees—to their local People's Council, and to the next higher People's Committee, or, for People's Committees at provincial and central municipal levels, to the Council of Ministers.[15]

All of this was roughly similar to the structures delineated in the 1959 Constitution. The 1959 Constitution had spoken in terms of People's Councils and Administrative Committees; the Administrative Committees (following terminology used in the 1940s and 1950s, when some of those groups exercised untrammeled and often dictatorial authority) became People's Committees in 1980 and earlier, with some altered jurisdiction.

ECONOMIC POLICY IN AN ERA OF SOCIALISM

The chapter on economic affairs stresses that Vietnam's 'central task' in the economic arena is 'socialist industrialization'. In Marxist terms, first pioneered in the Soviet Union and China, the constitution stipulates that Vietnam 'is advancing directly from a society in which small-scale production predominates to socialism, bypassing the stage of capitalist development'. Priority is given to the 'rational development of heavy industry on the basis of the development of agriculture and light industry'.[16]

The 1980 Constitution retains the 1959 Constitution's emphasis on '[t]he State sector play[ing] the leading role in the national economy' (article 18) and maintained an earlier provision for 'the socialist trans-formation of the private capitalist economy in both urban and rural areas' (article 26). However, in an era of centralised socialist economic policy, it also provided a constitutional basis for allowing—little at that time, and much more later—collective and individual use of land (article 20), the development of cooperatives under state guidance and assistance (article 23), individual work by farmers, handicraft workers and other self-employed people (article 24) and:

> protect[ing] the citizens' right to ownership of lawfully earned incomes, savings, housing, other personal possessions and the means of engaging in authorized private work (article 27).[17]

---

[15] 1980 Constitution, arts 121–6.
[16] 1980 Constitution, arts 15–16.
[17] 1980 Constitution, arts 18–27.

These provisions would be expanded in later constitutional texts, and dramatically expanded in practice and under party and government policy.

A new Chapter 3 of the 1980 Constitution provided a constitutional basis for party and state emphasis on culture, education, science and technology, including an endorsement for the 'strong develop[ment]' of 'social sciences, natural sciences, and technology'. In terms that would be debated later as the state began to retreat from the provision of education and health care, the 1980 Constitution also guaranteed that 'the State has sole responsibility for education' and 'is responsible for the protection and improvement of the people's health'.[18]

THE RIGHTS AND OBLIGATIONS OF CITIZENS

The provisions on the rights and obligations of citizens are generally similar to those provided in the 1959 Constitution. In this area— particularly in the rights arena—the constitution takes on an aspirational tone. Few of the rights guaranteed to citizens in 1959 and 1980 were actually enforceable, but even their mention in the text of the constitution may have given them a certain force in policy discussions and, in the 1990s and the first decade of this century, in attempts to detail those rights through specific laws, regulations, opportunities to participate in government and even, more recently, to challenge governmental action.[19]

The 1980 Constitution provides formal guarantees for citizens of equality before the law:

the right to vote beginning at the age of 18 and to stand for election in
    the National Assembly and local People's Councils at the age of 21;
the right and obligation to work;
the right and obligation to education;
the right to health care and housing;
legal equality for women;
the state's and society's obligation to care for children;

---

[18] 1980 Constitution, arts 41, 43 and 47.

[19] For further discussion of this point, see M Sidel, *Law and Society in Vietnam* (Cambridge, Cambridge University Press, 2008); and M Sidel, 'Analytical Models for Understanding Constitutions and Constitutional Dialogue in Socialist Transitional States: Re-interpreting Constitutional Dialogue in Vietnam' (2002) 6 *Singapore Journal of International and Comparative Law* 42.

freedoms of speech, the press, assembly, association, demonstration and religion;

protection from physical violence and arrest or detention without proper authority;

inviolability of residence and privacy of correspondence and communications;

freedom of movement;

the right to undertake research and literary, artistic and other such activities;

a specific provision guaranteeing intellectual property (the rights of authors and inventors) for the first time;

the right to lodge complaints and denunciations against government action and their prompt handling;

services for the disabled; and

the legitimate rights and interests of Vietnamese living abroad.

It also mandates the obligations of loyalty to Vietnam, military service, obedience to the constitution and paying of taxes.[20]

Several aspects of these rights and obligations are worth noting in somewhat more detail, particularly in cases where they became controversial later, or citizens tried to enforce them against a party and state wary of broader freedoms, or the government itself tried to retreat on particular constitutional guarantees. The 1980 Constitution provided in article 60 that '[t]he State gradually enforces free compulsory general education'. This and somewhat more general language in 1959 marked the beginning of constitutional language that would culminate in article 59 of the 1992 Constitution, which guaranteed that 'primary education is compulsory and dispensed free of charge'. In the 1990s, as the state retreated from the provision of basic education and localities began charging students' families in various ways, pressure built to reduce the state's commitment to free compulsory primary education. This was a major point of debate when the constitution was revised in 2001, as Chapter 6 shows. But it had its roots in the strengthening language of 1959 and 1980 expanding free compulsory primary education.

In very carefully worded language, the 1980 Constitution adapted similar provisions of the 1959 text providing that:

> Citizens enjoy freedom of speech, freedom of the press, freedom of assembly, freedom of association, and freedom to demonstrate in accordance

---

[20] 1980 Constitution, arts 55–80.

with the interests of socialism and of the people. The State shall create the necessary material conditions for the exercise of these rights. No one may misuse democratic freedoms to violate the interests of the State and the people.

These provisions typified the ambiguous nature of rights in the 1959, 1980 and even later Vietnamese constitutions. Broad rights were granted, and in constitutional form, including freedoms of speech, the press, assembly, association, demonstration and, in a separate article, religion. However, these rights were limited in several ways, the most important being similar provisions in 1959 and 1980 that (in the words of the 1980 document) 'no one may misuse democratic freedoms to violate the interests of the State and the people'.[21]

Yet the constitutional provision of these rights helped to fuel demands for their enforcement in the 1990s and beyond, including broad-based claims for laws and regulations that would serve to facilitate the emergence of these rights, particularly in the areas of press freedom, associational freedom and religious freedom. Chapter 7 discusses the demands for enforcement of this constitutional freedom, and the complex role of the state in elucidating it, in connection with the debate on the right of association in the 1990s and recent years.

THE ROLES OF THE COURTS AND PROCURACIES

Institutional arrangements for the courts and state prosecutors (procuracies) remained generally similar in the 1980 Constitution as in 1959. Without question, these were (and remain) party- and state-dominated organs; strengthening judicial autonomy is currently under debate in Vietnam, but most certainly was not in 1959 and 1980. The 1980 Constitution provided for a Supreme People's Court, local people's courts and military tribunals. In formal terms, the Supreme People's Court was made 'responsible and accountable' to the National Assembly, and to the Council of State during the frequent periods when the National Assembly was not in session.[22] In practice, the Supreme Court was responsible to party and state officials at the central level.

At the local level, people's courts were made 'responsible and accountable to the People's Councils at the same level'. Since those

---

[21] 1980 Constitution, art 67.
[22] 1980 Constitution, arts 128, 136.

People's Councils elected local judges, that meant in effect that local judges were responsible to and dominated by the local People's Council, itself dominated by the party. The Supreme Court was tasked only with supervising the work of the local people's courts with regard to trial proceedings, a limited delegation of authority within the court system itself. Having local courts report to—and be dominated by—local party and state leaders rather than part of a semi-autonomous vertical network reporting to the Supreme Court in Hanoi was, as intended, a major brake on judicial autonomy and independence.[23] Compared to the 1959 Constitution, Nguyen-Phuong Khanh found that:

> SRV central and regional organs of power and judicial organizations are very much the same as those provided for in the [1959] Constitution except that the functions and responsibilities of the present institutions are described with greater precision.[24]

This is true about much of the institutional arrangements discussed in the 1980 Constitution.

The 1980 Constitution provided for a limited principle of judicial autonomy in article 131, similar to that provided in 1959: 'During trials (*khi xet xu*), judges and people's assessors are independent (*doc lap*) and subject only to the law.'[25] As Vietnamese scholars such as Professor Nguyen Dang Dung, To Van Hoa and others have pointed out, even in rhetorical terms this principle applies only to judges as individuals rather than encompassing institutional court independence, and only during certain parts of the adjudication process rather than in all aspects of a court's or judge's work. The principle provided in the 1980 Constitution has been repeated in the 1992 Constitution and is now being tested as Vietnamese scholars and officials call for more robust protection of judicial autonomy, a wider concept of judicial independence and a

---

[23] 1980 Constitution, arts 115, 135 and 136.

[24] Nguyen Phuong-Khanh, 'Introduction to the 1980 Constitution of the Socialist Republic of Vietnam' (1981) 7(3) *Review of Socialist Law* 347.

[25] This formulation was similar to but not exactly the same as in the 1959 Constitution. The 1959 Constitution did not include the concept of people's assessors joining judges in rendering decisions. Perhaps more importantly, the 1959 Constitution's provision on autonomy may be translated as: 'During trial (*khi xet xu*), the People's Courts have the right to independence (*co quyen doc lap*) and are subject only to the law' (1959 Constitution, art 100). The difference between 'are independent' and 'have the right to independence' is perhaps small, but seems to imply a somewhat stronger autonomy right in the 1980 Constitution than in the 1959 Constitution—although this may also be merely overstating a quite possibly mere technical change in terminology.

reduction in party and government interference with judicial decision making.[26] In addition to the autonomy issue, 'people's assessors', chosen from among citizens who are not judges, were required to join judges in making determinations.

Although the courts and the procuracy[27] were paired in a chapter of the 1980 Constitution, they had vastly different power, jurisdiction and authority. The jurisdiction and power of the Vietnamese procuracy was very broad indeed, modelled after its counterpart in the Soviet Union's era of Stalin. The procuracy's power was much greater than that of the courts, and its views were usually dispositive in Vietnamese courts. For many decades, state prosecutors (procurators) in Vietnam have been called the 'standing judges' (*tham phan dung*) of Vietnamese courtrooms, a Vietnamese description of (and joke about) the role of the prosecutors that emphasises that they stand, rather than sit, but also that they have power at least equal to and often exceeding that of the 'sitting judges' on the bench.

In the 1980 Constitution, the procuracy was tasked as a kind of super-inspectorate, with:

> [the] control [of] the observance of the law by the ministries and other bod-
> ies under the authority of the Council of Ministers, local organs of power,
> social organizations, State employees, and all citizens; exercis[ing] the right
> of public prosecution; and ensur[ing] the strict and uniform observance of
> the law.

Only one of these functions—'public prosecution'—corresponded to roles in most other countries, and that function was formalised only in 1980. Local procuracies had the same broad roles in their jurisdictions, giving them wide authority over local state bodies. Furthermore, unlike the court system, procurators reported upward to higher procuracies and to the Supreme People's Procuracy in Hanoi, not to local People's Councils, giving them at least somewhat more autonomy and power in the Vietnamese system.[28]

---

[26] For further discussion of this issue, see ch 8. See also Nguyen Dang Dung (ed), *Nha nuoc va nha nuoc trach nhiem* (*The State and the Responsible State*) (Hanoi, National Political Publishing House, 2006); To Van-Hoa, *Judicial Independence* (Lund, Jurisförlaget i Lund, 2006); and Nguyen Dang Dung, *Y tuong ve mot Nha nuoc chiu trach nhiem* (*Thoughts on the Responsible State*) (Da Nang, Da Nang Publishing House, 2007).

[27] The procuracy is translated as 'people's control commission' in some versions of the 1980 Constitution, but the institutional term and concept is the same in Vietnamese as it was in the 1959 document.

[28] 1980 Constitution, arts 138 and 140.

The broad and powerful role of the procuracy would come under sustained attack in Vietnam beginning in the 1990s. Courts generally bowed to their (and police) decisions, and acquittals were rare. In the 1990s and lasting until now, Vietnamese reformers as well as party and state officials have tried to narrow the work of the procuracy toward criminal prosecution, and away from its role, as defined in the 1959 and 1980 Constitutions, as an inspector of legal compliance throughout the system (except for the party itself, which has its own discipline mechanisms).

KEY PROBLEMS IN IMPLEMENTING THE CONSTITUTION

In the wake of the adoption of the 1980 Constitution, it was clear that implementation and obedience to even this somewhat rhetorical effort would be a problem. The party issued a directive on implementing the new constitution in early 1981 that laid out some of the problems. Although the language was highly rhetorical, the problems identified were real:

> We must promptly expose and immediately take measures to rectify all violations of the Constitution and law … Administrative, legal and party disciplinary measures must be taken to resolutely deal with all violations … and all breaches of party discipline and state law. We must implement the principle that all men are equal before the law. Violations of the law anywhere by anyone must be exposed and severely and judiciously dealt with. The bad practices of protecting lawbreakers and persecuting and bullying the masses must be strictly prohibited.

Therefore, the constitution applied to everyone, and that was useful to say, although the mechanisms to ensure it—strong courts, an independent media and others—were not yet permitted. Another problem was the continuing overlap between party and government functions and the dominance of the party at every level of administration. The party's directive sought to address that continuing issue as well:

> We must strengthen the leadership of all party committee echelons in the implementation of the Constitution and law. The principle that the party is the leader, the people the master, and the state the manager must be promptly reflected more clearly at each level in the adoption of concrete regulations on the operational methods of party committee echelons, the state and the mass organizations. We must overcome the practice of party committee echelons doing the administrative work and belittling the role of the people's councils and people's committees. We must strive to build

the administrative apparatus, develop the role of the state apparatus in socioeconomic management and uphold socialist law.

A third significant problem of implementation was local party and state authorities going their own way, adopting policies and rules on their own without reference to what Hanoi was doing. In an editorial on the implementation of the constitution in April 1981, the party newspaper *Nhan Dan* also addressed this problem:

> Our party has adopted many decisions strictly prohibiting its organizations and members from unwarrantedly setting their own policies or regulations at variance with the Constitution and the law, or from arbitrarily disregarding state policies and law. Many [such] cases have been investigated and dealt with.

THE 1980 CONSTITUTION IN HISTORICAL PERSPECTIVE

Like all constitutions, the 1980 effort in Vietnam was a product of its times, a programme for political consolidation after lengthy and violent reunification, and a charter for economic construction in an era when traditional socialist principles still prevailed. It was drafted under the leadership of party and state leaders such as Le Duan; many such figures are now considered overly autocratic and insufficiently democratic by younger scholars and officials. Therefore, it should come as little surprise that the same Vietnamese scholars and lawyers regard the 1980 Constitution as one of the less impressive efforts in Vietnam's long modern history of constitutional drafting.

In Professor Nguyen Dang Dung's 200-page commentary and analysis of constitutional law in Vietnam, for example, published in the late 1990s for internal use by students and the faculty at the Ho Chi Minh City University Faculty of Law, the 1980 Constitution merits but one page of description and analysis, and the analysis is dismissive. 'Like the 1959 Constitution', Professor Dung writes from the perspective of the 1990s, when the considerably more detailed and reformist 1992 Constitution had been promulgated:

> the 1980 Constitution included a number of provisions of a centralized, bureaucratic and subsidy-based system and some of our old concepts on socialism.[29]

---

[29] Nguyen Dang Dung and Ngo Duc Tuan, *Luat Hien phap Viet Nam* (*Vietnamese Constitutional Law*) (Ho Chi Minh City, Ho Chi Minh City University Law Department, c 2000).

The 1980 Constitution fares a bit better in other analyses, but that may be because they were openly published and emphasised description rather than commentary. It merits a full discussion here because of its historical place in Vietnam's constitution-making and as the sole constitutional document in force in the important period from 1980 to 1992, spanning the start of the *doi moi* reforms. In a volume on fields of law published by the Department of State and Law in the Ho Chi Minh National Political Academy (the party school) in 2004, the 1980 Constitution merits a longer description and a more neutral analysis:

> The provisions on the political system, economic system, culture, education, science and technology in the 1980 Constitution systematized a centralized ... revolutionary socialist line of the Vietnamese Communist Party, affirming the goals and orientation for construction and development of the state and society, establishing structures to implement to ensure that the authority of the people was consistent with the nature of the socialist state system[30] (HCM Political Academy, 2004).

The party school analysis also emphasises some elements that were introduced in the 1980 Constitution and later expanded in the 1992 Constitution and its 2001 revision. These include, for example, the roles of the Vietnam Fatherland Front, the Confederation of Trade Unions and other mass organisations stipulated in articles 9 and 10. For while those may seem overly formal and centralising today, in an era when Vietnam is debating much more active roles for civil society, in 1980 such provisions were the first direct mentions of a role for even mass organisations under direct party control. Similarly, the party school analysis mentions article 4 on the leading role of the party, including the provision in that article that party organisations 'operate within the framework of the Constitution'.

Elsewhere, the analysis emphasises the concept of a diversified economy, drafted very carefully and gingerly into the 1980 Constitution, the mention of protection for the rights of authors and inventors in article 27 and that the 1980 Constitution 'for the first time provided for a relatively complete structure of principles for the organization and activities of the State'—certainly more structured than in the 1959

---

[30] Ho Chi Minh National Political Academy, Department of State and Law, *Mot so nganh luat trong he thong phap luat Viet Nam* (*Branches of Law in the Vietnamese Legal System*) (Hanoi, Political Theory Publishing House, 2004, 2 vols).

Constitution. 'Compared to the 1959 Constitution', the party school commentators wrote:

> the structure of state institutions in the 1980 Constitution specifies some changes and marks a step forward with respect to the functions, tasks, powers and duties and the overall structure of the state apparatus

as the Vietnamese Party and state faced and led a reunified Vietnam in 1980.[31]

FURTHER READING

The 1980 Constitution of the Socialist Republic of Vietnam (adopted by the National Assembly of the Socialist Republic of Vietnam, 18 December 1980).

Nguyen Phuong-Khanh (1981) 'Introduction to the 1980 Constitution of the Socialist Republic of Vietnam' 7(3) *Review of Socialist Law* 347 (including the text of the 1980 Constitution).

Nicholson, P (2007) *Borrowing Court Systems: the Experience of Socialist Vietnam* (Leiden, Martinus Nijhoff).

Pham Van Bach and Vu Dinh Hoe (1984) 'The Three Successive Constitutions of Vietnam' 1 *International Review of Contemporary Law* 105.

Sidel, M (2008) *Law and Society in Vietnam* (Cambridge, Cambridge University Press).

To Van-Hoa (2006) *Judicial Independence* (Lund, Jurisförlaget i Lund) (particularly Pt V, chs XVI–XIX).

---

[31] Ibid.

5

The 1992 Constitution: A Charter for Renovation (Doi Moi)

———◆———

B Y THE LATE 1980s, the 1980 Constitution was considered hopelessly out of date in Vietnam. In large part that was because of the major changes that had begun in the mid-1980s under the policy framework of *doi moi*, or renovation. The economy was being liberalised to allow far freer private, corporate, individual, cooperative and other forms of business; discussions of national policy were expanding beyond the party and the highest reaches of the state to a more energetic National Assembly, livelier newspapers and magazines, and people's councils and people's committees were expanding their work at the local level.

Social life was beginning to emerge from the watch of the authoritarian state; intellectuals were discussing foreign models of cultural, political and economic life (although always within limits); science and social science were beginning to re-emerge from decades of war and state control; and a new generation of research institutions, policy centres and other groups with more space from party and state control were taking form and expanding.

For those responsible for constitutional issues in the party, state and National Assembly, it became clear that a new constitution was needed for a new era of renovation. Drafting of that new constitution began in the late 1980s under the direction of a Constitutional Revision Committee led by senior party, state and National Assembly officials and including political and legal officials and a few academics. From the beginning, it was assumed that this would be a new constitution, not merely some scattered amendments of the 1980 document. That understanding led to assiduous research, discussion and drafting by the Constitutional Revision Committee, accompanied by detailed discussion with senior party and government officials, culminating in the release of a draft constitution to party and state officials in 1991, and then to the general public later in the year.

THE FRAMEWORK OF THE 1992 CONSTITUTION

The 1992 Constitution that emerged from this long period of research, debate and drafting is the charter that, with additional amendments in 2001, remains in force in Vietnam today. It was adopted by the National Assembly on 15 April 1992, going into effect immediately and supplanting the 1980 Constitution. The amendments to the 1992 Constitution, which are discussed in the next chapter, were adopted by the National Assembly in December 2001.

The 1992 Constitution is the longest and most detailed of the DRV's or SRV's constitutions in the modern era. Its role is clearly stated, as it was in the 1980 Constitution:

> The Constitution of the Socialist Republic of Vietnam is the fundamental law of the State and has the highest legal effect. All other legal documents must conform to the Constitution.[1]

The 1992 Constitution consists of a preamble, chapters on the political system; the economic system; culture, education, science and technology; national defence; the fundamental rights and duties of citizens; the state President (President of the Socialist Republic of Vietnam); the government; people's councils and people's committees at the provincial and local levels; the courts and procuracy; the national flag, emblem, anthem, capital and national holiday; and the effect of the constitution and procedures for amending it.[2]

THE PREAMBLE: SETTING THE STAGE BY REVIEWING
VIETNAMESE HISTORY AND THE ROLE
OF THE CONSTITUTION

Constitutional preambles are a useful lens into the mindset of constitutional drafters, their vision of their nation's history and political system, and their reasons for drafting a new or amended constitution.

---

[1] 1992 Constitution, art 146.

[2] In addition to this chapter, useful commentaries in English on the 1992 Constitution include RHK Heng, 'The 1992 Revised Constitution of Vietnam: Background and Scope of Changes' (2002) 4:3 *Contemporary Southeast Asia* 221; and Ngo Ba Thanh, 'The Constitution and the Rule of Law' in C Thayer and D Marr (eds), *Vietnam and the Rule of Law* (Canberra, Australian National University Political and Social Change Monograph, 1993).

The 1992 Constitution was drafted at a time when Vietnamese militancy had turned largely to maintaining the dominant political role of the Communist Party, building economic prosperity through diversification away from central planning, but with state-owned enterprises still centering a multifaceted economic system, and locating a peaceful space for Vietnam in the world so that it could carry out domestic economic construction and reintegration with the world after several decades in which the socialist community was virtually its only friend and partner.

The preamble set that tone, setting out the Vietnamese people's core goal to 'renovate, build and defend their motherland'. It began with a short review of Vietnamese history, far briefer and less politically militant than in the 1959 or 1980 Constitutions, emphasising that:

> the Vietnamese people, working diligently, creatively and fighting courageously to build their country and defend it, have forged a tradition of unity, humanity, uprightness, perseverance and indomitableness for their nation and have created Vietnamese civilization and culture.[3]

Certainly, some revolutionary politics still remained, because Vietnam could not discuss its history without it. The preamble emphasised the leadership of the Communist Party, the revolutionary struggle from 1930 to 1945, the Declaration of Independence in 1945 and the establishment of the Democratic Republic of Vietnam and the 'uninterrupted struggle' over the next several decades:

> defeat[ing] the two wars of aggression by the colonialists and the imperialists, liberat[ing] the country, reunify[ing] the motherland, and br[inging] to completion the people's national democratic revolution.

The 'precious assistance of friends throughout the world' was recognised, but without explicitly mentioning the Soviet Union (which had ceased to exist by 1992) or China, as had occurred in the 1980 Constitution (positively with regard to the Soviet Union, highly negatively on China). The preamble did specifically mention assistance provided by 'the socialist countries and neighboring countries'. Similarly, the United States was not mentioned by name; part of the reference to the 'colonialists and ... imperialists' clearly referred to the United States, but this was now put in a historical context and Vietnam sought much better relationships with its former enemy.[4]

---

[3] 1992 Constitution, Preamble, para 1.
[4] 1992 Constitution, Preamble, para 2.

The key background for drafting the 1992 Constitution was explicitly stated in the preamble:

> Starting in 1986, a comprehensive national renewal advocated by the 6th Congress of the Communist Party of Vietnam has achieved very important initial results. The National Assembly has decided to revise the 1980 Constitution in response to the requirements of the new situation and tasks.

The description of the constitution itself was largely apolitical, save for the role of the Party

> This Constitution establishes our political regime, economic system, social and cultural institutions; it deals with our national defence and security, the fundamental rights and duties of the citizen, the structure and principles regarding the organization and activity of State organs; it institutionalizes the relationship between the Party as leader, the people as master, and the State as administrator.

The preamble closed, and the remainder of the constitution opened, on a stirring and, in historical context, less political rhetoric:

> In the light of Marxism-Leninism and Ho Chi Minh Thought, carrying into effect the programme of national construction in the period of transition to socialism, the Vietnamese people vow to unite millions as one, uphold the spirit of self-reliance in building the country, carry out a foreign policy of independence, sovereignty, peace, friendship and cooperation with all nations, strictly abide by the Constitution, and win ever greater successes in their effort to renovate, build and defend their motherland.[5]

THE POLITICAL SYSTEM: THE ROLE
OF THE COMMUNIST PARTY

The 1992 Constitution defined the Socialist Republic of Vietnam as 'a State of the people, from the people, for the people', consciously echoing language used by Ho Chi Minh and his colleagues back to 1945 and before.

> All State power belongs to the people and is based on an alliance between the working class, the peasantry, and the intelligentsia.

Contrast this to the much more highly politicised and revolutionary formulation for the definition of the Vietnamese state in the 1980

---

[5] 1992 Constitution, Preamble, paras 3, 4 and 5.

Constitution: 'The Socialist Republic of Vietnam is a State of proletarian dictatorship'.[6]

What is the role of the state? By 1992, it was largely unobjectionable, and except for some initial nod to socialist theory it would have been at home in most countries:

> The State guarantees and unceasingly promotes the people's mastery in all fields, and severely punishes all acts violating the interests of the motherland and the people; it strives to build a rich and strong country in which social justice prevails, all men have enough to eat and to wear, enjoy freedom, happiness, and all necessary conditions for complete development.

Again, contrast this to the harder and more politicised formulation for the role of the state in the 1980 Constitution, just 12 years earlier but far removed in terms of the policies of the Vietnamese Party and state:

> The State ensures the continuous perfection and consolidation of the working people's collective mastery in the political, economic, cultural and social fields; collective mastery in the whole country, and in each unit; collective mastery over society, over nature, and over oneself.[7]

After the definition of the nation and the state came the definition of the role of the party, the single most criticised and controversial element of the 1992 Constitution among domestic political and overseas Vietnamese dissidents. Given those criticisms, the famous article 4 is worth quoting in full:

> The Communist Party of Vietnam, the vanguard of the Vietnamese working class, the faithful representative of the rights and interests of the working class, the toiling people, and the whole nation, acting upon the Marxist-Leninist doctrine and Ho Chi Minh Thought, is the force leading the State and society *(la luc luong lanh dao Nha nuoc va xa hoi)*. All Party organizations operate within the framework of *(hoat dong trong khuon kho)* the Constitution and the law.

This formulation of the role of the Communist Party is subtly different from the wording used in 1980, and that change of wording in turn resulted from broad and serious debate among the drafters of the 1992 Constitution. The 1980 Constitution referred to the Communist Party as

---

[6] 1992 Constitution, art 2; and 1980 Constitution, art 2.
[7] 1992 Constitution, art 3; and 1980 Constitution, art 3. The reference to 'all men have enough to eat and to wear' in the 1992 Constitution reflects the official Vietnamese translation of the 1992 Constitution into English and is a mistake; the official Vietnamese version clearly uses the term for 'people' or 'person' in Vietnamese *(nguoi)*.

'the *only* force leading the State and society',[8] and by 1992 the term 'only' had been deleted from the constitution. This one word shift may not seem important to the foreign reader, but it was important in Vietnam—the party was 'the force leading the State and society', but it need not be the only such force, opening the door for very gradual moves to begin strengthening and differentiating the role of the government and the National Assembly, and to begin recognising the positive roles that business, mass organisations and other sectors of society might have.[9]

To domestic and overseas critics, this was but a small point—to them, there was no substantive difference between the Communist Party as 'the force leading the State and society' and 'the only force leading the State and society'. And for those critics this shift in language was also minor because of historical precedent: the hard-line Constitution of 1959 had contained no 'force leading' language in the text of the constitution itself (although it had clearly recognised the monopoly role of the party in the 1959 preamble), and the party had gone unmentioned as a leading force in the broad-based Constitution of 1946. However, these constitutional wordings are crucially important, and the Vietnamese Party was acknowledging—eagerly by some leaders, begrudgingly by others—that other forces could come to play some sort of significant role in Vietnamese state and society without supplanting the leadership role of the party.

The other shift in article 4 in 1992 was in the often-ignored second paragraph, which states that: 'All Party organizations operate within the framework of the Constitution and the law.' There were two differences between this formulation and the wording of the 1980 Constitution. First, in the 1992 formulation, the idea that party organisations must 'operate within the framework' of 'the law' was new; article 4 of the 1980 Constitution had stated that '[t]he Party's organizations operate within the framework of the Constitution' without mentioning operating within the framework of the law. Secondly, the 1980 text had spoken rather generically of 'the Party's organizations', while the 1992 formulation emphasised—using a clear and different terminology in Vietnamese—that it covered 'all' party organisations.[10]

---

[8] 1980 Constitution, art 4 (emphasis added here). In Vietnamese, the 1980 formulation was '*la luc luong duy nhat lanh dao Nha nuoc, lanh dao xa hoi*' (art 4).

[9] See also ch 1 on the role and dual existence of state and party constitutions.

[10] The 1992 formulation could also be translated even more strongly than the official English translation of 'all Party organizations'. It could also be translated as: 'Every Party organization operates within the framework of the Constitution and the law.'

These may seem to domestic and overseas critics, once again, like the smallest of formal concessions to a new era without changing the basic point—that the Communist Party rules Vietnam and, in their view, stands above the law. It must be re-emphasised that these textual changes did not, in any way, change the ruling power and dominance of the Communist Party in Vietnam. However, again, the wording is different, and the new formulation does indeed emphasise—at least in rhetorical terms—that 'all' or 'every' party organisation operates within the framework of the constitution and the law.

What is meant by 'operates within the framework of' the constitution (1980) or the constitution and the law (1992)? Why not just say 'abides by', 'observes' or 'obeys' the constitution? That language was certainly available to the drafters of the 1992 Constitution; they use it but five paragraphs earlier, in the preamble, where the Vietnamese people are adjured to 'strictly abide by the Constitution', and eight articles later, when state institutions, the military and citizens are required to 'strictly observe the Constitution and the law'. Furthermore, that kind of language is used several times in the 1980 Constitution as well.

'Operate within the framework of the Constitution' (or the constitution and the law) is an awkward formulation, but more importantly it is a more flexible and largely non-legal formulation that does not recognise clearly and strictly the legal hierarchy of the constitution (or the constitution and the law) over the party in the way that 'abide by', 'observe' or 'obey' would require. It is a formulation considerably less specific and largely unsusceptible to judicial or other review, one that emphasises structure and behaviour rather than law, a formulation that can both require the party to 'operate within the framework of the Constitution and the law', while also maintaining the party's predominance in the first paragraph of that same article.

THE POLITICAL SYSTEM: INSTITUTIONAL ELEMENTS

The chapter on the political system in the 1992 Constitution also refers to 'equality, solidarity and mutual assistance' among Vietnam's nationalities in stronger terms than in 1980; begins the process of defining the role of the National Assembly, people's councils and people's committees; retains a right to recall members of the National Assembly, people's councils or people's committees; maintains a strongly worded article against official bureaucratism, arrogance and arbitrariness and adds corruption to the list of those evils; and defines the role of the

Vietnam Fatherland Front (the umbrella organisation for Vietnam's party-related mass organisations).[11]

The 1992 Constitution also recognises the role of the trade unions, emphasising their role 'in looking after and safeguarding the rights and interests of cadres, workers, employees and other labouring people' in stronger terms than the 1980 Constitution, in recognition of the changing role of trade unions in Vietnam. It defines the basic role of citizens and state institutions; requires state institutions and citizens to oppose threats to Vietnam's 'independence, unity, sovereignty, and territorial integrity'; and sets forth a foreign policy of 'peace and friendship' and to:

> expand … relations and cooperation with all countries in the world regardless of political and social system on the basis of respect for each other's independence, sovereignty, and territorial integrity

a far cry from the 1980 Constitution's prioritisation of strengthening 'fraternal friendship, militant solidarity and cooperation in all fields' with 'the Soviet Union, Laos, Cambodia and other socialist countries', followed by developing friendly relations and peaceful coexistence with other nations.[12]

THE ECONOMIC SYSTEM

The 1980 Constitution emphasised the building of socialism, socialist industrialisation, the centrally run economy, the leading role of the state sector in the national economy, state monopoly in foreign trade and foreign economic relations, the 'socialist transformation of the private capitalist economy' and a subservient role for private, cooperative and other forms of business. By 1992, six years after *doi moi* began, the situation was different. The 1992 Constitution emphasised the building of a 'multi-component commodity economy functioning in accordance with market mechanisms under the management of the State and following the socialist orientation'—a clause laden with political terminology that nonetheless clearly recognised the emerging role of market forces and mechanisms together with the socialist tradition of central planning, and helped to lead to a new generation of laws governing foreign investment, domestic business and other economic legislation.[13]

---

[11] 1992 Constitution, arts 5–9.
[12] 1992 Constitution, arts 10–14.
[13] 1992 Constitution, art 15.

The constitution recognised state ownership, collective ownership, private ownership and other forms of economic activity, and state monopoly on the management of land along with entrusting land to organisations and individuals for usage, together with 'the right to transfer the land entrusted to them by the state, as determined by law'—a complex formulation that recognised the state's crucial role in land management, but left open increasingly private usage arrangements that multiplied throughout the 1990s. It stressed that 'the state sector shall … play the leading role in the national economy', while recognising and encouraging the rapidly growing roles of the collective sector, private sectors and the family economy, joint ventures and partnerships—both domestic and with foreign entities.[14]

The 1992 Constitution takes a much firmer position against nationalisation of 'lawful property' than the 1980 charter, requiring compensation that takes into account market prices when forcible purchases of property are required; the 1980 Constitution did not require compensation. In addition, the new constitution guaranteed 'right to lawful ownership of funds, property and other interests by foreign organizations and individuals' and that 'enterprises with foreign investments shall not be nationalized'. Both were new formulations. The chapter on the economic system also sought to prohibit:

> all illegal production and trading activities, all acts wrecking the national economy and damaging the interests of the State, the rights and lawful interests of collectives and individual citizens.[15]

The chapter on the economic system was arguably the most important portion of the 1992 Constitution, for it sought to delineate and govern—in general terms to be further specified in other legislation—the legal contours of a transition to a socialist market economy—what article 15 called, awkwardly but following the ideology of *doi moi*:

> a multi-component commodity economy functioning in accordance with market mechanisms under the management of the State and following the socialist orientation.

Law would have trouble keeping up with the rapid transition toward a market economy, and in 2001 the constitution would be revised again to keep pace with these rapid changes, as discussed in the next chapter. However, the tenor of the chapter on the economic system in the 1992

---

[14] 1992 Constitution, arts 15 and 18–22.
[15] 1992 Constitution, arts 23, 25 and 28.

Constitution was one of rapid change, yet hopefully, in the eyes of the drafters and the party, constrained by party and state policy.

CULTURE, EDUCATION, SCIENCE AND TECHNOLOGY

In the arena of culture, education, science and technology, the 1992 Constitution sought to recognise and solidify the liberalisation in these fields since the beginning of the *doi moi* era in 1986, while maintaining the state's primary role and political control over the administration of these important activities. So the state preserves and develops Vietnamese culture, while it also forbids 'reactionary and depraved thought and culture' and 'superstitions and harmful customs'; it fosters and invests in literature and the arts; promotes the press, radio, television, cinema, publishers, libraries and other communications channels, while banning activities 'detrimental to national interests, and destructive of the personality, morals, and fine lifestyle of the Vietnamese'; and preserves and develops Vietnam's cultural heritage and punishes damage to historical sites, art and preserved landscapes.[16]

Several articles state the government's commitment to developing education and training as 'top-priority policies' and several more reiterate the same commitment to science, technology and public health. Priority investment for education and health is to be given to those who live in the highlands, national minorities and other special groups.[17]

RIGHTS AND DUTIES OF CITIZENS

The 1992 Constitution broadens and simplifies the overall declaration of citizens' rights compared to the 1980 Constitution. Gone is language about the 'collective mastery of the working people', 'harmonious combination of the requirements of social life and legitimate individual freedoms' and 'identity of interests between the State, the collective and the individual'. Now the basic article on rights states:

> In the Socialist Republic of Vietnam human rights in the political, civil, economic, cultural and social fields are respected. They are embodied in the citizen's rights and are determined by the Constitution and the law.[18]

---

[16] 1992 Constitution, arts 30–34.
[17] 1992 Constitution, arts 35–40.
[18] 1992 Constitution, art 50; and 1980 Constitution, art 54.

That simpler statement broadens the overall conception of rights in a rhetorical sense only; it gives no detail or clue to their implementation other than the limiting language set forth in article 50 itself—such rights are 'determined by the Constitution and the law'. The constitution carries forward the traditional relationship between rights and duties:

> The citizen's rights are inseparable from his duties. The State guarantees the rights of the citizen; the citizen must fulfil his duties to the State and society.[19]

On specific rights, the constitution mentions the right to 'participate in the administration of the State and management of society', including rights to send petitions and 'vote in referendums organized by the State', a conscious reference to and tie back to the 1946 Constitution. The constitution also:

guarantees the right to vote at the age of 18 and to stand for the National Assembly and People's Councils at the age of 21;

guarantees the right and duty to work;

requires the state to establish labour protection standards; provides for 'freedom of enterprise';

includes a significantly expanded 'right of ownership [of] lawful income, savings, housing, goods and chattels, means of production, funds and other possessions in enterprises or other economic organizations';

guarantees rights of inheritance; and

guarantees the right to receive education and training, including free primary school education—an issue that would re-arise in 2001, when most primary education had become *de facto* fee paying.[20]

The constitution maintains the protection of citizens' rights to undertake scientific and technical research, literary and artistic creation and criticism, and protects copyright and industrial property rights, largely a continuation of the provision of the 1980 Constitution on these issues. It protects:

the right to health care;

'the right to build dwelling-houses according to zoning regulations and the law', including rights of lessees and lessors;

---

[19] 1992 Constitution, art 51.
[20] 1992 Constitution, arts 53–9.

gender rights and gender equality;

family and marriage rights;

children's rights in a general provision; and

preferential treatment for 'war invalids, sick soldiers, and the families of fallen soldiers and revolutionary martyrs'.[21]

The 1992 Constitution expands the 1980 provision guaranteeing freedom of movement and residence. The 1980 provision had limited and qualified those freedoms 'in accordance with the law', but the 1992 Constitution deletes the qualification. The 1992 provision includes the new stipulation that '[t]he citizen … can freely travel abroad and return home from abroad in accordance with the provision of the law'—a provision impossible under the 1980 conditions of escape and boat people.[22]

The clause on basic political freedoms in the 1992 Constitution comes only at article 69, after the other freedoms mentioned above, and reflecting Vietnamese prioritisation of other forms of individual, economic, family and other rights before political rights. At the same time, the 1992 Constitution somewhat expands—in textual form—the political freedoms available for speech, the press, 'the right to be informed', assembly, association and demonstration. They remain limited, to be sure, using the now-standard qualification 'in accordance with the provisions of the law', but that limitation is itself textually narrower than the very broad limitation of the 1980 political freedoms clause. In the 1980 Constitution, similar political freedoms were limited by the qualification 'in accordance with the interests of socialism and of the people'. This difference, as in other provisions of the 1992 Constitution, also indicates a graduate 'legalisation' of constitutional terms. Freedoms may still be limited, for example, but their perhaps still broad limitations are expressed in terms of law rather than in terms of politics ('the interests of socialism and of the people').[23]

Religious freedom is also guaranteed in formal terms in the 1992 Constitution, through the provision of article 70 that '[t]he citizen shall enjoy freedom of belief and of religion; he can follow any religion or follow none'. Although enforcement of the religious freedom clause remains a significant problem, the clause itself was expanded from the 1980 Constitution to include a constitutional statement that '[a]ll religions

---

[21] 1992 Constitution, arts 60–67.

[22] 1992 Constitution, art 68; and 1980 Constitution, art 71.

[23] 1992 Constitution, art 69; and 1980 Constitution, art 67.

are equal before the law' and '[t]he places of worship of all faiths and religions' are protected. Inevitably, there is an important qualification to the religious freedom clause, given continuing actions by the Vietnamese state against independent Buddhist groups, house churches and some other religious groups. The limiting clause states that 'no one can misuse belief and religions to contravene the law and State policies'.

The 1992 Constitution also guarantees 'inviolability of the person and the protection of the law with regard to … life, health, honour and dignity'. The 'inviolability' clause has also been expanded from the 1980 Constitution, primarily by a provision limiting the cases in which arrests can be made without judicial or prosecutorial sanction. The 1980 Constitution allowed arrests subject to later ratification by the procuracy, while the 1992 Constitution allows arrests without judicial or procuracy approval only for 'flagrant offences', and adds a provision, absent in 1980, that '[t]aking a person into, or holding him in, custody must be done with full observance of the law'. Harassment, coercion, torture and violation of honour and dignity are also prohibited. As with the religious freedom clause, textual guarantees are not enforcement, and enforcement of these freedoms is the continuing issue.[24]

The 1992 Constitution also provides for the presumption of innocence, compensation for damages from arrest, detention, prosecution or trial in violation of law and punishment for those committing such acts, inviolability of domicile, security of correspondence and communications, searches only under authority of law, and the right to file complaints and denunciations 'against the illegal [acts] of State organs, economic bodies, social organizations, units of the people's armed forces, or … any individual' and the principles for dealing with such cases.[25]

The constitution also broadened the provisions for protecting the rights of Vietnamese residing abroad, a complex and controversial topic within Vietnam. The 1980 Constitution had stated in summary fashion that: 'The State protects the legitimate rights and interests of overseas Vietnamese.' As part of a new policy of gradually reaching out to the Vietnamese diaspora around the world, the new constitution expanded that stipulation to provide that:

> The State shall protect the legitimate rights and interests of Vietnamese living abroad … [and] shall create the necessary conditions for Vietnamese

---

[24] 1992 Constitution, art 71; and 1980 Constitution, art 69.
[25] 1992 Constitution, arts 72–4.

residing abroad to maintain close ties with their families and native land and to contribute to national construction.

As discussed in the next chapter, the 2001 revision to the 1992 Constitution expanded the overseas Vietnamese provision of the constitution by re-emphasising their role in the transnational Vietnamese community:

> Overseas Vietnamese make up a part of the Vietnamese nationalities community. The State protects the legitimate rights and interests of Vietnamese residing abroad

and adds that the state 'encourages and creates conditions for Vietnamese residing abroad to preserve ... Vietnamese cultural identity', in addition to maintaining close ties and contributing to national construction.[26]

Duties come after rights, and the 1992 Constitution requires citizens to be loyal to Vietnam, calling betrayal of the country 'the most serious crime', to defend the nation and fulfil military obligations, to respect and protect state property and the public interest, 'to obey the Constitution and the law' and to pay taxes and perform labour in the public interest. Foreigners are specifically enjoined to 'obey the Constitution and law of Vietnam'.[27]

THE NATIONAL ASSEMBLY

The 1992 Constitution maintained and sought to enhance the role of the National Assembly as 'the highest representative organ of the people' and 'the only organ with constitutional and legislative powers', both reflecting and contributing to a gradual rise in the standing and role of the Assembly in the more than 20 years since the *doi moi* (renovation) era began. It adds 'the country's national defence and security issues' to the list of matters decided upon by the Assembly, although the transition to a fully participatory role in those matters is still very much in process.

Article 84 sets out the specific obligations and powers of the National Assembly, which include:

making and amending the constitution and laws;
exercising 'supreme control [or supervision] over conformity to the Constitution, the law and the resolutions of the National Assembly';

---

[26] 1980 Constitution, art 75; and 1992 Constitution, art 75 and revised art 75.
[27] 1992 Constitution, arts 76–81.

examining the reports of executive, legislative, judicial and prosecutorial
    bodies;

deciding on plans for social and economic development;

deciding on financial and monetary policies, budgets and taxes;

determining nationalities policy;

'regulat[ing] the organization and activity; of the Assembly, the State
    President, the government, the judiciary, procuracy and local
    administration;

electing and removing all central state, legislative, government, judicial,
    procuracy and other officials (including members of the National
    Assembly itself);

establishing and eliminating government ministries and agencies,
    provincial and centrally administered city boundaries;

proclaiming amnesties, military and diplomatic titles and ranks;

deciding issues of war and peace;

proclaiming states of emergency;

deciding on foreign policy; and

holding referenda.

Many of these powers are similar to those in the 1980 Constitution,
although in some cases they have been somewhat expanded—and in
a few cases, like the referendum power, they have been re-added to
the constitution.[28] In formal and textual terms, the expansion of the
National Assembly's role in the 1992 Constitution makes Vietnam
look somewhat like a system of parliamentary supremacy, but the
Vietnamese know that core power still lies with the party, and readers
outside Vietnam should continue to remind themselves of that as well.

The National Assembly has a term of five years, with a new Assembly
elected at least two months before the new term. It meets twice a
year, and for special meetings called by the State President, the Prime
Minister or one-third of the Assembly. A full range of legislative, executive, judicial, procuracy and other groups may submit draft laws to the
Assembly. The 1992 Constitution includes a new provision allowing
National Assembly delegates to 'present motions concerning laws and
draft laws' to the Assembly, and requires that procedures for dealing
with legislation be established by law. A majority of the Assembly is
needed to adopt law and resolutions, with special actions such as constitutional amendments requiring a two-thirds vote.[29]

---

[28] 1992 Constitution, arts 83 and 84.
[29] 1992 Constitution, arts 85–8.

Since the 1950s, the Vietnamese National Assembly has had a powerful Standing Committee (or a body with a similar function), which has come to conduct most of the National Assembly's work given the unwieldy size of that group and its occasional meetings, until recently gathering but twice a year. The 1992 Constitution defines the Standing Committee as the 'permanent committee' of the National Assembly, but that understates its role. Its specific duties and powers, enumerated in article 91, give a clearer idea of its standing in the Vietnamese legislative process, including its crucial role in the Vietnamese constitutional process. The Standing Committee calls and presides over Assembly elections, prepares for, convenes and presides over Assembly sessions, 'interpret[s] the Constitution, the law, and decree-laws', enforces decrees, 'exercise[s] supervision and control over the implementation of the Constitution, the law, the resolutions of the National Assembly' and other legislative, executive, judicial and procuracy activities, including suspending execution of orders of the central government, judiciary and procuracy that 'contravene the Constitution' laws or Assembly resolutions, exercising supervision and control over local people's councils, the committees of the National Assembly, proclaiming a state of war when the Assembly is not in session, ordering mobilisations of troops, proclaiming states of emergency and 'organiz[ing] a referendum following decision by the National Assembly'.[30]

The constitution also makes provision for the role of the Chairman of the National Assembly, the Assembly's Nationalities Council and committees, requires government ministers and other senior officials, including the heads of the judiciary and procuracy, to report to the Assembly and specifies that National Assembly deputies 'represent[] the will and aspirations of the people, not only of his [or her] constituency but of the whole country'. National Assembly deputies may question the State President, the Prime Minister, government ministers and the heads of the judiciary and procuracy, as well as government agencies and other bodies.[31]

THE STATE PRESIDENT

The role of the President of Vietnam has been complex since the days when Ho Chi Minh held the position, from the 1940s until his death

---

[30] 1992 Constitution, arts 90 and 91.
[31] 1992 Constitution, arts 92–8.

in 1969. After Ho's death, a collective presidency, called the Council of State, was specified in the 1980 Constitution, serving both as the Standing Committee of the National Assembly and as the collective presidency for the nation. In time, that structure was considered unwieldy and ineffective—the legislative roles of a Standing Committee not meshing well with the executive and foreign relations role of a president—and so the two functions were split in the 1992 Constitution. The functions of the Council of State relating to the functioning and supervision of the National Assembly and the legislative process became the province of the renewed and strengthened Standing Committee of the National Assembly, while the renewed State President—last stipulated in the 1959 Constitution—'represents the Socialist Republic of Vietnam internally and externally'.[32]

In formal terms, the President is elected by the National Assembly from its members and reports to the Assembly, although the party plays the key role in selecting the President. The President's duties and powers include:

promulgating (formally releasing into force) the constitution, laws and decree-laws;
'hav[ing] overall command of the armed forces' and serving as Chairman of the National Defence and Security Council;
proposing the election and removal of the Vice President, Prime Minister and the presidents of the Supreme People's Court and Procuracy;
appointing and dismissing the Deputy Prime Ministers, ministers and other senior government officials based on resolutions of the National Assembly;
proclaiming a state of emergency and amnesties;
appointing and removing senior national judges and prosecutors;
conferring military and diplomatic ranks and titles and national honours; and
appointing ambassadors and concluding international agreements, including submitting them to the National Assembly for ratification.

In addition to articles on the President's role in the National Defence and Security Council, permitting the President to attend National Assembly sessions and government meetings, and to issue orders and decisions to accomplish the President's duties, the constitution has little more to say

---

[32] 1992 Constitution, art 101.

on the role of the President.[33] In recent years, the role of the President has to some degree depended on the political strength of the person holding that office, national needs and party decisions, leading to work not specifically mentioned in the constitution. For example, as of 2008 the current President and the one right before him headed the Judicial Reform Steering Committee, which is responsible for undertaking significant reforms in the court system, since the President is a highly placed member of the party (always a member of the party's Political Bureau) and is well placed to work with and direct the courts, procuracy, National Assembly, police and security forces and others on judicial issues.

THE GOVERNMENT

The government of the Socialist Republic of Vietnam is defined in the 1992 Constitution as 'the executive organ of the National Assembly, the highest organ of State administration'. It is responsible for all of the 'political, economic, cultural, social, national defence, security and external duties' of the Vietnamese state, although of course the party plays a central role in all of these activities as well, and the relationship between party and state tasks has been an enduring issue in both pre-renovation days and the *doi moi* era as well. The constitution also makes the government responsible for 'ensur[ing] respect for and implementation of the Constitution and the law', in addition to the National Assembly and other bodies. The government is 'accountable' to the National Assembly and reports to the National Assembly, the Assembly's Standing Committee and the President of Vietnam.

By constitutional mandate, the Vietnamese Government consists of a Prime Minister, Deputy Prime Ministers, cabinet ministers and other senior officials. The government's formal duties and powers are common to most executive branches around the world. They include:

directing the work of ministries and other agencies, including local
    People's Councils and People's Committees;
ensuring the implementation of the constitution and the law;
drafting legislation for the National Assembly to consider;
managing the economy and national fiscal policies;
promoting socio-economic development, education, culture, science
    and technology;

---

[33] 1992 Constitution, arts 102–8.

protecting citizens' rights;
protecting the environment;
strengthening national defence;
proclaiming states of emergency when needed;
fighting corruption;
managing foreign relations; and
implementing policies on nationalities and religion.

Governments in Vietnam normally have terms of five years, co-terminous with those of the National Assembly.[34]

Of these tasks for a national government, perhaps the least familiar to Western readers would be the duty to 'ensure respect for and implementation of the Constitution' as stated (in slightly different terms) in articles 109 and 112 of the 1992 Constitution. As To Van Hoa and other Vietnamese scholars have noted, since the 1950s Vietnam's political leaders and constitutional drafters have made a range of institutions, including the National Assembly and the government, responsible for ensuring implementation of the constitution, partly to avoid assigning the power of constitutional review to the judiciary or to a constitutional court. The result is a fragmented set of mandates for constitutional implementation involving the National Assembly, the Assembly's Standing Committee, the government, government agencies and even People's Councils and People's Committees—a system that is now under sustained attack, discussed in Chapter 9, as Vietnam discusses very different models for constitutional review and ensuring obedience to the constitution.[35]

The Prime Minister's role in this system will also not surprise observers of most other executive branch systems. He directs the work of the government, proposes the appointment and removal of senior government officials to the National Assembly for decision, appoints and dismisses officials at deputy minister rank, approves election and dismissal of the chairs and vice chairs of the People's Committees of provinces and centrally administered cities (Hanoi, Ho Chi Minh City, Hai Phong and Da Nang), has a direct role in suspending or annulling decisions, directives, circulars and resolutions of cabinet ministers, other government members, People's Councils and People's

---

[34] 1992 Constitution, arts 109–13.
[35] See To Van-Hoa, *Judicial Independence* (Lund, Jurisförlaget i Lund, 2006) (particularly Pt V, chs XVI-XIX); and Bui Ngoc Son, *Bao Hien o Viet Nam* (*Constitutional Protection in Vietnam*) (Hanoi, Judicial Publishing House, 2006).

Committees 'that contravene the Constitution, the law, and other formal written documents of superior State organs' and makes regular reports to the Vietnamese people, among other tasks. Both the government and the Prime Minister are empowered to issue resolutions and decrees (in the case of the government), and decisions and directives (in the case of the Prime Minister) in furtherance of their work.

Cabinet ministers and other senior government officials are responsible for state management in their fields of authority and 'ensur[ing] … autonomy in production and business activities of establishments according to the provisions of law'. This provision was strengthened and broadened in 2001 to indicate that business activities should also be protected. Ministers and other senior officials may issue decisions, directives and circulars in support of their work. They report to the Prime Minister and the National Assembly.[36]

LOCAL PEOPLE'S COUNCILS AND PEOPLE'S COMMITTEES

The 1992 Constitution divides the nation into provinces and cities under direct central administration (which include Hanoi, Ho Chi Minh City, Hai Phong and Da Nang). Provinces are further divided into districts, provincial cities and towns, with cities under direct central administration being divided into urban districts, rural districts and towns. In turn, rural districts are divided into communes and townlets, and urban districts into wards. People's Councils are legislative organisations for the local level in Vietnam; they are the analogue to the National Assembly at the national level and adopt local resolutions to implement the constitution and national laws, local socio-economic development plans and budgets, and other economic and administrative measures. People's Councils consist of deputies elected in direct elections at the local level; they have the right to question local executive, judicial and procuracy officials.

The People's Committee is the 'executive organ' of the People's Council, 'the organ of local state administration'. It implements the constitution, national law, the orders of higher executive bodies and the resolutions of the local People's Council, and it may issue decisions and directives on its own authority to undertake its administrative work.[37]

---

[36] 1992 Constitution, arts 114–17.
[37] 1992 Constitution, arts 118–24.

The role of the People's Councils and People's Committees has been under virtually constant discussion in Vietnam since the *doi moi* era began, particularly because the Communist Party's role remains very strong at the local level, leaving three institutions with authority in local areas. The People's Councils—like the National Assembly in Hanoi—are often weak legislative institutions, and have sought more authority over local affairs. People's Committees have been called both too restrictive and too relaxed at different times and in different places. The role of the party vis-à-vis both is complex and not yet fully worked out. Vietnamese observers of the People's Councils and the People's Committees expect that these continuing discussions, and the evolution of these legislative and executive bodies, will require significant constitutional amendment when the 1992 Constitution is again revised, in 2011 or 2012—an issue to which we will return in the conclusion.

THE COURTS AND THE PROCURACY

The 1992 Constitution defines the role of the people's courts and the procuracy as to:

> within the bounds of their functions, safeguard ... socialist legality, the socialist regime and the people's mastery, the property of the State and the collectives, [and] the lives, property, freedom, honour and dignity of the citizen.

That formulation is similar to the definition of judicial and procuratorial roles in the 1980 Constitution, but the 1980 document also provided a second broad and highly politicised function that was deleted from the 1992 document. The 1980 Constitution had required that:

> [a]ny act encroaching upon the interests of the State or the collective or the legitimate interests of citizens must be dealt with in accordance with the law.

The constitution defines the judicial organs to include the Supreme People's Court, local people's courts, military tribunals and other courts established by law, including special tribunals established under special circumstances by the National Assembly—a provision that could be used, in future, to set up a constitutional court or a constitutional tribunal within the Supreme Court, as some Vietnamese have advocated. The constitution requires the use of non-judge people's assessors in people's and military courts, lay judges with a status equal to that of a judge during trials.[38] The system of people's assessors has had both defenders and attackers in Vietnam (as in China), and may at some point be eliminated as the judicial corps becomes more professionalised. People's assessors are chosen from among trusted local citizens, most if not all party members. To proponents of the system, it serves to provide a citizen's perspective on court cases and a reality check on judicial decision making. To opponents, it symbolises lack of legal professionalism in judicial decisions, a further opportunity for pressure or corruption and another way for local party and government officials to control case outcomes.

As discussed later, in Chapter 8 on judicial independence, the 1992 Constitution requires that 'at trial, the judges and assessors are independent and shall only obey the law'. This relatively clear but limited guarantee and concept of judicial independence is now coming under energetic discussion in Vietnam, as further discussed below.

The constitution defines the Supreme People's Court as 'the highest judicial organ of the Socialist Republic of Vietnam' and stipulates that it 'supervises and directs the judicial work of local People's Courts and military tribunals'. There is a limitation here that is clear to Vietnamese eyes, but may not be so clear to foreign readers: the Supreme Court supervises and directs the 'judicial work' of local and military courts. However, it does not supervise or direct the administrative work of those local and military courts, nor does it appoint their judges. Those tasks are the responsibility, respectively, of local people's councils or of the military. The next article makes explicit that while '[t]he President of the Supreme People's Court is responsible and makes his reports, to the National Assembly', the reporting relationship of local people's courts is not upward to the Supreme People's Courts, except in technical and legal elements of 'judicial work'. Instead, as article 135 provides, '[t]he President of the local People's Courts is responsible, and makes his reports, to the National Assembly'.[39] This dual reporting problem, and the continuing influence of local party and state officials on court appointments and judgments, is the topic of continuing and energetic debate in Vietnam and a topic in the ongoing judicial reform approved by the party in 2005. It is discussed further in Chapter 8 on judicial independence, including a specific case in which these issues were raised directly.

---

[38] 1992 Constitution, arts 126–9; and 1980 Constitution, art 127.
[39] 1992 Constitution, arts 134 and 135.

Courts hold their hearings in public, 'except in cases determined by law'; defendants have a right to defence, and 'an organization of barristers' is specified:

> to help the defendant and other parties in a law case to defend their rights and legitimate interests and contribute to the safeguarding of socialist legality.

Minority nationalities are guaranteed that they may use their own languages and writing systems in court.

Finally, but importantly, the constitution attempts to help in resolving the continuing problem of government institutions, economic organisations, military units and individual citizens ignoring the judgments rendered by local, appellate and national courts. Article 136 provides that:

> The sentences and decisions of the People's Court which have acquired legal effect must be respected by State organs, economic bodies, social organizations, people's armed units and all citizens; they must be seriously implemented by the individuals and organs concerned.[40]

The constitutional and political trend in Vietnam has been to strengthen the role of the judiciary over time—very gradually, to be sure, under strict party control, and with much difficulty, a task still much closer to its beginning than its end in Vietnam given the weaknesses of judicial power and capacity and the continuing strength of national and local party and state officials over judicial affairs. The constitutional and political trend with regard to the procuracy—that curious institutional artefact of Soviet and Chinese practice that found its way to Vietnam—has been to narrow the role and functions of this institution.

In 1980, when the role of the procuracy may have reached its height and greatest expanse, the constitution required that the procuracy:

> shall control the observance of the law by the ministries and other [executive] bodies, local organs of power, social organizations, State employees, and all citizens, exercise the right of public prosecution; and ensure the strict and uniform observance of the law.

This gave the procuracy not only the chief role in public prosecutions that is perhaps most familiar to readers of this volume, but also a powerful role as a kind of inspector-general in ensuring that government and other agencies and citizens observe the law, including enabling the procuracy to serve as both prosecutor in court and ensuring that the courts implement the law as it believed necessary.

---

[40] 1992 Constitution, arts 131–3 and 136.

The 1992 Constitution initially gave the procuracy a similar mandate. The Supreme People's Procuracy[41]:

> supervises and controls obedience to the law by ministries [and other government agencies]; local organs of power, social organizations, people's armed units and citizens; it exercises the right to initiate public prosecution, [and] ensures a serious and uniform implementation of the law.

Throughout the 1990s—and, it must be said, even when the 1992 Constitution was discussed and adopted—the role of the procuracy was coming under sustained discussion and attack. Executive, legislative and judicial forces decried the low quality of its work and its overly powerful role as inspector-general for obedience to law for virtually all other state agencies, and they and legal reformers called for narrowing the procuracy's role to that of public prosecutions.[42]

That process began with the 2001 amendments to the 1992 Constitution. After significant debate, including attempts by the Supreme People's Procuracy to beat back attempts to narrow its authority, the National Assembly approved an amended article 137, which states:

> The Supreme People's Procuracy shall exercise the right to public prosecution and inspection of judicial activities, thus contributing to ensuring that laws are strictly and uniformly observed.

A related amendment narrowed the scope of reporting by local heads of procuracies to their respective people's councils—away from the broad reporting to the people's councils 'on the situation in law enforcement in … respective localities' under the 1992 Constitution, which involved reporting on the work of the judiciary, and toward reporting solely on their own work with a focus on public prosecution.[43] Yet even the substantial narrowing of the amended article 137 from the procuracy's earlier mandates was still far too broad for some delegates and commentators, who continued to advocate for restricting the procuracy's role to public prosecution alone. Since 2001, extensive discussion has continued on the role of the procuracy and improving the quality, accuracy and consistency of public prosecutions. The procuracy (and the police) have also come under regular attacks for cases of false imprisonment and false

---

[41] The Supreme People's Procuracy is termed the People's Office (or Organ) of Supervision and Control in some translations of the constitution and relevant laws, but the terms procuracy and Supreme People's Procuracy are used throughout this volume to refer to this important institution.

[42] 1992 Constitution, arts 137 and 138.

[43] 1992 Constitution, revised arts 137 and 140.

conviction that continue to be uncovered in Vietnam. These cases are taken as examples of the need for upgrading the quality and accuracy of prosecutions and—because the power of the procuracy is regularly blamed for cases of false imprisonment and false conviction—narrowing the role and power of the procuracy at national and local levels.

THE NATIONAL FLAG, EMBLEM, NATIONAL ANTHEM, CAPITAL AND NATIONAL DAY

The constitution defines the national flag of Vietnam, the national emblem, names the national anthem, *March to the Front (Tien quan ca)*, defines the capital of Vietnam as Hanoi and names 'the day of the Declaration of Independence', 2 September 1945, as National Day.[44]

THE ROLE OF THE CONSTITUTION AND ITS AMENDMENT

The constitution's clearly stated role has been mentioned earlier:

> The Constitution of the Socialist Republic of Vietnam is the fundamental law of the State and has the highest legal effect. All other legal documents must conform to the Constitution.

However, this clause does not indicate, for example, the party's relationship to the constitution. To the degree that that is addressed in the constitution, it is specified in the famous article 4, discussed earlier. Constitutional amendment is the province of the National Assembly, and amendments must be approved by two-thirds of the Assembly.[45] A new constitutional amendment process will begin in Vietnam in approximately 2010, leading to what is expected to be a revised constitution in 2011 or 2012. We return to that process in the conclusion.

THE CONTENTIOUS 1990s IN VIETNAM AND THE CONSTITUTION

In the years that followed the promulgation of the 1992 Constitution, political dissidents at home and overseas Vietnamese dissident

---

[44] 1992 Constitution, arts 141–5.
[45] 1992 Constitution, arts 146 and 147.

activists began to challenge elements of the constitutional regime. Their criticisms—sometimes couched in open letters to the party leadership by dissidents in Vietnam, and essays, articles and diatribes from outside the country—dwelt on the continued primacy of the party under article 4, the weaknesses of the courts and of the guarantee of judicial independence in article 130, the continued centrality of socialist, state-owned enterprises in the constitutional framework, the absence of a constitutional court or other mechanism for deciding on constitutional claims (beyond the National Assembly, which had been formally given this task, but had never been allowed to take it up) and other issues.

Within Vietnam, these were small bands of intellectual dissidents largely isolated from other scholars and everyday citizens, but they included some prominent figures, and their criticisms, while not addressed in constitutional redrafting and law-making, were certainly heard. The criticisms of the overseas Vietnamese dissidents were watched as well, but tended to be less sophisticated and more focused on the party's role under article 4 as the core issue of what the overseas dissidents thought of as Hanoi's false constitutionalism.

Vietnam embarked on a constitutional amendment process in the late 1990s that culminated in a major revision to the constitution in 2001. As the next chapter discusses, that process was driven by a sense that Vietnamese society and the economy had moved beyond the circumstances regulated and described in the 1992 Constitution; a revised constitution was needed to keep up with the changes in Vietnamese society. Although the party, National Assembly and the Constitutional Revision Commission would not admit it, the drafting and discussions of constitutional amendments beginning in 2000 indeed benefited from the contentious criticisms levelled by both domestic and overseas dissidents throughout the 1990s.

Few of their primary demands were taken up—article 4 on the primacy of the party was not to be revised to weaken the party's role, for example, nor would a constitutional court or commission make it onto the agenda for constitutional amendment in 2001. However, the angry domestic and overseas voices of the 1990s were still heard in party and state leadership and drafting circles, even where some of those critics were detained, arrested, imprisoned in Vietnam or, in the case of the overseas Vietnamese, barred from returning or deported if they dared to come back. The next debate on Vietnamese constitutionalism, the discussions of 2000 and 2001, would draw on the 1992 Constitution, its eight years in force and the criticisms of it.

FURTHER READING

The 1992 Constitution of the Socialist Republic of Vietnam (as revised by Resolution No 51/2001/QH 10 of 25 December 2001 Amending and Supplementing a Number of Articles of the 1992 Constitution of the Socialist Republic of Vietnam).

Heng, RHK (2002) 'The 1992 Revised Constitution of Vietnam: Background and Scope of Changes' 4:3 *Contemporary Southeast Asia* 221.

Ngo Ba Thanh (1993) 'The Constitution and the Rule of Law' in Thayer, C and Marr, D (eds) *Vietnam and the Rule of Law* (Canberra, Australian National University Political and Social Change Monograph).

Nicholson, P (1999) 'Vietnamese Legal Institutions in Comparative Perspective: Constitutions and Courts Considered' in Jayasuriya, K (ed) *Law, Capitalism and Power in Asia: The Rule of Law and Legal Institutions* (London, Routledge).

Quinn, BJM (2002) 'Legal Reform and Its Context in Vietnam' 15 *Columbia Journal of Asian Law* 219.

Sidel, M (2002) 'Analytical Models for Understanding Constitutions and Constitutional Dialogue in Socialist Transitional States: Re-interpreting Constitutional Dialogue in Vietnam' 6 *Singapore Journal of International and Comparative Law* 42.

—— (2008) *Law and Society in Vietnam* (Cambridge, Cambridge University Press).

To Van-Hoa (2006) *Judicial Independence* (Lund, Jurisförlaget i Lund) (particularly Pt V, chs XVI–XIX).

6

Revising the 1992 Constitution: Debates and Decisions after Fifteen Years of Renovation (Doi Moi)

⟶◦⟵

B
Y THE LATE 1990s, the 1992 Constitution was already showing its age. Numerous and rapid developments in the Vietnamese
process of *doi moi* (renovation) pushed the Vietnamese Party and
state to begin the process of revising and amending the constitution—
in particular, the rapid diversification and resurgence of the economy—
especially the emergence of the private economy, and changing patterns
of governance, including a strengthened role for the National Assembly
and the growth of provincial and local power.

In this context, some provisions of the 1992 Constitution began to
look somewhat passé. They included the sections that focused on the
state-run economy and slighted the role of cooperative and private
forces, articles providing incomplete or out-of-date descriptions of the
role of the National Assembly and other institutions of government;
out-of-date discussions of the role of law, of the Vietnam Fatherland
Front and other party-supported mass organisations, foreign investment, education, science and technology, the powers and duties of the
National Assembly and its Standing Committee, and the role of the
Supreme People's Procuracy. And so the Vietnamese Communist Party
and legislative institutions turned toward a process of updating the 1992
Constitution.

THE IMPLICATIONS OF CONSTITUTIONAL DEBATE

However, there were also other issues at work, and the Communist
Party was determined to keep some of those out of any constitutional redrafting process. Most important was article 4 of the 1992

Constitution, which states that '[t]he Communist Party of Vietnam ... is the force leading the State and society' and that '[a]ll Party organizations operate within the framework of the Constitution and the law'. Overseas Vietnamese opponents of the party, and some domestic dissidents, had persistently called for the removal of article 4 from the 1992 Constitution or its substantial revision. Dissidents at home and abroad also called for the inclusion of a multiparty system in the constitution, direct elections of party and state personnel, a sharply enhanced role for the National Assembly and other aspects of political reform.

So the party and constitutional re-drafters were faced on one hand with a constitutional document that increasingly appeared out of date, and on the other hand with dissident and liberal forces calling for rapid political reform through constitutional change. After a lengthy and hotly debated process that included those forces as well as others who pressed, no less strongly, for other changes, the Vietnamese National Assembly amended and revised its constitution in 2001 in ways approved by the political leadership. This process was controlled by the Communist Party and was not allowed to result in far-reaching amendments on political reform and constitutionalism. However, at the same time this process of constitutional dialogue, debate, revision and amendment significantly broadened the scope of constitutional debate in Vietnam and served as a fulcrum for airing some of the most important and controversial constitutional issues since the promulgation of the 1946 Constitution.

Why did the Vietnamese Party and state not just leave the constitution alone, avoiding a lengthy and potentially disruptive national debate that threatened at times to spill over into demands for significant political and constitutional reform? The same could be asked of China, where the 1982 Constitution has been revised and amended a number of times over the past 25 years. The answer appears to be that the Vietnamese political and legislative leadership were concerned about a constitution that would increasingly appear irrelevant to governing Vietnamese society, out of touch with Vietnamese realities and not reflecting current party and state policies—and that they firmly believed that they could manage a revision and amendment process without allowing the process to get out of hand in demands for political reform. As discussed earlier in this volume, the constitution and constitutional law are at the apex of law and legal reform in Vietnam. The notion of an increasingly and embarrassingly irrelevant constitution at a time when the legal system was developing rapidly was unacceptable—it could pose a threat to the legitimacy of the constitution itself, and to the process of building a 'state governed by law' that the Vietnamese Party and state were engaged in.

The party also understood that discussions of revising and amending the 1992 Constitution would become a wide-ranging debate on the political, economic and social arrangements for Vietnam as a transitional state. The process of revising and amending the Vietnamese constitution in 2001 became just such a forum for dialogue, although it was moderated, bounded and ultimately controlled dialogue.[1]

THE PROCESS OF REVISING THE 1992 CONSTITUTION

The 1992 Constitution was formally amended in December 2001, 10 years after the enactment of the 1992 document. The development of those amendments began earlier, when the party and state established a Constitutional Amendment Commission in early 2001 to draft the amendments and exploratory documentation.

The constitutional amendment process was aimed at:

> bring[ing] the constitutional and legal framework into line with the country's shift from a centrally planned economy to a socialist-oriented market system

as the government noted in 2001. This concept of constitutional revision was largely reactive, focusing on adapting the constitution to a rapidly emerging market economy, strengthening the state machinery, reforming Vietnam's cumbersome and often corrupt national and local administration, reducing and shortening government procedures, decentralising decision making, reducing the size of government bureaucracy, making administration more responsive to citizens and upgrading the civil service. In a slightly broader formulation, the constitutional amendment process aimed for a 'clarification of the responsibilities, functions and relations among legislative, executive and juridical bodies in conformity with the new situation'.

Initially, some legislators, reformers and intellectuals called for a 'fundamental revision' of the constitution or even the drafting of a new constitution. Other legislators and intellectuals called for a discussion

---

[1] For more on this process, see M Sidel, *Law and Society in Vietnam* (Cambridge, Cambridge University Press, 2008) (especially ch 8); and M Sidel, 'Analytical Models for Understanding Constitutions and Constitutional Dialogue in Socialist Transitional States: Re-interpreting Constitutional Dialogue in Vietnam' (2002) 6 *Singapore Journal of International and Comparative Law* 42, portions of which have been updated for this chapter.

of a mechanism for enforcing the constitution and constitutional rights, the concept of 'constitutional protection' (*bao ve Hien phap*) discussed in considerable detail in Chapter 9. Both of these were sensitive topics. The calls for a fundamental revision of the constitution or drafting a new constitution were sensitive because they would open up a range of issues—such as the role of the Communist Party and of non-Communist parties, and other political and economic reforms—which the party and state were not willing to address. The calls for discussing and formulating a structure for constitutional enforcement were sensitive because Vietnam has never had a system in which the judiciary or the legislature plays a significant role in enforcing constitutional rights, and the party deemed it too early to engage in that complex debate.

Party and government leaders, and more conservative legal scholars, rejected these calls for a fundamental revision or a new constitution, and for a discussion of such sensitive areas as methods to protect constitutional rights. They sought to limit debate to key areas in which the 1992 Constitution had clearly fallen behind the times. Those primary topics for discussion and drafting were:

(i)   reflecting economic reform and economic changes in the constitution;
(ii)   the role, functions and authority of the National Assembly;
(iii) improving and reforming aspects of local governance;
(iv)   the role of the 'procuracy', the system of state prosecutors; and
(v)   issues of social justice and the constitution.

The Vice Chairman and senior legal official of the National Assembly led the efforts to corral the debate:

> The recent Ninth Party Congress came to a conclusion [on these matters] and we … have a duty to systematize the viewpoints and line decided by the … Congress. So we must revise the chapters on state organization, and some economic, scientific and technology issues … and on the state machinery. We cannot just separately legislate on separation of power and the powers of the state machinery … first and foremost because we must ensure the reality of the effectiveness of the state.[2]

---

[2] '*Quoc hoi tiep tuc thao luan ve noi dung sua doi, bo sung Hien phap nam 1992*' ('The National Assembly continues to discuss the substance of the revision and supplementation of the 1992 Constitution') *Bao Lao Dong* (27 June 2001).

Yet another leader re-emphasised the limited nature of the revision and amendment process:

> This amendment … of certain articles in the 1992 Constitution must … continue to affirm the … form of the state machinery currently in effect and concentrate only on amending some articles that are really necessary and urgent.[3]

In June and July 2001, the Constitutional Amendment Commission finished drafting most of the amendments and their rationales. On 15 August 2001, the Commission released a draft of the proposed amendments asking for comments from citizens and organisations throughout Vietnam as well as overseas by 15 September. The proposed amendments were published in domestic newspapers, including the main party newspaper *Nhan Dan*.

The comments that resulted from this process provide us with an unprecedented window into constitutional debate in Vietnam. Commentary on the amendments and the revision process were sent to the National Assembly, which posted a selection on its website, and appeared in newspapers around Vietnam. Other, often much harsher comments were posted by overseas Vietnamese on websites outside Vietnam. These focused primarily on the question of article 4 stipulating the leading role of the Communist Party, as well as related issues of political structure and reform. Many of the individual and organisational comments published by the National Assembly or in domestic newspapers focused on individual amendments. Some organisations sought heightened constitutional attention (including, at times, formal identification in the constitution) for their groups.

BROADENING THE DEBATE

Despite the attempts to channel the drafting and comment process into the specific areas of constitutional amendment, some of the domestic commentary sought to broaden the range of potential constitutional amendments, establish an agenda for broader reform or put deeper constitutional and political issues on a longer-term agenda. For example, in a frank commentary published in September 2001, a senior

---

[3] Nguyen Van Yeu of the National Assembly, quoted in *Nguoi Dai bieu Nhan dan*, 1 August 2001.

government official called for considerably broader constitutional change in the relationships among state, legislative, judicial and prosecutorial institutions.

> Who stands at the head of the legal system? ... Legal institutions should not belong to the executive system ... What is the position of the public prosecutor? ... The organization of the court system is inappropriate ... So in these amendments to the Constitution ... we must study issues such as establishing a legal commission with an attorney general as chair (standing at the head of the legal system); establishing a public prosecutors' office belonging to the Government in place of the [traditional Soviet] procuracy; and organizing the courts in accordance with jurisdiction over trials, and not based on administrative levels, and strengthening the function of the administrative courts.[4]

Other commentators raised even broader and deeper issues of constitutionalism.

The prominent constitutional scholar Nguyen Dang Dung wrote that the constitution is not an ordinary law, and called for a clear recognition of the differences between constitutional and statutory drafting so as to:

> permit the Constitution a long life, and so it can serve as the basis for other laws, because constitutional stability is one of the fundamental measures of the stability of a political system.[5]

A senior official at the National Assembly harkened back to the 1946 Constitution, with an implicit slap at all the constitutions thereafter, when he wrote that the amendment process should:

> inherit the essence of the progressive and scientific terminology and arrangement of the 1946 Constitution ... For example, some of the substantive terms that ensure democracy, on holding referenda, testimony before the National Assembly.[6]

---

[4] Diep Van Son, '*Sua doi Hien phap tao dieu kien cai cach he thong tu phap*' ('Revising the Constitution and creating the conditions for judicial reform') *VnExpress.net* (5 September 2001).

[5] Nguyen Dang Dung, '*Can quan triet hon nua ky thuat lap hien*' ('We must pay more attention to constitutional drafting') *Bao Nhan Dan* (11 September 2001), reprinted on the National Assembly constitutional amendment comment site at <http://www.na.gov.vn>.

[6] Do Van Tri, '*Hien phap phai mang tinh khoa hoc, khai quat, van phong chuan xac*' ('The Constitution must embody the spirit of science, conciseness, and accuracy') *Bao Van Hoa* (29 September 2001), reprinted on the National Assembly constitutional amendment comment site at <http://www.na.gov.vn>.

Among the most far-reaching individual comments were those made by the noted legal policy specialist and scholar Nguyen Van Thao. Professor Thao raised the difficult and controversial question of implementing and enforcing the constitution, supposedly the province of the National Assembly and its Standing Committee. This issue had been put aside by the Constitutional Amendment Commission as inappropriate for the 2001 revision process:

> In nearly ten years of Constitutional implementation, we have never once seen the National Assembly or its Standing Committee abrogate, cancel or suspend ... a single document issued by the President, the Government or the Prime Minister. The system of monitoring is almost never exercised by the Government or the Prime Minister with respect to the ministries or local authorities, despite the fact that some legal documents issued by ministries and local authorities clearly violate the Constitution or the laws.

For Thao, the fundamental reason for these failings was clear: 'The 1992 Constitution did not delegate to any institution judgment on the constitutionality of laws', and it remained vague on the extent of the National Assembly's powers in this area. For Thao and some others, the question of constitutional enforcement and implementation should now be on the agenda for debate. However, the Constitutional Amendment Commission, the leadership of the National Assembly, and the party did not agree, for a full and frank discussion of those issues would bring into play the question of allowing the Vietnamese judiciary to adjudicate the constitutionality of government laws, regulations and acts (which it has no power to do), or establishing a constitutional court, or a constitutional commission under the National Assembly—the political leadership declined to address these controversial and political risky questions.

Thao moved from constitutional enforcement to personal rights, objecting to the Constitutional Amendment Commission's rather brief and, in his view, weak proposal to add wording to the constitution that 'a defendant's right to counsel is guaranteed'. 'This is insufficient', Thao wrote, quoting directly from and relying on the International Covenant on Civil and Political Rights:

> [W]e must clearly declare that defendants have the right to counsel, and that adjudicative institutions must guarantee that defendants are able to exercise this right.

Thao then went a step further, coming close to demanding that the provisions of the Covenant be noted as a form of constitutional legislative history in domestic law so that the origins and basis for a right to counsel would be clear.[7]

CHANNELLING THE DEBATE AND AGREEING ON
CONSTITUTIONAL AMENDMENTS

Quite obviously, the party, National Assembly and Constitutional Amendment Commission were faced with the already complex task of deciding upon, drafting and defending proposed amendments to the constitution while fending off repeated sallies from intellectuals, legal reformers, workers, overseas critics and others to broaden substantially the revision and amendment process as a means of moving toward deeper legal and political reform. The leadership sought to re-channel discussion back toward the formal amendments under consideration in the limited number of official and important areas that the party and the Commission had authorised for the revision process. It worked quickly in October 2001 to digest the comments received and determine whether they should have any effect on the amendments scheduled to go before the National Assembly.

However, before the draft constitutional amendments could go to the National Assembly, there was another crucial step. Not surprisingly, given the primacy of the Vietnamese Communist Party in Vietnamese political and legal life, the amendments proposed by the Commission first had to be discussed and approved at the highest levels of the Communist Party, through meetings of the Party Central Committee and its even smaller, and higher, Political Bureau—the key decision-making group within the party that has existed for many decades.

Those meetings were held in November 2001. At the Central Committee meeting to discuss the constitutional amendments, the General Secretary of the party reaffirmed that discussion and drafting of constitutional amendments should be limited to certain key, approved areas and these should not be strayed beyond. 'Revising the Constitution is a must', General Secretary Nong Duc Manh told party officials and others around the nation in widely publicised remarks:

> but for the time being efforts should focus only on urgent issues which have already been clearly decided and approved by a majority.

---

[7] Nguyen Van Thao, '*Ve kiem tra tinh hop hien, hop phap cua van ban phap luat va cac co quan tu phap*' ('On supervising the constitutionality and legality of legal documents and legal institutions') *Bao Khao hoc va Phat trien* (3 October 2001), reprinted on the National Assembly constitutional amendment comment site at <http://www.na.gov.vn>.

The General Secretary's closing statement at the Central Committee meeting once again closed the door on broader constitutional revision. 'The question is not posed as to the comprehensive revision of the Constitution', but only specific amendments.[8]

CONTINUING THE DEBATE AT THE NATIONAL ASSEMBLY

Nine days after the party approved draft amendments, they were presented to the National Assembly. The Assembly Chairman opened the proceedings with clear instructions:

> Only amend and supplement certain articles that are truly urgent and necessary, and that have sufficient foundation and high unanimity; do not undertake the issue of fundamental revision, or of the entire Constitution.[9]

He was only partly successful. The Assembly debated the key proposed amendments—new language to reflect economic reform and privatised markets; the changing role of the public prosecutors; the role of state subsidies for primary education and other areas—but discussion could not entirely be limited to the areas set out by the party and assembly leadership. Reaching considerably beyond the channelling and narrowing efforts of the party leadership, some National Assembly delegates raised issues of constitutionalism far beyond the boundaries set by the party. For example, an Assembly delegate and senior legal official in Ho Chi Minh City called for establishment of a constitutional court (*toa an Hien phap*) to 'defend the Constitution ... against the many forms of constitutional violation that at present cannot be investigated or adjudicated'.[10] Most assuredly, this was not on the party's and Commission's agenda for constitutional amendment in 2001.

After months of party, National Assembly, media and overseas debate, the National Assembly met in December 2001 to review, debate and vote on the proposed amendments. Despite months of sharp controversy, the Constitutional Amendment Commission's draft revisions, shaped in conjunction with and approved by the party, won the day on virtually all issues.

---

[8] '*Thong bao Hoi nghi lan thu tu Ban Chap hanh Trung uong Dang khoa IX*' ('Communique of the Fourth Session of the Ninth Central Committee') *Bao Nhan Dan* (13 November 2001).

[9] '*Quoc hoi nghe to trinh ve viec sua doi, bo sung mot so dieu cua Hien phap nam 1992 va mot so thuyet trinh, bao cao*' ('The National Assembly hears the proposal on amending and supplementing certain articles of the 1992 Constitution and [related] speeches and reports') *Bao Nhan Dan* (21 November 2001).

[10] '*Can co hinh tuc bo phieu bat tin nhiem*' ('There must be a method for voting no confidence') *Bao Lao dong* (1 December 2001).

THE 2001 REVISIONS TO THE 1992 CONSTITUTION

The amendments made to the 1992 Vietnamese Constitution made in December 2001 after this long discussion and debate included the following main revisions.

Vietnam's Patriotic Traditions

The Preamble to the 1992 Constitution was amended to emphasise Vietnam's 'tradition of patriotism' and national solidarity as a means for seeking greater internal unity and reaching out to overseas Vietnamese.

Strengthening a 'State Governed by Law' and Government Coordination (Not Separation of Powers)

The definition of the state of Vietnam and of the state's powers were amended to emphasise the party and state policy of developing Vietnam's legal system, by adding to the constitution a definition that Vietnam is a 'state governed by law', and to stress that 'state powers are unified and decentralized to state bodies, which shall coordinate with one another in the exercise of ... legislative, executive and judicial powers'.[11]

This idea of a 'state governed by law' emerged with increasing importance in the 1990s, becoming a significant enough priority that it was added to the very important article 2 that defined the nature of the Vietnamese state. Within Vietnam and beyond, the meaning of 'state governed by law' (which is not the same formulation as 'rule of law') has been much discussed and somewhat controversial. Given the continuation of the party's role in Vietnam, the addition of the idea of a 'state governed by law' is somewhat ambiguous and remains to be worked out in the coming years. It does not, Vietnamese political officials and commentators agree, mean that Vietnam is moving to a system of separation of powers as in some Western political systems (despite the wishes of some Vietnamese officials and scholars).

---

[11] 1992 Constitution, revised art 2.

Strengthening the Constitutional Discussion of Corruption, Bureaucratism and Officials' Links to Citizens

Article 8 of the revised constitution strengthened an earlier provision on the responsibilities of state institutions, officials and institutions toward citizens, a response to enormous popular dissatisfaction with corrupt and authoritarian behaviour by party and state officials. In the new, tougher formulation:

> all State agencies, cadres, officials and employees must show respect for the people, devotedly serve the people, maintain close contact with the people, listen to their opinions and submit to their supervision; resolutely struggle against corruption, extravagance and all manifestations of bureaucracy, arrogance, and authoritarianism.

Gradually Increasing Recognition of Social Organisations

After a decade in which various forms of 'social organisations'—including incipient non-governmental organisations, social policy institutes, research organisations, clubs and other such groups—had formed by the hundreds, the constitution recognised this diversification of Vietnamese social organisation in the definition of the umbrella Vietnam Fatherland Front. The amendments redefined the Fatherland Front as:

> a political alliance and a voluntary union of political organizations, socio-political organizations, social organizations and individuals representing their social classes and strata, nationalities, religions, and overseas Vietnamese.[12]

Economic Reform, the Private Economy, Markets and International Economic Integration

The amendments recognised the rapid process of economic reform within Vietnam and international economic integration with new language that recognised both the changing nature of economic life and a concern that neither marketisation nor globalisation damage Vietnam's independence and sovereignty.

---

[12] 1992 Constitution, revised art 9. See also ch 7.

> The State builds an independent and sovereign economy on the basis of bringing into full play … internal resources and actively integrating into the international economy, and carries out … national industrialization and modernization.

It further recognised the process of economic reform and the strength of the private economy that had developed since 1992, explicitly recognising the private economy in the constitution in the definition of the economic structure and somewhat de-emphasising the earlier focus on 'socialist orientation'. The amended paragraph read:

> The State consistently implements the policy of developing a socialist-oriented market economy. The multi-sector economic structure with diversified forms of production and business organization is based on the regime of the entire people's ownership, collective ownership and private ownership, in which the entire people's ownership [state ownership] and collective ownership constitute the foundation.[13]

The amendments went on to make explicit the party's and state's endorsement of business and markets, and citizens' rights to engage in private market activities by adding new language:

> All economic sectors are important constituents of the socialist-oriented market economy. Organizations and individuals of all economic sectors are allowed to conduct business and/or production activities in branches and trades not banned by law and to be jointly engaged in long-term development, cooperation and healthy competition according to law.

Additional support for the private economy—including private, small business and family forms—was also provided in the revised charter.[14]

In the 1992 Constitution, the state economic sector was referred to as 'play[ing] the leading role in the national economy'. That reference was amended in 2001 to refer to the state-owned sector as 'together with the collective economic sector, becom[ing] an ever firmer and firmer foundation of the national economy'—bringing in the collective economy into this definition of the 'foundation of the national economy' and softening the concept of the state economic sector from

---

[13] 1992 Constitution, revised art 15. The original art 15 in the 1992 Constitution provided: 'The State promotes a multi-commodity economy functioning in accordance with market mechanisms under the management of the State and following the socialist orientation. The multi-component economic structure with various forms of organization of production and trading is based on a system of ownership by the entire people, by collectives, and by private individuals, of which ownership by the entire people and by collectives constitutes the foundation.'

[14] 1992 Constitution, revised arts 16 and 21.

playing the 'leading role' to being a 'firm foundation'. The new article 19 provided:

> The State economic sector shall be consolidated and developed, particularly in key branches and domains, play the leading role in the national economy and, together with the collective economic sector, become an ever firmer and firmer foundation of the national economy.[15]

A Renewed Emphasis on Science and Technology

The constitution strengthened an emphasis on science and technology, adding language that called 'development of science and technology … a top national policy'.[16]

Enhancing the Role of Foreign Investment

The revised constitution sought to strengthen both the rhetorical and the legal protection for foreign investment in Vietnam.[17]

Strengthening the State Commitment to Education at a Time of Rapid Economic Reform

The revised constitution, in articles 35 and 36, redefined 'development of education' as a 'top national priority', sought to encourage the development of multiple forms of 'state-founded and people-founded' schools, as well as investment in education by diverse groups.

Strengthening Outreach to Overseas Vietnamese

The 2001 amendments re-emphasised the role of overseas Vietnamese as part of the broad community of Vietnamese in Vietnam and around

---

[15] The original art 19 in the 1992 Constitution provided: 'The State sector shall be consolidated and developed, especially in key branches and areas, and play the leading role in the national economy. The State-run enterprises enjoy autonomy in production and trading and shall guarantee that production and trading are to yield effective results.'

[16] 1992 Constitution, revised art 37.

[17] 1992 Constitution, revised art 25.

the world, at a time when the party and state were seeking stronger relationships with overseas Vietnamese, encouraging investment and remittances, and unprecedented numbers of overseas Vietnamese were returning to Vietnam to work, live or study. The amended article 75 on overseas Vietnamese stated:

> Overseas Vietnamese make up a part of the Vietnamese nationalities' community. The State protects the legitimate interests of overseas Vietnamese … The State encourages and creates conditions for overseas Vietnamese to preserve the Vietnamese cultural identity, maintain close ties with their families, and contribute to national construction.[18]

Strengthening Government Accountability—Votes of Confidence on Government Officials in the National Assembly

The 2001 constitutional amendments recognised, as had the 1992 Constitution, that government ministers and other high officials are responsible to the people, the National Assembly and the Prime Minister. However, except for the 1946 Constitution, there had been no formal and public procedure for the elected representatives of the people in the National Assembly to remove senior government officials or express dissatisfaction at their performance. After substantial debate, the 2001 amendments added to the powers of the National Assembly that it may 'cast votes of confidence on persons holding positions elected or approved by the National Assembly'.

That group of 'persons holding positions elected or approved by the National Assembly' includes the President and Vice President of Vietnam, the Chairman, Vice Chairmen and members of the Standing Committee of the National Assembly, the Prime Minister, the Chief Justice of the Supreme Court and Procurator-General of the Supreme People Procuracy, Deputy Prime Ministers, ministers and 'other members of the government'—a long list of appointees all of whom would now be subject to votes of confidence by the National Assembly.[19]

To the uninitiated, this provision of a procedure for votes of confidence on government officials by a national legislature may seem like

---

[18] The original art 75 in the 1992 Constitution provided: 'The State shall protect the legitimate interests of Vietnamese people residing abroad. The State shall create the necessary conditions for Vietnamese residing abroad to maintain close ties with their families and native land and to contribute to national construction.'

[19] 1992 Constitution, revised art 84.

a small matter, but it was one of the most important accomplishments of the 2001 constitutional amendment process, for it directly reflected popular demand for the accountability of government officials. It was also a hard-won achievement, for there was significant opposition to even this relatively attenuated form of accountability.

Clarifying the Roles of the National Assembly, the Government and the Prime Minister

In several amendments, the revised constitution also sought to clarify and strengthen gradually the role of the National Assembly in deciding state budget policies and allocations, nationalities policy, religious policy, and to update the duties and powers of the government and the Prime Minister.[20]

Narrowing the Jurisdiction and Functions of the Supreme People's Procuracy

Traditionally, the procuracy, headed by the Supreme People's Procuracy, had had an enormously powerful role in Vietnam's legal system and in the adjudication of criminal and civil cases—far more powerful, for example, than the role of the courts themselves. Furthermore, the scope of the procuracy's responsibilities had encompassed not only prosecuting criminal offences, but also inspecting the work of ministries and other government agencies—including the courts—as well as local institutions, economic institutions, social organisations and the military to 'supervise and control [their] obedience to the law' and 'ensure a serious and uniform implementation of the law'. In effect, the procuracy was not only the prosecutor of criminals, but also a kind of all-encompassing inspectorate over the entire government and legal system with the duty to ensure that those agencies acted in accordance with law.

By the 1990s, there was substantial opposition to these overly broad overlapping roles of prosecutors and inspectors, and efforts began—as they also began in China in the 1980s—to narrow the scope of the procuracy's work. This was a hotly debated topic in the 2001 constitutional amendment process, with the procuracy and the Supreme

---

[20] 1992 Constitution, revised arts 84, 91, 103, 112, 114 and 116.

People's Procuracy in Hanoi seeking to head off proposals to narrow the jurisdiction and functions of the procuracy. In the end, however, those advocating reform and narrowing of the procuracy won out, and won new institutional arrangements that were memorialised in article 137 of the revised constitution:

> The Supreme People's Procuracy shall exercise the right to prosecution and investigating justice-related activities, thus contributing to ensuring that laws are strictly and uniformly observed. The local people's procuracies and the military procuracies shall exercise the right to prosecution and investigating justice-related activities within the scope of their responsibilities prescribed by law.[21]

To non-Vietnamese eyes, this may still look like a very broad remit, especially the duty to 'investigate justice-related activities'. However, in fact it was the beginning of a restriction in procuratorial activities; the earlier delegation of tasks to the procuracy had been considerably broader and enabled the procuracy to have a hand in the legal work of virtually any part of the government, including the judiciary.

DEALING WITH DIFFICULT AND
CONTROVERSIAL AMENDMENTS

Some amendments initially proposed were not agreed to, and those are also worthy of mention. Perhaps the most prominent example is that the Constitutional Amendment Commission had proposed revising a provision of article 59 of the 1992 Constitution which states that '[p]rimary education is compulsory and dispensed free of charge' to eliminate the 'free of charge' provision. In the intervening years since the 1992 Constitution, charging for primary education had become an unfortunate norm in many parts of Vietnam, and the amendment's advocates sought to bring the constitution in line with the reality that the parents of many elementary schoolchildren were in fact paying

---

[21] A related amendment narrowed the scope of local procuracy reporting responsibilities to local People's Councils (art 140). The original art 137 on the role of the procuracy in the 1992 Constitution provided: 'The Supreme People's Office of Supervision and Control supervises and controls obedience to the law by ministries, organs of ministerial rank, other organs under the Government, local organs of power, economic bodies, social organizations, people's armed units and citizens; it exercises the right to initiate public prosecution, [and] ensures a serious and uniform implementation of the law. Local Offices of Supervision and Control and the Military Offices of Supervision and Control supervise and control obedience to the law and exercise the right to initiate public prosecution within the bounds of their responsibilities as prescribed by law.'

tuition and fees. However, this proposal ran into a buzz-saw of opposition from the public, intellectuals and others, and it became clear that it could not pass at the National Assembly level, so it was shelved before the final consideration of the draft amendments.

THE AFTERMATH OF THE CONSTITUTIONAL AMENDMENT PROCESS

After all of the fierce debate, the amendments adopted by the National Assembly in December 2001 reasonably closely matched those proposed by the Constitutional Amendment Commission and the party earlier that summer. They had been the subject of months of spirited dialogue, but in only one significant case—the proposed amendment eliminating the 1992 provision for free primary education—was a proposed amendment overturned by public opinion and the National Assembly. However, to focus on this single refusal would be to miscomprehend the importance of the constitutional revision process in 2001. Despite the fact that, in the end most of the proposed amendments were adopted, the amendment process became a debate on constitutional legitimacy and substance unprecedented in Vietnam since 1946.

The party, National Assembly and Constitutional Amendment Commission managed this process in several ways. Some particularly controversial issues—such as revising the article 4 affirmation of the party's leading role—had been firmly taken off the political agenda in advance and, despite the loud voices of overseas Vietnamese dissidents, such a proposal would have been unlikely to pass in any case.

Other issues were clearly raised, more publicly than they had ever been before, and were taken off the agenda for the time being, but would clearly return. Such issues included constitutional enforcement and the protection of constitutional rights—what is called 'constitutional protection' in Vietnam, the related calls for establishing a constitutional court or commission, and broader calls for reforming the Vietnamese legislative, executive and judicial structure. These were not acted upon in 2001, but clearly had enough support that party leaders could not label them as taboo for future discussion. Furthermore, of course, management of this debate also included concretising some calls for greater political accountability in the constitutional amendments that were adopted—especially the provision for National Assembly votes of confidence on senior government officials.

In the end, the Vietnamese constitutional amendment and revision process of 2001 served two worthy aims: it helped to 'modernise' the constitution by bringing it into line with rapid and significant changes in Vietnamese society, so that the apex of Vietnamese law under which all other laws and regulations are promulgated would not appear behind the times. The amendments strengthening the role of economic reform, private market activity, emphasising the state governed by law, recognising the role of social organisations and enhancing outreach to overseas Vietnamese all fell into this category of matching a 1992 document to a rapidly changing set of political, economic and social circumstances.

The second aim was responding to demands from society. The amendments recognising and promoting the role of economic reform, private market activity and international economic integration; introducing a right for the National Assembly (and, by extension, the citizenry) to hold senior government officials accountable through the newly enacted provision for votes of confidence on senior government officials; and the narrowing of the role, jurisdiction and functions of the procuracy all reflected and responded to citizen demands for economic autonomy, political accountability and an adjustment in the role of agencies long regarded as having too much power.

At the same time, many issues were raised during the constitutional amendment process that were then left to later discussion and action. A few of those matters have consistently earned the opposition of the party—such as altering the article 4 recognition of the party's leading role—and are unlikely to be adopted. But others, including constitutional enforcement and the protection of constitutional rights ('constitutional protection'); the related calls for establishing a constitutional court or commission; broader calls for reforming the Vietnamese legislative, executive and judicial structure; and calls for strengthening judicial independence would resonate in the years after the 2001 constitutional amendment process, becoming the next fora for debate and reform in Vietnamese constitutional law.

In 2008, as this volume is being finished, Vietnam is planning to revise the 1992 Constitution once again, most likely in 2011 or 2012. The issues will likely be different from those debated and drafted in 2000 and 2001. They will include ongoing issues of controversy such as the formation of a constitutional court or some other provision for constitutional review; amending the constitution to provide more clearly for the private economy; perhaps greater recognition of individual freedoms; probably significant redrafting on the structure, jurisdiction and functions of the courts and procuracy; redrawing the map and roles of the National Assembly; extensive revision of the troubled system of

People's Councils and People's Committees, the institutions of administration at the local level; and other key issues.

Most importantly, however, the next process of constitutional revision and amendment in Vietnam will provide an opportunity for wide-ranging elite and public discussion of the purposes of the constitution and precisely what it should contain. That process, like the debates summarised here from 2000 and 2001, will be an opportunity for Vietnam to consider the position of a constitution in a rapidly changing nation, and the basic principles that the Vietnamese Communist Party and other actors in Vietnamese society, both institutional and individual, will focus on in the years ahead.

FURTHER READING

The 1992 Constitution of the Socialist Republic of Vietnam (as revised by Resolution No 51/2001/QH 10 of 25 December 2001 Amending and Supplementing a Number of Articles of the 1992 Constitution of the Socialist Republic of Vietnam).

Sidel, M (2002) 'Analytical Models for Understanding Constitutions and Constitutional Dialogue in Socialist Transitional States: Re-interpreting Constitutional Dialogue in Vietnam' 6 *Singapore Journal of International and Comparative Law* 42.

—— (2008) *Law and Society in Vietnam* (Cambridge, Cambridge University Press).

To Van-Hoa (2006) *Judicial Independence* (Lund, Jurisförlaget i Lund) (particularly Pt V, chs XVI–XIX).

7

Implementing Constitutional Guarantees: The Problem of Associational Rights

T HE RHETORIC—and the lack of implementation—of constitutional rights is an enduring problem for modern Vietnamese constitutionalism. Until the late 1980s, the fact that constitutional guarantees went unenforced was not a political problem for Vietnam's Communist Party leadership. However, in the late 1980s, and episodically in the 1990s and into the decade after 2000, Vietnamese political and legal reformers and dissidents began to point directly to the gap between rhetorical rights and real rights in each successive constitution.

Several examples illustrate the different ways in which the Vietnamese polity has dealt with the increasing contradictions between rhetorical rights and their implementation. This chapter discusses how Vietnam has struggled with the constitutional grant of freedom of association. The next chapter discusses interference in the judiciary through a major recent case. And chapter 9 recounts a battle fought by citizens in 2006 and 2007 against restrictions on motorcycles in urban Hanoi—a battle fought on broad constitutional grounds, by the public, perhaps the first time that constitutional appeals have formed the basis for public resistance to state authority in the history of the SRV.

FREEDOM OF ASSOCIATION AND ITS IMPLEMENTATION IN VIETNAM

All of Vietnam's modern constitutions, those of 1946, 1959, 1980 and 1992, have guaranteed a right to form associations (*quyen lap hoi*) in formal terms. In the most recent formulation, the 1992 Constitution stipulated in article 69 that:

> The citizen shall enjoy freedom of opinion and speech, freedom of the press, the right to be informed, and the right to assemble, form associations and hold demonstrations in accordance with the provisions of the law.

In the early years of regulation of associations between 1957 and the early 1990s, through a series of regulatory documents issued in 1957 and again in the late 1980s, the party and state responded to that ostensible constitutional guarantee with legislation that severely restricted the exercise of the constitutional right under the guise of 'implementing' it.[1]

However, resistance to implementing a constitutional right by restricting its exercise grew. In the 1990s, and particularly after 2000, legislators, intellectuals and legal reformers increasingly lobbied for statutes and regulations that directly implemented and facilitated the constitutional guarantee of freedom of association and to form associations. Party and state law drafters sought to channel and limit the role of associational life and freedom through registration, reporting and other mechanisms while encouraging state-supported groups to form and operate in support of the state's economic, social and cultural policies and to take burdens of service provision off the state.

The drafting of Vietnam's first Law on Associations (*Luat ve Hoi*), intended both to implement the constitution's guarantee of freedom of association and protect order by delimiting the exercise of that freedom, began in 1992. Over the ensuing 17 years Vietnamese drafters, legislators, legal scholars and political officials have struggled toward a formulation of that law that balances the multiple views at stake on freedom of association and political order in Vietnam.

These debates accelerated in 2005 and 2006, when the drafting of the Law on Associations appeared to be drawing to a close and to legislative adoption. Vietnamese scholarly, trade, legal and other associations and groups struggled to orient Vietnam's drafting of the Law on Associations to implement more directly the guarantee of freedom of association in the constitution. This energetic campaign was carried out through conferences, the press, alliances with legislators and party and government officials, and—particularly noteworthy in Vietnam—the drafting of a full, alternative draft statute by unofficial, non-legislative and non-governmental actors for the first time in Vietnam's legislative history. The associational sector threatened to bring that alternative draft statute to the national legislature if its concerns were not fully heard.

---

[1] For further information on this history, see M Sidel, 'The Emergence of a Voluntary Sector and Philanthropy in Vietnam: Functions, Legal Regulation and Prospects for the Future' (1997) 8 *Voluntas: International Journal of Nonprofit and Voluntary Organizations* 283; and M Sidel, 'Vietnam: The Ambiguities of State-Directed Legal Reform' in Tan (ed), *Asian Legal Systems: Law, Society and Pluralism in East Asia* (Sydney, Butterworths, 1997).

These reformers battled against a draft that retained many of the administrative and bureaucratic hurdles to forming associations and other civil society groups that had characterised the regulations of the past. The official drafters of the Law on Associations explicitly sought to implement the constitutional right while retaining substantial state power to limit registration and operations of associations and other groups.

The efforts of reformers to explicitly implement the constitutional guarantee of freedom of association in less restrictive ways has been unprecedented in modern Vietnamese constitutional history, and relied on direct appeals to the wording and primacy of the constitution. However, the reformers also worked carefully to avoid appeals to constitutional values that widely separated themselves from the party and state, seeking to avoid a heightened battle that would put them at political odds with those authorities by being perceived as autonomous and independent interpreters of constitutional rights. In short, reformers fought actively on the important but bounded issue of legislation implementing associational rights, rather than challenging the political position of the party and Vietnam's political system.[2]

THE ROLE OF ASSOCIATIONS AND OTHER VOLUNTARY ORGANISATIONS

In recent years, Vietnam's emerging and diversifying voluntary sector has expanded rapidly to provide social services and public needs from which the Vietnamese state is rapidly retreating, to undertake policy research and advocacy, and to play other roles in Vietnamese society. This emerging voluntary sector includes party-related mass organisations, business, trade and professional associations, policy research groups, social activist and social service groups, religious groups, clans, charities, private and semi-private universities, social and charitable funds, and other institutions. Many are closely related to or dominated by the Communist Party, but others operate with considerably more

---

[2] For more information on Vietnam's association sector, see B Kerkvliet, Nguyen Quang A and Bach Tan Sinh, *Forms of Engagement Between State Agencies & Civil Society Organizations in Vietnam: Study Report* (Hanoi, VUFO-NGO Resource Centre, December 2008); I Norlund, *Filling the Gap: The Emerging Civil Society in Viet Nam* (Hanoi, 2007); and B Kerkvliet, Russell HK Heng and David WH Koh (eds), *Getting Organized in Vietnam: Moving In and Around the Socialist State* (Singapore, Institute of Southeast Asian Studies, 2003).

autonomy. By 2007 and 2008, hundreds or thousands—depending on definitions—of such organisations were operating within Vietnam, and if local, more informal groups are counted—such as water user groups in the countryside—then there are thousands.

The party and state have sought carefully to encourage the growth of these social organisations, at least partly to compensate for the inability of the state to keep pace with social needs in a period of rapid reform. At the same time, of course, Vietnam's Communist Party retains management and control over the growing voluntary sector at a level more detailed and specific than in many other countries. That management and control of associations has a long history of decrees and regulations dating back to 1957.

The important 1957 decree on forming associations, as well as laws and documents in the 1980s and 1990s, were issued in the guise of 'implementing' constitutional guarantees in the Constitutions of 1946, 1959 and 1980 on the freedom to form associations. Furthermore, they did allow the formation of carefully selected and approved groups. They also subjected voluntary groups to onerous and highly discouraging registration and reporting requirements, restrictions on activities and 'dual management' by both state 'line' ministries in particular areas of work (such as health, education or the environment), as well as the national Ministry of Home Affairs (MOHA and its predecessors), which is responsible for policy toward social organisations at the national level.[3]

Beyond those regulatory efforts, the Vietnamese state has also taken punitive action against a relatively small number of organisations that challenge the state in political, religious or human rights terms. That harsher and swifter control is generally the responsibility of national police and security forces. For the vast majority of the thousands of formal and informal organisations now active throughout the country, the Vietnamese state generally acquiesces in and even encourages their day-to-day activities, while retaining a detailed regulatory structure and making clear that the state and party remain generally in control of the pace and direction of growth in non-profit activity.

Since 1992, Vietnam has struggled to enact a Law on Associations that would govern much of this rapidly emerging voluntary sector. In formal terms, that Law on Associations—like earlier legislation and

---

[3] Sidel, n 1 above.

regulation governing the associational sector—implements article 69 of the 1992 Constitution of Vietnam. Article 69 stipulates that:

> The citizen shall enjoy freedom of opinion and speech, freedom of the press, the right to be informed, and the right to assemble, *form associations* and hold demonstrations in accordance with the provisions of the law (emphasis added).[4]

In recent years, that legal drafting process has been enveloped in a significant and contentious struggle for power and authority. The Communist Party, powerful government ministries, national associations flexing new muscles in interest representation, the National Assembly, intellectuals, lawyers and other forces have joined battle in an attempt to shape, through law, the institutional arrangements that will govern relationships between the Vietnamese state and its voluntary sector for many years to come, as well as the burdens and obstacles organisations must overcome to achieve registration and legalisation. In this process, the legal status of a number of powerful party-related associations that have long been administered directly by the party under separate statutes have come into question as reformers have struggled to bring such powerful 'mass organisations' within a law on associations as well, raising rather directly the problem of party organisational obedience to a rule of law.

This chapter points to the rising interests at stake and the interest groups that have staked their claims to particular drafting positions, providing a window into newly contentious legal drafting conflicts in a transitional socialist country and pointing to the debates over institutional authority, constitutional freedoms and the role of law that are likely to dominate debates in Vietnam and other transitional socialist countries in the years to come.

CONTROL MECHANISMS IN THE LEGAL REGULATION OF SOCIAL ORGANISATIONS, 1946–90

Legal regulation of the voluntary sector in any country can range on a spectrum from encouragement of sectoral activity and autonomy to stricter control of the registration and operations of social organisations.

---

[4] The Vietnamese text of article 69 is '*Cong dan co quyen tu do ngon luan, tu do bao chi; co quyen duoc thong tin; co quyen hoi hop,* lap hoi, *bieu tinh theo quy dinh cua phap luat*' (emphasis added).

Vietnam's political and legal history since the establishment of the Democratic Republic of Viet Nam in 1945 clearly shows that the party and state began, particularly after 1954, with a distinctly restrictive approach to associational rights, very much at one end of the spectrum between control and encouragement, an approach at odds with provisions in the 1946, 1959, 1980 and 1992 Constitutions guaranteeing freedom to form associations. In more recent years, the state has recalibrated its position to be somewhat more flexible on associational life, but not nearly fast enough for non-governmental organisation (NGO) activists, some policymakers, activists, academics and others.

In 1946, during a period of alliance between Ho Chi Minh's revolutionary forces and other political groups, Ho's coalition government promulgated a statute that both permitted and fairly strictly regulated the development of voluntary organisations, ostensibly implementing the 1946 constitutional provision of a right to form associations. Under that 1946 statute, the state held the primary role in authorising voluntary groups, was the sole grantor of rights and retained continuing control and authority over them. This pattern would be repeated in later legislation.

After years of fighting against the French, the victory at Dien Bien Phu in 1954, the retaking of Hanoi and several years of party rule, the mid-1950s saw rapid land reform along a Chinese model and growing resistance in intellectual and political circles to increasing party authoritarianism. In late 1956, Vietnam experienced its own version of the Chinese 'Hundred Flowers Movement', an outpouring (at least within relatively narrow circles of intellectuals) of demands for tolerance and gradual democratisation.

In late 1956 and early 1957, the party shattered the Vietnamese Hundred Flowers, closed reformist magazines and newspapers, halted broader conversations within and outside the party over Vietnam's future, imprisoned a number of intellectuals and cultural figures and severely curtailed emergent civil activity. In mid-1957, the party promulgated a new law on associations and implementing regulations that severely limited rights to form civic organisations, reflecting tightened policies. Although Vietnamese social and civic life was to change dramatically in the next several decades, and particularly after the *doi moi* era began in the mid-1980s, the 1957 law on associations have not yet been abrogated and remain in effect until a new Law on Associations is adopted by the National Assembly.

Between 1957 and the mid-1980s, decades of war and intense poverty in the north were accompanied by strict party control. Social organisations other than directly controlled party mass organisations and labour unions had no significant role in Vietnamese society. However, after wars, a long period of autarkic economic, political and social policies, and the beginning of rapid economic reform and social change in the mid-1980s, the role, number and variety of Vietnamese social organisations of various types has now expanded rapidly in a process still managed by the Communist Party, but with considerably more flexibility than at any point since at least 1954.

These changes in the role of social organisations and in party and state policy toward them quickly outstripped the legal provisions applicable to the sector; the growing number and role of social organisations has consistently outsped attempts at regulation since 1986. In 1989, three years after the *doi moi* process took hold, the Vietnamese party and government issued new policy documents encouraging the growth of a social organisational sector within continuing strict political controls and limits set by the state. The restrictive 1957 law and regulations remained in force, but the 1989 policy documents were a political attempt, through administrative documents, to balance continued close state control with a careful but noticeable move along the spectrum toward state encouragement of at least some voluntary activity.[5]

One key marker in the relative strictness or flexibility of non-profit legal systems is whether the formation of organisations must be approved by political authorities, or whether organisations are generally allowed to register without seeking approval. In Vietnam, even the somewhat more encouraging 1989 policy document maintained the traditional process by which associations were established, requiring approval (*cho phep*) by the party and state rather than moving toward a registration (*dang ky*) system that would provide less state intervention in the process of establishing social organisations. Arguably, a registration system rather than an approval process would better effectuate the freedom guaranteed in Vietnam's constitution to form associations. But Vietnam would not begin to cross the important line from a *cho phep* to a *dang ky* system until a careful initiative for research and scientific organisations in 1992 undertaken by a reformist branch of the government—and only then for a narrow category of elite organisations.

In mid-1990, the party and state recalibrated control back toward even more rigorous restriction. Between early 1989 and mid-1990, the party and government apparatus had become considerably more concerned about the activism and growing political role of a few groups,

---

[5] Council of Ministers, Instructions 01-CT on the Organisation and Activities of Mass Organisations (5 January 1989).

as well as its increasing inability to keep track of the growing number and range of social organisations. Prominent among such groups was the Club of Former Resistance Fighters, which demanded better conditions for veterans and began to take their demands into the political realm. A government document issued in June 1990 (once again, formally implementing the 1957 law and regulations, which remained on the books) sought once again to stiffen controls on social organisations.[6]

OPENING CHANNELS FOR SOCIAL ORGANISATIONS
THROUGH THE TRANSITION FROM 'APPROVAL'
TO 'REGISTRATION' IN THE 1992 SCIENCE
AND TECHNOLOGY DECREE

The early 1990s were a period of rapid growth in policy research institutes, social service and social activist organisations, new and voluntary cooperatives, and other forms of voluntary organisations. Their increasing diversity also had one important commonality: virtually all operated publicly without formally registering with the state and, in most cases, were largely satisfied with that ambiguous legal status.

However, ambiguity could not grow a voluntary sector quickly enough, and in 1992 the relatively reformist Ministry of Science, Technology and the Environment opened a considerably more flexible window for some social organisations to seek a fully legalised, formal, state-recognised and registered status. Seeking to encourage and motivate scientific talent, raise funds for basic and applied science and technology research, and help scientists remain in the basic and applied sector, the ministry promulgated regulatory documents endorsing and encouraging organisations promoting scientific and technological innovation and exchange. A number of urban voluntary organisations, including some of the most important policy research, social service and social activist organisations then operating in Vietnam, understood the legalisation that became possible through the relatively flexible and welcoming window provided by the 1992 Science and Technology Decree (Decree 35 of 1992), taking the opportunity to register with the ministry under those Regulations.[7]

The 1992 Science and Technology Decree and its implementing regulations helped to provide a measure of legalisation and legitimacy

---

[6] Council of Ministers, Instructions 202-CT on the Implementation of State Regulations on the Formation of Associations (5 June 1990).

[7] Ministry of Science and Technology, Decree 35-HDBT on the Management of Science and Technology (28 January 1992); and Implementing Regulations to Decree 35 (Joint Circular 195-LB, 13 November 1992).

to a number of voluntary organisations. It also gave them some measure of protection through affiliation with the powerful science, technology and environment system within the government—also providing the mantle of science and technology in a nation that had long declared its primacy and power. Groups such as the Centre for Gender, Family and Environment in Development in Hanoi and the Social Development Consulting Group in Ho Chi Minh City found legitimacy through the 1992 Science and Technology Decree. Throughout the 1990s, the Science and Technology Decree was regularly cited throughout urban Vietnam as important support for the formation of new civil organisations. Although control was still sought and retained, the pendulum continued to swing gradually toward encouragement and flexibility in the several years after the 1992 decree was promulgated. Hundreds of new voluntary groups were formed, including many voluntary agricultural cooperatives to replace the involuntary or mobilised cooperatives formed during the period of central planning in the countryside.

The statutory language in question may not seem revolutionary to Western eyes; it may even appear quite statist at first glance. But it came closer to implementing the constitutional right to form associations than any legislation in modern Vietnamese history. Article 1 of the 1992 Decree stipulated:

> All state institutions, military units, economic organizations, social organizations and each citizen have the right *(quyen)* to organize and undertake science and technology activities.

Furthermore, under article 15:

> science and technology organizations ... established at the provincial or municipal level, or by collectives or individuals, must register *(dang ky)* their activities [not apply for approval] at the provincial or municipal science and technology office.[8]

The drafters of the 1992 Decree understood the sea change they were effecting and the space they were opening, as did the organisations that found legalisation through this new step. For 'the first time', wrote Professor Vu Cao Dam, a key drafter of Decree 35:

> a new democratic idea was found in a State document on science and technology: that the State acknowledges the 'right' *(quyen)* of 'citizens,' instead of the commonly-used term 'permission' *(cho phep)* in earlier legal documents

to organise science and technology activities and social organisations.

[8] Decree 35 (1992).

In Decree 35, Professor Dam continues:

> the traditional conception that the State is the superior body 'granting permission' to carry out science and technology activities that was commonly found in official documents was replaced by a democratic spirit that recognized the 'right' of each individual and social organization to carry out science and technology activities.

He noted that the Decree moved toward:

> abolishing ... the right of bureaucratic 'examination and approval' of the administrative system, limiting the administrative function to approving the 'registration' form supplied by citizens. The result, as we all know, is that today it is difficult to be able to count precisely how many science and technology research, training and service organizations were established by citizens and social organizations through the spirit of Decree 35/HDBT. And so the terms '35 Center' and '35 Institute' appeared ... As we reflect on it today, the Decree was issued under the limited framework of an administrative system, but it really played the role of a *democratic charter* for science.[9]

RECOGNITION OF SOCIAL ORGANISATIONS
IN THE 1995 CIVIL CODE

The 1992 Science and Technology Decree was a watershed for the Vietnamese associational sector, particularly the intellectual and professional sector based in the cities. However, it was also what Vietnamese legislators and scholars sometimes call an 'under-law', a legal document issued by one ministry and applicable to that organisation, not throughout the country by all government authorities. It could not fulfil the full constitutional guarantee of associational rights. Further recognition in the form of a full national law was given to the expanding social organisation sector in 1995, when the Civil Code of the Socialist Republic of Vietnam was adopted by the National Assembly. The Civil Code formally recognised economic and social organisations, social and charitable foundations (funds) and other voluntary groups as legal entities.[10]

Of course, hundreds or thousands of social organisations of various types had existed during the 10-year period of reform preceding the promulgation of the Civil Code—the Code certainly did not initiate the

---

[9] Vu Cao Dam, 'On the Occasion of the Tenth Anniversary of the Promulgation of Decree 35-HDBT by the Government' (Hanoi, 2002).
[10] Civil Code of the Socialist Republic of Vietnam (1995), arts 114 ff.

emergence of the sector. But the recognition of legal personality was important at the level of national legislation rather than ministerial regulation. The Code sought to remove still significant legal, economic and political obstacles to participation in the voluntary sector, in part by enabling voluntary groups to pursue bank loans with greater ease and flexibility, for example, and it sought to protect members' personal assets from risk due to losses or negligence of members acting in their organisational roles. Finally, by recognising social and professional organisations and funds in a key piece of national legislation, the Code opened the door both to facilitating and restrictive implementing legislation at the national, ministerial and provincial levels, a chapter in the tale of social organisations in Vietnam that would play out over the next decade.[11]

THE LONG ROAD TOWARD THE CONSTITUTIONAL GUARANTEE OF FREEDOM OF ASSOCIATION: THE LAW ON ASSOCIATIONS IN VIETNAM

In the early 1990s, a drafting group began work in Hanoi on a national Law on Associations to replace finally the restrictive 1957 law regulations on associations that were still in effect, and under the rubric provided by article 69 of the 1992 Constitution. Those drafting efforts involved a range of government ministries as well as the Vietnam Fatherland Front, a national party-led coalition of mass organisations, and continued for a number of years. They were bogged down in the late 1990s over a range of difficult issues in state management, registration, coverage and other problems relating to the associational sector, an early signal of the even more significant difficulties to come when drafting of the Law on Associations re-accelerated several years later.

Both in the 1990s, and since the drafting process to formulate a Law on Associations was reinitiated several years later, drafters sought to implement the article 69 right to form associations by replacing the 1957 associational regulations with a law that maintains state control of the associational sector and clarifies an increasingly confused environment while also providing encouragement to a range of associations

---

[11] The special problems in regulating voluntary agricultural cooperatives are dealt with at some length elsewhere, but are not treated here. Similarly, most religious organisations are outside this stream of regulation. On religious organisations, see P Taylor (ed), *Modernity and Re-Enchantment: Religion in Post-Revolutionary Vietnam* (Singapore, Institute of Southeast Asian Studies, 2007).

and other social organisations that fulfil party- and state-favoured goals. From the beginning of the drafting of the Law on Associations, it was understood that the new law would continue to require the registration and approval of voluntary organisations as well as continuing controls on activities, reporting requirements, financial affairs and other important areas to impose some discipline—or at least give the state the ability to impose some order—on this burgeoning sector. However, the process has been long, subject to debate on complex and politically sensitive issues, and in recent years has been sharply affected by the growing power of national business, trade and professional associations and the increasing power and restive activity of the National Assembly and its delegates and committees.[12]

As this conflict began to develop, however, lower-level law-making on the sector continued. Individual decrees and regulations were employed to regulate parts of the associational sector that have developed particularly quickly, were subject to little formal state regulation in the past and that have caused regulatory headaches for the state—such as the proliferation of 'funds' (*quy*, sometimes termed 'foundations') for a variety of social, charitable, artistic and cultural, educational and other activities.

THE BATTLEGROUND OF THE 2003 DECREE ON THE ORGANISATION, OPERATION AND MANAGEMENT OF ASSOCIATIONS

The drafting of a Law on Associations continued to drag on while the social organisation sector continued to grow very rapidly, and required detailed regulation on a scale unimagined in 1957 when the original regulations were issued by the Vietnamese authorities. With a Law on Associations still far on the horizon, the government promulgated a decree providing more detailed provisions on the organisation and management of associations, both to govern the burgeoning sector and to preview and test the approaches and provisions that might be utilised in a full law.

Decree 88 on the Management of Associations, drafted by the Ministry of Home Affairs and promulgated by the government in July 2003, provided this updated framework for associational activities—but

---

[12] On the role of business associations, see, eg J Stromseth, 'Business associations and policy-making in Vietnam' in B Kerkvliet et al (eds), *Getting Organized in Vietnam: Moving In and Around the Socialist State* (Singapore, Institute of Southeast Asian Studies, 2005).

also became a lightning rod for criticism of government efforts to restrict formation of associations beyond the constitutional guarantees. The 2003 Decree also played a major role in fuelling increased conflict between the ministry, which sought to retain control as well as to keep the 'dual management' system of Ministry and line ministry authority, and the increasingly strong efforts of national associations to maintain distance from government ministries.

The 2003 Decree on Associations defined associations broadly as:

> voluntary organizations of citizens, Vietnamese organizations of the same professions, the same avocations, [or] the same gender, with the common purpose of gathering and uniting their members, conducting regular activities, seeking to protect the legitimate rights and interests of their members, supporting each other in effective activities, contributing to the nation's economic and social development, which are organized and conduct their activities in accordance with this Decree and other relevant legal documents.

However, like all earlier legislation, the 2003 Decree explicitly excluded the mass organisations under the party from its scope. These organisations—the Vietnam Fatherland Front, Labour Confederation, Ho Chi Minh Communist Youth Union, Vietnam Peasants Association, Vietnam War Veterans Association and the Vietnam Women's Union— have long been governed directly by the party and by their own statutes. The party and state are considerably less concerned about managing the few but important mass organisations than the thousands of emerging associations and social organisations, although increasingly powerful national associations now openly complained of the special treatment accorded to the traditional mass organisations. The 2003 Decree retained the 'dual management' structure of the Home Ministry, which exercised 'uniform management with respect to associations throughout the country', and line (functional) ministry control under which associations were beginning to chafe under their new-found fiscal and operational freedom in practice. The Decree also continued to give the authorities broad discretion to approve registration, bar groups for 'purposes or activities that violate the law' and de-register organisations. The state also retained a wide range of other traditional powers: to approve organisational charters and to approve establishment, division or separation, merger, consolidation or dissolution of associations. Associations were required to report on (among other matters) organisational annual and other important meetings, changes in officers, establishment of offices in other localities and annual financial reporting, all subject to administrative, civil and criminal sanctions. The government and the Ministry of Home Affairs would seek to retain all of these prerogatives in the accelerated drafting of the formal Law on Associations that was to come; in turn, many in the associational sector would seek to weaken some of these management and control mechanisms.

Under the 2003 Decree, associations were permitted a wide range of activities, including providing information on their goals and purposes, representing their members and protecting their interests, organising membership activities, providing 'advice and criticism on matters within the association's scope of activities', contributing views on drafts of laws and regulations, raising funds for operations (including from 'business or services in accordance with the provisions of law') and receiving 'lawful support' from organisations and individuals at home and abroad. Other provisions provide detailed rules on the division, separation, merger, consolidation and dissolution of associations, with a focus on ensuring that associational assets do not end up in the pockets of individuals.[13]

However, the drafting of the 2003 Decree was also an initial battle-ground for later debates on the role of the state. In a concession to demands from the associational sector, fuelled by references to the 1992 Constitution's guarantee of freedom of association, the traditional approval requirements and discretionary powers were accompanied by a new requirement that the examining state agencies must issue receipts for organisational applications, reply to 'complete' and 'lawful' petitions within 60 days and provide 'clear reasons' if the application is denied. In turn, activists and more liberal officials failed in their attempts to include an even stronger provision that would have granted automatic approval of associational applications if a decision was not communicated within the 60-day time period, or a right to judicial appeal of administrative decisions.

Thus, these complex drafting discussions, which presaged the far broader debates on the Law on Associations in the years which followed, emerged in a compromise that retained the examination and approval system rather than moving toward a considerably less discretionary registration system—together with a minor bow to the concerns of the associational sector expressed through time limits on consideration of applications and providing clear reasons for denial, but not going so far as to provide for automatic registration if the government failed to respond to applications, or for judicial review of those administrative decisions.

---

[13] Decree 88/2003/ND-CP of the Government on the Organisation, Operation and Management of Associations (2003).

DEBATING THE CONSTITUTIONAL GUARANTEE:
THE CONFLICTS OVER THE LAW ON ASSOCIATIONS

The 2003 Decree on Associations was promulgated both to provide some order in the burgeoning world of Vietnamese associations and to serve as an experiment for the future drafting and promulgation of a national Law on Associations. Drafting of the Law on Associations gathered steam once again in 2003 and 2004, as the number of social and other non-governmental organisations of various kinds grew rapidly.[14] These activities began with a series of drafting meetings and workshops to review foreign experience in non-profit law. However, the National Assembly pointed out the complications of this process, noting that:

> this is a difficult law ... Moreover, the ... development of associations and social organizations in Vietnam is very complex [in keeping with] the level of social development. So new factors in the sphere of associations and social organizations continue to appear.[15]

After a lengthy process of drafting to govern the formation, management, supervision, operations, internal structure, funding and other aspects of the work of Vietnamese associations and other social organisations, the eighth draft of the Law on Associations was released by the Office of the Government in Hanoi in early December 2005 for comment, setting off a firestorm of reaction from national associations representing intellectuals and business sectors. The draft law generally tracked the provisions of Decree 88 on Associations (2003), which had been regarded by the Vietnamese associational sector as unnecessarily restrictive and limiting, both in its dual management and control structure and in effecting approval and registration through line ministries and the Ministry of Home Affairs. But national business, professional and intellectual associations also lobbied for legal verification of their status and the status of hundreds of associations around Vietnam through law.

---

[14] On recent developments in this field in Vietnam, see the sources noted above in n 2.
[15] For more detail on the drafting debates, see M Sidel, 'Associational Rights and Freedom of Expression in Vietnam', paper delivered to the Conference on the Protection of Constitutional Rights (Pescara, Italy, December 2007); and M Sidel, 'Changing Dynamics of Law Formation in a Transitional Socialist State: Conflict, Power and Resistance in the Debates over the Law on Associations and State-Nonprofit Relations in Vietnam', paper presented to the Association for Asian Studies (March 2007).

The official draft law that emerged in late 2005 retained many of the most criticised elements of Decree 88 and earlier drafts. The draft law continued the dual management and control structure by both line (functional) ministries and the Ministry of Home Affairs. In a gesture to increasingly vocal opponents of the traditional approval system for organisations, the law now referred to registration—but the shift was formal rather than substantive, for 'registration' under the draft law required compliance with a complex, lengthy, multi-stage system for formation of associations and other social organisations that retained virtually all of the characteristics of the 1957 and 2003 approval systems. The six key party-related mass organisations were also excluded from the law, prompting fierce calls from other national associations for equal treatment and the inclusion of the mass organisations in the draft law.

That draft law, largely written by the drafting committee chaired by the Ministry of Home Affairs, was brought to the government for formal approval and forwarding to the National Assembly in December 2005—and it was rejected by the office of the Prime Minister because of continuing controversies and opposition from a wide alliance of national professional and business associations and intellectuals, who stated more boldly than ever that government attempts to legislate in this area violated the freedom of association guaranteed in the 1992 Constitution. The draft was formally sent back for further discussions, an unexpected victory in the formal process for critics that further emboldened national associations and intellectuals.

By late December 2005, the debate reached a point previously unknown in modern Vietnamese legislative history, when a team of specialists convened and supported by the Vietnamese Union of Science and Technology Associations drafted their own alternative Law on Associations in response to the official draft law, threatening to take the alternative draft Law on Associations to the floor of the National Assembly in spring 2006 and formally propose it for adoption. That alternative bill reached its fifth draft by mid-January 2006; it was the first time in modern Vietnamese history that opposition to a government-drafted law had reached a level where a 'rebellious' alternative law was presented for discussion.

The alternative draft opened with an explicit reference to article 69 of the constitution guaranteeing freedom to form associations and boldly situated the draft law in the realm of the protection of constitutional rights rather than the administration of citizens' organisation. The draft provided alternative approaches on virtually every question under debate. It stipulated a much simplified procedure for forming and registering associations that was much closer to a registration model than an approval model, and a single system of state management (Home Ministry at the national level; People's Committees at the level of provinces and below), with specified roles for state management; a much simpler reporting mechanism for associations; and it differentiated clearly among types of associations.

The alternative draft also made specific provisions for the legal treatment of 'unions' or 'federations' of associations (like the Vietnam Union of Science and Technology Associations (VUSTA) and the Vietnam Union of Literary and Arts Associations (VULAA)); sought to initiate a national register of associations; broadened the rights of associations, particularly relating to advocacy and participation in public affairs; introduced the concept of particular privileges for a category of public benefit organisations; and, in procedural terms, provided more time limits for and greater opportunities to challenge administrative action.[16]

By 2005 and 2006, the key issues in the draft Law on Associations were centred on the following important controversies.

Should Party-Related Mass Organisations be Subject to the Law on Associations?

The six mass organisations—the Vietnam Fatherland Front, Vietnam General Labour Confederation, Ho Chi Minh Communist Youth Union, Vietnam Peasants Association, Vietnam War Veterans Association and the Vietnam Women's Union—lobbied strongly and vociferously, including through high party and state channels, to remain outside the scope of the law. The stakes were high, both for the mass organisations, which had long enjoyed a special political status and at least some continuing central funding, and for other major associations (such as VUSTA, the Union of Literary and Arts Associations, the Vietnam Chamber of Commerce and Industry (VCCI) and the Lawyers Association), which sought to level the playing field by bringing the

---

[16] The drafts of the Law on Associations are available at <http://www.vibonline. com.vn> accessed 26 February 2009. For discussion of the various drafts, see M Sidel, 'Changing Dynamics of Law Formation in a Transitional Socialist State: Conflict, Power and Resistance in the Debates over the Law on Associations and State-Nonprofit Relations in Vietnam' (Association of Asian Studies, March 2007).

mass organisations into parity with other major national associations—
or, perhaps, even to join the six political mass organisations with an
exemption from the law.

The official 2005 draft law explicitly kept the six mass organisations
outside the scope of the law, sparking extensive opposition from other
national associations and intellectuals. In December 2005 and January
2006, the situation became politically more complicated when intellectuals associated with VUSTA and other groups dramatically increased
the temperature of the debate by accusing the drafters, and implicitly the
party, of relegating intellectuals to second-class status by making them
subject to the draft law while privileging non-intellectual groups.

Should the 'Dual Management' Role of the State be Maintained?

The second major conflict erupted when the drafting committee led by
the Ministry of Home Affairs recommended in the 2005 draft law that
line ministries as well as the Home Ministry would continue to manage
the voluntary sector, including individual associations. In general terms,
the 'dual management' structure provided that the line (functional)
ministries would retain operational and professional authority over
associations within their functional realm (ie the Ministry of Health
over health organisations), while the Ministry of Home Affairs would
regulate non-specialised organisational issues.

This continuing dual management formulation has produced substantial controversy in the national associational sector, which understands
the need for Home Ministry administration, but has sought, since at
least the mid-1990s, to expand and preserve autonomy from direct
supervision by an individual line ministry in what was consistently, and
pejoratively, referred to as the '*bo chu quan*' or 'ministry-in-charge' patterns of an earlier and more conservative era.

For its part, the Home Ministry preferred to maintain a strong role
for the line ministries, fearful that it could not maintain knowledge and
control of the operations and activities of thousands of associations and
needing the line ministries to play that role as partners in the control
process. Conseqently, the official 2005 draft law retained the dual management structure, including a strong role for the line ministries, using
statutory wording that infuriated national associations and intellectuals
who believed that it would bring back unlamented days of direct line
ministry control, reinvigorating and returning their formerly subordinate relationship to resurgent government ministries.

How Complex and Cumbersome Should Registration of Associations Be?

The official 2005 draft Law on Associations provided for 'registration' of associations through a complex multi-staged process that largely tracked the procedure utilised in the 2003 Decree 88 on Associations and closely resembled—except for the word 'registration'—the examination and approval requirements of the past. Due to the highly cumbersome process that requires at least two submissions by the association to the relevant state authority and at least two approvals by the relevant state authority, it could take more than 180 days to form an association through all of these steps. The official draft law provided few guidelines or limitations on state discretion in rejecting an application or at other points in the approval process. Furthermore, it did not provide an opportunity to appeal or seek judicial resolution of such complaints. In both failing to provide effective limits on the exercise of state discretion in the application process other than requiring an application receipt and providing time limits for state action, the registration process largely tracked the 2003 Decree.

This cumbersome and fully discretionary process, and the continued reliance on approval mechanisms even if now termed 'registration', engendered strong opposition from national associations and other social organisations. They demanded a single system of state management under the Ministry of Home Affairs and a simplified formation and registration process that did not cede as much discretion to MOHA and line ministries and provided for limits in the registration process.

The Problem of Geographic Restrictions on Registration

Another problem concerned whether more than one association should be allowed to operate in a functional field in a defined geographic area. Earlier official drafts had repeated a traditional position that no more than one association operating in a particular field (such as health or education) should be approved for formation in a particular defined geographic area, such as a township. The Ministry of Home Affairs and security forces appeared to support such geographic restrictions in order to ease the management of the associational sector, but increasingly associations themselves came to view geographic restrictions as limiting innovation, competition and the provision of social services.

Should Non-Resident Vietnamese, Foreigners and Foreign-Invested Enterprises in Vietnam be Permitted to Join Vietnamese Associations?

Earlier drafts had assumed that membership in Vietnamese associations would be limited to Vietnamese citizens and organisations registered in Vietnam. However, increasingly powerful national associations—including scientific and business groups—insistently asked why non-resident Vietnamese, foreigners and foreign-invested enterprises in Vietnam should not be permitted to join Vietnamese associations.

DETAILING THE CONSTITUTIONAL GUARANTEE: THE ALTERNATIVE DRAFT LAW ON ASSOCIATIONS (2005–06)

The separate and unofficial draft Law on Associations composed by legal scholars in Hanoi and others affiliated with the Vietnam Union of Science and Technology Associations—an unprecedented event in Vietnamese modern law-making—provided different procedures and remedies for each of these issues. On the issue of the mass organisations, the alternative draft law made them subject to the law rather than allowing them separate political status outside the statute. The alternative draft law eliminated the traditional 'ministry-in-charge' structure of dual management of associations, leaving management and administration of the associational sector solely with the Ministry of Home Affairs (and provincial authorities for lower-level associations).

The alternative draft replaced the official draft's cumbersome, long and complex 'registration' procedure with a streamlined procedure; reduced geographic restrictions on associations; allowed non-resident Vietnamese and foreigners to join associations; and simplified reporting requirements—all based on an explicitly stated idea that the Law should implement and enforce constitutional guarantees of freedom to form associations.[17]

CONFLICT, DENOUEMENT—AND BEGINNING AGAIN

Two drafts—one official, one unofficial and unauthorised—as well as outspoken debate in newspapers and through government reports

---

[17] The full text of the VUSTA alternative draft of the Law on Associations is available at <http://www.vibonline.com.vn> accessed 26 February 2009.

was the situation faced by the Ministry of Home Affairs in the winter of 2005 and spring of 2006, when the government rejected the official December 2005 draft and sent it back to the drafting committee for further discussion of unresolved issues. For the first time in modern Vietnamese legislative history, a 'rump' group of lawyers, researchers and civil society activists had drafted their own law intended to give substance to a constitutional guarantee, and had threatened to bring that much more liberal law to the floor of the national legislature, the National Assembly—where it would have had substantial support.

In accordance with standard Vietnamese law-making practice, the Home Ministry, as the lead drafting agency responsible for the law, prepared the government's official Proposal to the National Assembly of the Draft Law on Associations, on behalf of the government. The government submitted that Proposal to the National Assembly in April 2006 over the signature of the Minister of Home Affairs on behalf of the Prime Minister and government.

The official Government Proposal on the draft Law on Associations recognised explicitly that the Law on Associations was intended to give substance to a constitutional right, and that:

> this is a draft law that is exceptionally complex, relating to the rights and obligations of citizens and organizations and the responsibilities of [various] state agencies. In addition, as we further democratize social activities ... our understanding of associations has also undergone some changes.[18]

On several of the key issues in the law—including the status of the party-based mass organisations and the role of line ministries in administering associations—the ministry and government were forced to present different views and alternative draft language to the National Assembly, since it had proven impossible in the highly charged debates over the law in late 2005 and early 2006 to resolve the key issues. Those issues on which the government's proposal provided alternative language included: the scope of the statute, and particularly whether the mass organisations were included within it; whether the law applied to foreign commercial and trade associations and to foreign individuals as associational members; and the methods of government oversight.

In each case the government advised the National Assembly of the draft language that it preferred and found appropriate, but provided

---

[18] Government Proposal to the National Assembly on the Draft Law on Associations, 17 April 2006, available at <http://www.vibonline.com.vn> accessed 26 February 2009 (*Chinh phu To trinh len Quoc hoi Du an Luat ve Hoi*).

alternative draft language reflecting the deep and bitter disagreements. In turn, the National Assembly could not agree on the key issues they faced—there was continuing disagreement between the Assembly's Law Committee, Standing Committee and delegates over the scope of the law (particularly whether it should include the party-related mass associations), the problem of dual state management (on which there was continuing, bitter controversy), procedures to establish associations, whether individuals abroad (including overseas Vietnamese) should be allowed to join Vietnamese associations (and organisations), government subsidies and financial policies toward associations and other matters.

AWAITING THE CONSTITUTIONAL GUARANTEE OF FREEDOM OF ASSOCIATION

In the end, under pressure from party officials, the National Assembly declined to resolve these difficult conflicts in 2006 and did not pass the Law on Associations—after 14 years of research, drafting and discussion. In the end, the myriad of controversies surrounding the law might have been resolvable at the National Assembly. However, the 'colour revolutions' that erupted in 2003 in Georgia and then expanded into the Ukraine and Kyrgyzstan (with ripples into other post-Communist states) in 2004 and 2005 worried party officials greatly, combining with reluctance to give too wide an imprimatur to the formation of associational entities, and thus the party decided that the Law on Associations should be delayed.

IMPLEMENTING THE CONSTITUTIONAL GUARANTEE: KEY ISSUES FOR THE FUTURE

When the Law on Associations and other regulatory documents affecting civil society return to the fore in Vietnam, a number of important issues will remain unresolved. They include the following.[19]

---

[19] See also M Sidel, *Law and Society in Vietnam* (Cambridge, Cambridge University Press, 2008) ch 6; and M Sidel, 'Changing Dynamics of Law Formation in a Transitional Socialist State: Conflict, Power and Resistance in the Debates over the Law on Associations and State-Nonprofit Relations in Vietnam', paper presented to the Association of Asian Studies (March 2007).

Prohibited Purposes and Activities and the Scope of Constitutional Guarantees to Form Associations

The prohibited purposes and activities of associations is one continuing point of division. The draft Law on Associations defined 'prohibited activities' very broadly and in ways that gave significant, largely unfettered discretion in interpretation and enforcement. In language similar to that of the 2003 Decree 88 on Associations, the draft Law prohibited:

> illegal activities which jeopardize the legitimate interest of organizations, individuals and communities, and the great unity of the entire people, [or which] violate national security [or] social order and safety

and associational names that 'conflict with the national tradition, culture, and ethical and moral practices'.

The associational sector criticised such provisions as overbroad, internally contradictory and confusing, although only rarely did the sector use constitutionalist appeals in these debates. These provisions also allowed no opportunity to challenge state decisions, either in the administrative or judicial realm. One might therefore expect the duelling draft prepared by specialists associated with the Vietnamese Union of Science and Technology Associations to prohibit a narrower range of activities and to provide for less state discretion in applying such principles. Yet the VUSTA alternative draft also gave the state broad discretion to prohibit associational purposes and activities. In a tactical concession to the party and state, the alternative draft tracked the relatively broad formulation of organisations and acts that states may prohibit contained in the 1966 Covenant on Civil and Political Rights, arguably even providing for greater state discretion in this area.

Should the 'Dual Management' Role of the State be Maintained?

How will the state 'manage' or 'administer' the associational sector under the framework of the new Law on Associations? Successive drafts of the law have provided for a continuing dual management structure in which (for associations at the national level) the Home Ministry would manage the sector in terms of organisation on behalf of the government, and government ministries and ministerial-level agencies would be responsible for management of the activities of associations operating in their professional sectors. (At the provincial level, the draft law provided for management of the association sector by the People's Committees of provinces and directly administered municipalities.)

This continuing dual management formulation at the national level (management of associations by both MOHA and ministries) has produced substantial controversy in the national associational sector, which understands the need for Home Ministry administration, but disagrees on the role of line ministries. For its part, the Home Ministry prefers to maintain a role for the ministries, but indicates that the role envisioned is somewhat different from the 'ministry-in-charge' relationship of the past. For their part, large national associations such as the Vietnamese Union of Science and Technology Associations (VUSTA) and others are concerned that maintaining the traditional formulation of the relationship between the state and associations would reinvigorate their subordinate relationship to government ministries that has been fading in recent years. The issue of where associations report and how detailed and cumbersome that regulation is will need to be resolved in some form before a draft law can emerge that hopes to substantiate the constitutional guarantee of freedom of association.

Will Party-Related Mass Organisations be Subject to the Law?

Whether the six key party-founded and -led Vietnamese mass organisations will be subject to the Law on Associations, or outside its scope, has never been resolved. These six organisations have high stakes in this debate, for they have long had a special political status and at least some continuing central funding. Similarly, the stakes are high for other national associations, such as VUSTA, the Literary and Arts Associations, the Vietnam Lawyers Association and the Vietnam Chamber of Commerce and Industry (VCCI), which seek to level the playing field by requiring that the mass organisations be subject to the law like them, or that they join the six political mass organisations in being exempted.

How Complex and Cumbersome Should Registration of Associations Be?

The draft Law on Associations provides for registration of associations through a complex multi-staged process that largely tracks the complex procedure that has been utilised in the 2003 Decree 88 on Associations.

That highly cumbersome process requires at least two submissions by the association to the relevant state authority and at least two approvals by the relevant state authority, and it could take more than 180 days to form an association through all of these steps. Furthermore, the official draft law provided few guidelines or limitations on discretion of the relevant state authority in rejecting an application or at other points in the exercise of state discretion, nor an opportunity to appeal or seek judicial resolution of such complaints. Nor does the draft law provide effective guidelines or limitations on the exercise of state discretion in the application process, other than requiring an application receipt and providing time limits for state action.

This cumbersome and discretionary process, and the continued reliance on approval mechanisms even if now termed registration, caused substantial opposition from national associations and other social organisations. They demanded a single system of state management under the Ministry of Home Affairs and a simplified formation and registration process that did not cede as much approval authority to MOHA and line ministries.

Geographic Restrictions on Registration

Geographic restrictions on registration of associations have also proven a problem. One of two clearly defined drafting options in the eleventh draft of the law provides that 'the proposed area of operation is not coincident with the major area of operation of another association'—and the other option omits this geographic restriction on registration. Including such a limitation would discourage multiple groups from serving in citizens and social development (and discourage competition to provide good services or other activities and to raise organisational quality).

Organisational Membership: Non-Resident Vietnamese, Foreigners and Foreign-Invested Enterprises in Vietnam

Should non-resident Vietnamese, foreigners and foreign-invested enterprises in Vietnam be permitted to join Vietnamese associations? There was widespread and continuing debate on these issues, and the later drafts of the law contained numerous drafting options on this point reflecting a lack of consensus among drafters and government agencies. One option is to allow foreign-invested enterprises to join Vietnamese business associations; another would have not specifically named such enterprises as eligible. Another drafting option would allow Vietnamese resident abroad and foreign individuals to join associations; a fourth option was silent on that issue. All of these options reflected continuing debate on the role of these three important and sensitive groups, and remained unresolved in 2006 when the final adoption of the law was delayed.

The Special Role of Government Appropriations

How should associations be financed? A significant problem in many non-profit law-drafting processes is whether the state allows associations and other non-profit organisations to engage in income-producing activities—and, if income-producing activities are allowed, what kinds are allowed, and if they are taxed. For example, must income-producing activities be related to the non-profit mission of the association? The draft Law on Associations is vague on this issue, an increasingly important concern for social organisations in Vietnam as they struggle to raise revenue. The draft law permitted associations to engage in 'raising funds from membership fees and other sources of revenue in accordance with the law' and speaks of 'legitimate revenues gained from the Association's activities'. It remained unclear, in later drafts of the law, whether associations are allowed to engage in revenue-producing activities and, if so, of what kinds.

The alternative draft law was somewhat more flexible, although still vague, in treatment of income. This issue is complicated because the draft law also contemplates that associations can establish 'affiliated legal entities' (art 37). However, it is not clear whether such entities are intended primarily to produce revenue (regardless of their legal form), rather than providing services or associational activities. If so, there is a very significant danger that associations will be formed primarily to take advantage of the formation of 'affiliated legal entities' that will produce revenue under an associational 'umbrella', thereby, in effect, providing an advantaged 'cover' for business activities. This has occurred in a number of other countries.

However, in the final pre-delay draft of the law, the question of government appropriations emerged. One drafting option would have included the language 'government budget as stipulated by law' among 'the revenues of an association', while another option omitted governmental budgetary outlays as potential associational revenue. Once again, this important issue remained unresolved.

The Scope of Advocacy Allowed to Associations

The draft law permitted associations to conduct (in one draft) 'advocacy on its objectives' or, in a perhaps more accurate translation of the Vietnamese text, 'to publicize the objectives of the association'. This limited scope for advocacy and participation in public affairs has been criticised by opponents of the draft law, and the alternative draft provided a broader scope for such work. In recent years, the role and extent of advocacy and participation by non-government groups in law-making and public policy in Vietnam has become a significant issue, and discussion of this issue is expected to continue to increase.

The Role of Taxation in Associational Formation and Regulation

The various drafts of the Law on Associations have virtually ignored the tax issues that become increasingly important for non-profit sector development as national prosperity increases, focusing instead in issues of registration and governance. This is consistent with early drafting in a number of other developing countries. The 2006 draft of the Law on Associations provided only that 'those associations that work for humanitarian and charity purposes or for public interest shall enjoy preferential tax rates according to the Law' (art 57). The alternative draft bill is slightly more specific and introduces the concept of special privileges for public benefit organisations.

FIGHTING FOR CIVIL SOCIETY? CONSTITUTIONALISM AND THE CONFLICT OVER THE LAW GOVERNING FREEDOM OF ASSOCIATION

The debate over the Vietnamese Law on Associations illuminates conflicts that have plagued the relationship between the state and the associational sector in both China and Vietnam. In China, the party and state have managed these conflicts by retaining control through a variety of mechanisms—including dual management structures and approval mechanisms for a range of non-profit activities, and other measures—while permitting the sector to expand rapidly to fulfil pressing needs in Chinese society without directly challenging the party.

In Vietnam, the rapidly emerging strength of the business, trade and professional sector, represented most clearly by the Vietnam Union of Scientific and Technological Associations (VUSTA) and the

Vietnam Chamber of Commerce and Industry (VCCI), sparked the major conflict in 2005 and 2006 discussed here over the extent and scope of governmental control over the emerging associational sector. That conflict went further, in legislative terms, than has occurred in China: in Vietnam, it resulted in the drafting of the alternative Law on Associations discussed in this chapter, and the threat to seek to bring that alternative draft law to the floor of Vietnam's National Assembly.

This is in part a conflict among elites. Here, large and increasingly powerful associations representing Vietnam's business and intellectual elites seek to protect their autonomy from a state that attempts to use modes of management regarded as a legacy of the past, particularly the 'dual management' of a Ministry of Home Affairs and a line ministry. They join with smaller research, advocacy and service groups to form a relatively powerful coalition. The state's opponents here cannot be ignored, nor, like rural peasants or ethnic minorities, can they be suppressed in the interests of national policy. The party and state need both centralised modes of control, but also the initiative and autonomy that organisations and intellectuals bring to the reform process. All of this comes together in the battle over the Law on Associations.

In these debates, Vietnamese reformers sought to re-emphasise constitutional guarantees to form organisations through explicit reference to article 69 of the Vietnamese Constitution, and through an explicit reorientation of the legal drafting process toward implementing constitutional rights rather than the state's focus on administering troublesome associations. Yet the reformers' work on the Law on Associations—carried out through liberal legal scholars, scientific, literary and trade associations, and the media—was also highly measured and nuanced. Reference to constitutional guarantees was made, but reformers struggling with state administrators over the level of control and restriction over associations avoided isolating themselves and radicalising their cause, through autonomous constitutional appeals that might ally them with Vietnam's small but vocal community of democratic dissent.

While this campaign and the associational actors and individual drafters who led it sought to implement constitutional guarantees, they also worked carefully to avoid appeals to constitutional values and guarantees that widely separated themselves from the party and state, seeking to avoid a heightened battle that would put them at political odds with those political authorities by being perceived as autonomous and independent interpreters of constitutional rights.

As in China, Vietnam is likely to come to a compromise that allows for both a level of control that satisfies the party and state, and a level of autonomy that temporarily satisfies powerful associational actors while allowing for some flexible expansion in the future. Of perhaps more import for the future—although little discussed in 2005 and 2006—is how these debates and compromises may affect smaller and weaker community-based organisations that may seek to defend the economic and other rights of forces less powerful than large companies and Hanoi- and Saigon-based intellectuals. If the result of the 2005 and 2006 debates is that control is applied more flexibly to the large and powerful business and intellectual actors and much more rigorously to less powerful community and advocacy groups, then the constitutional guarantee will have been applied unevenly and unfairly, and these battles may need to be fought again in the future.

FURTHER READING

Civicus and Vietnam Institute of Development Studies (2005) *The Emerging Civil Society: An Assessment of Civil Society in Viet Nam* (Hanoi, Civicus), <http://www.undp.org.vn> accessed 26 February 2009 and <http://www.civicus.org> accessed 26 February 2009.

Hannah, J (2007) *Local Non-Governmental Organizations in Vietnam: Development, Civil Society, and State-Society Relations* (PhD dissertation, University of Washington).

Kerkvliet, B, Heng, R and Koh, D (eds) (2003) *Getting Organised in Vietnam: Moving In and Around the Socialist State* (Singapore, Institute of Southeast Asian Studies).

Sidel, M (1997) 'The Emergence of a Voluntary Sector and Philanthropy in Vietnam: Functions, Legal Regulation and Prospects for the Future' 8 *Voluntas* 283.

—— (1997) 'Vietnam: The Ambiguities of State-Directed Legal Reform' in Tan (ed) *Asian Legal Systems: Law, Society and Pluralism in East Asia* (Sydney, Butterworths).

—— (2008) *Law and Society in Vietnam* (Cambridge, Cambridge University Press).

8

The Problem of Judicial Independence in a Party–Dominated State

J UDICIAL INDEPENDENCE IS a sensitive topic in Vietnam, and has always been in the Communist Party-dominated states and legal systems. This is an area in which reality differs sharply from the words in constitutional texts. Each of Vietnam's twentieth-century constitutions—1946, 1959, 1980 and 1992—guaranteed a form of judicial independence or autonomy in reasonably strong terms. The 1946 Constitution provided that judges would be appointed by the government and that '[i]n administering justice, judges shall obey only the law. Other agencies shall not interfere'.[1] The 1959 Constitution stipulated that '[i]n administering justice, the People's Courts are independent, and shall obey only the law'. This formulation used the term *quyen doc lap*, meaning right to independence, which is possibly a slightly stronger term than in constitutional texts before and after.[2]

The 1980 Constitution maintained the guarantee, also using the term *doc lap* for independence: 'In administering justice, judges and people's assessors are independent and shall obey only the law.'[3] Furthermore, the 1992 Constitution, the constitution of the *doi moi* (reform) era, also retained the guarantee and used the same formulation: 'In administering justice, judges and assessors are independent and shall only obey the law.' The only difference between the formulations in 1980 and 1992

---

[1] Article 69 of the 1946 Constitution states: '*Trong khi xet xu, cac vien tham phan chi tuan theo phap luat, cac co quan khac khong duoc can thiep.*' The Vietnamese text of these provisions on judicial independence is provided here to facilitate detailed comparison and analysis in the text.

[2] Article 100 of the 1959 Constitution states: '*Khi xet xu, Toa an nhan dan co quyen doc lap va chi tuan theo phap luat.*'

[3] Article 131 of the 1980 Constitution states: '*Khi xet xu, tham phan va hoi tham nhan dan doc lap va chi tuan theo phap luat.*'

was that the term for 'people's assessors' in 1980 had become 'assessors' in 1992.[4]

However, the real state of judicial independence in Vietnam has been very different from the rhetoric of the constitutional guarantees. Courts and judges in Vietnam have always been beholden to the party and government, and political and administrative interference in judgments has been common. Political and administrative control of and interference with the judiciary in Vietnam has taken two broad forms. First, local and national political authorities have often had direct control over courts at their respective levels, either alone or in cooperation with national authorities.

The 1959 Constitution provides a clear illustration of this structural form of control.

> The Supreme People's Court supervises (*giam doc*) the judicial work of local People's Court, military courts, and special courts ... The Supreme People's Court is responsible to the National Assembly and reports to it (*chiu trach nhiem va bao cao cong tac*), or when the National Assembly is not in session, to its Standing Committee. The local People's Courts are responsible to the local People's Councils at corresponding levels and report to them.[5]

Similar provisions were at work in 1980. By 1992, the constitution stated that 'the Supreme People's Court ... supervises and directs the judicial work of local People's Courts and Military Tribunals'.[6] In terms of reporting relationships:

> The President of the Supreme People's Court is responsible and makes his reports to the National Assembly and, when the latter is not in session, to its Standing Committee and to the State President. The President of the local People's Court is responsible, and makes his report, to the [local] People's Council.[7]

These strict control provisions have long stirred debate in Vietnam. The result is that both national and local courts are subject to extensive control not only by other state bodies at both national and local levels, but also by the Communist Party at various levels. This is not a hidden fact in Vietnam; it is well known and widely discussed.

---

[4] Article 130 of the 1992 Constitution states: '*Khi xet xu, Tham phan va Hoi tham doc lap va chi tuan theo phap luat.*' On the differences among the Vietnamese constitutions on this important issue, see also To Van-Hoa, *Judicial Independence* (Lund, Jurisförlaget i Lund, 2006) (particularly Pt V, chs XVI–XIX).

[5] 1959 Constitution, arts 103 and 104.

[6] 1992 Constitution, art 134.

[7] 1992 Constitution, art 135.

An important second dimension of control and interference is direct interference in the trial process. This is harder to measure, but reports indicate that interference with the judiciary occurs in Vietnam from local levels to national levels, and in a wide variety of criminal, civil and more sensitive political cases. In these ways, judicial independence in Vietnam has remained severely compromised by linked structural and political factors. Since the mid-1990s, efforts have been underway to upgrade the skills, status and conditions available to the judiciary in order to provide them with the tools for better work and more autonomy. These efforts have resulted in a better trained judiciary, and in some cases with better facilities, but it is difficult to know how much more autonomy the judiciary has in a variety of cases.[8]

In recent years, the Vietnamese Communist Party has outlined a plan to strengthen and reform the court system, including through revamping of the jurisdiction of the courts. This plan is part of a party-drafted programme for strengthening judicial reform adopted in June 2005 and known as Resolution 49 on Judicial Reform Strategy toward 2020. Resolution 49 barely speaks of judicial independence, although a form of autonomy is stipulated in the constitution itself; it is striking how little attention is given to judicial independence in the primary judicial reform document now in force in Vietnam.

The gulf between the constitutional rhetoric of judicial independence and the reality in Vietnam, at local, provincial and national levels, makes the process of achieving more judicial autonomy in Vietnam a long and arduous task. There has been some external pressure on the party, state and judiciary to strengthen autonomy and the quality of judicial work—pressure that has come from the National Assembly, in connection with the annual reports on the judiciary made by the Chief Justice of the Supreme People's Court, as well as from domestic and foreign dissidents and, occasionally, from the press.

THE DO SON LAND CASE AND THE EMERGENCE OF JUDICIAL INTERFERENCE ONTO THE PUBLIC STAGE

Rarely, however, have instances of interference with the judiciary and the violation of the constitutional norm that 'judges ... are independent

---

[8] On this issue see, eg P Nicholson, 'Judicial Independence and the Rule of Law: The Vietnam Court Experience' (2001) 3 *Australian Journal of Asian Law* 37; and P Nicholson, *Borrowing Court Systems: The Experience of Socialist Vietnam* (Leiden, Martinus Nijhoff, 2007).

and shall only obey the law' become a major public and political issue in Vietnam. In 2005 and 2006, however, a significant case of judicial interference by high-ranking party and state officials broke into the mainstream Vietnamese media, illuminating both the scale of the problem and the difficulties in reducing judicial interference. This case helps to illustrate the gaps between the constitutional rhetoric of judicial independence and reality, but also may help to indicate some ways forward for Vietnam in seeking to reach more judicial autonomy.

On 2 April 2004, the People's Committee of Hai Phong Municipality, a major eastern Vietnamese city on the coast, issued Decision No 807, signed by the Vice Chairman of the Municipal Party Committee. Among the hundreds of administrative decisions issued by a municipal-level Vietnamese entity in that year or any other, this one would not normally have elicited much notice. Under existing Vietnamese law, the decision allocated plots of land to over 100 local citizens and others. By law and policy, such land was supposed to go to local residents, with priority being given to the poor, disabled, war wounded, veterans and other vulnerable social groups.[9]

The plots were issued in an area under Hai Phong's administration called Do Son—an area of already valuable and still growing land values, near the coast, with a casino nearby and numerous other tourism and recreation projects on the drawing board. One newspaper estimated the land as worth in the thousands of dollars per square metre, with resales of land already going for far higher amounts. It was, in the words of a national newspaper, 'land with beautiful views, and value in the billions of *dong*'.

This decision drew interest because of who received the land. Among the more than 60 households that received land, at least nine of those were members of the Standing Committee of the Do Son Communist Party Committee of the local county seat or other local high-ranking officials, all of whom were not entitled to such land under national regulations for the allocation of land. They received parcels ranging from 60 to 300 square meters. They included: Vu Duc Van, Secretary of the Do Son Party Committee, in the name of one or more family members, who received 314.2 square metres; Dinh Xuan Thenh, Deputy Secretary of the Party Committee, who received 120 square metres; and

---

[9] This account of the Do Son case is drawn from multiple articles in Vietnamese newspapers and web news services during this period, including *Thanh Nien*, *Lao Dong*, *VnExpress* and *Tuoi Tre*.

members of the household of Hoang Anh Hung, Chairman of the Do Son People's Committee, who received over 700 square metres.

In addition to these allocations, the decision issued on 2 April 2004 also recommended that Hai Phong Municipality approve allocations of 22 parcels of land ranging from 120 to 250 square metres to senior officials working in a number of departments of Hai Phong Municipality, including the Bureaux of Construction, Finance, Planning and Investment, the Organisation Department of the municipal Party Committee, several departments of local Party Committees, and officials working in public security, justice, health and education in Hai Phong—all specifically named.

As local citizens began to talk about this flagrant land grab by officials, a retired local official, public security colonel Dinh Dinh Phu, learned of these land transfers and began to complain loudly and unceasingly to local and national authorities and media. In the words of the Vietnamese online newspaper *VnExpress*, Colonel Phu engaged in a 'firm struggle, holding his ground, leveling accusations of negative actions, including meeting with a number of eminent people'. Colonel Phu would become the only real hero in an increasingly complex story of corruption and judicial interference that would, eventually, lead to the highest levels of the party in one of Vietnam's largest cities, Hai Phong.

Colonel Phu's complaints and other reports of the land transfer were originally published in the nationally read *Youth* (*Thanh Nien*) newspaper and quickly picked up by other national media. They sparked a wave of public opposition and an investigation undertaken by the Government Inspectorate (*Thanh tra Chinh phu*) at the urgent request of the Deputy Prime Minister responsible for anti-corruption matters. The inspectorate concluded that the procedures used for deciding on the allocation of the land were completely lacking in integrity, official reporting had been untruthful and investigators had been interfered with. Responsibility both for the corrupt allocation of the land and for interference in the investigation process was laid directly at the feet of the local Party Committee and important local party and state officials.

The Government Inspectorate asked the central Party Secretariat in Hanoi and the Deputy Prime Minister to force the Hai Phong Party Committee to make amends and punish local officials. However, with regard to the untruthful reports, provision of falsified files and other issues, the inspectorate also noted that those actions likely constituted violations of land law and other laws and regulations, and suggested to the Deputy Prime Minister that he refer these matters to the Ministry of Public Security for investigation and possible charges.

In response, the Hai Phong Party Committee formed a group of senior officials to handle the matter and to determine, together with the Standing Committee of the local Do Son Party Committee, collective and individual responsibilities in the allocation of the land. Nine members of the Standing Committee of the Do Son Party Committee wrote self-criticisms and undertook personal responsibility for the violations. The party issued internal disciplinary penalties under the party constitution and rules, raising questions about the dual applicability of overlapping constitutional and legal documents, as first discussed in Chapter 1. Similar self-criticisms were made and similar internal discipline was issued to officials in the Hai Phong Bureau of Natural Resources and Environment, who had engaged in corrupt behaviour, 'causing the municipal People's Committee to allocate land in error'.

The Deputy Party Secretary of Hai Phong in charge of the group handling the problem—a process that was being watched carefully by Hanoi—noted that:

> some of the individual leaders' understanding of their errors is still childish, and does not reflect understanding of the seriousness of their errors.

He also announced that the disciplinary process would end within a month, by 13 May 2005. The Hai Phong Party Committee issued a collective warning to the Standing Committee of the Do Son Party Committee, and issued warnings to and removed five key local party and state officials from office.

Most or all of this was posturing to end the investigations and to protect higher officials. This posturing included the mild penalty of disciplinary warnings within the party against officials at the local Do Son Party Committee and local party and state agencies. The Deputy Prime Minister in charge of the investigation at the central level, Truong Vinh Trong, who had become known as a sort of anti-corruption fighter, was not assuaged by these local moves to end the scandal. He responded to the Government Inspectorate report by accepting the recommendation to refer information to the Ministry of Public Security for investigation of potential crimes, instructing the ministry to carry out an investigation and to 'issue charges in the case in accordance with law where there is clear evidence of a crime'.

The Ministry of Public Security carried out its investigations in May and June of 2005 and announced in early July that it had lodged charges of abusing functions and power in the Do Son case with a notice of those charges to local authorities and defendants. Attempts to forestall more serious charges continued, for example through the removal of more local officials. However, none of this could forestall criminal charges: on 11 August, the investigative police under the Ministry of Public Security in Hanoi filed charges against three Do Son officials—Party Secretary Vu Duc Van, People's Committee Chairman Hoang Anh Hung and Vice Chair Luu Kim Thai—for:

> using their position and powers to carry out an incorrect decision to allocate land in the Do Son township (Hai Phong), causing widespread anger among the people.

A month later, charges were filed against a fourth official, Chu Minh Tuan, the former Director of the Hai Phong Bureau of Natural Resources and Environment, for his involvement in the affair.

There the matter lay, at least in terms of press coverage, until early 2006. Under Vietnamese criminal procedure, the charges levelled by the Ministry of Public Security went next to the procuracy with the recommendation of an indictment. The procuracy brought formal indictments against the officials in 2006. In August, three of the four charged defendants—Vu Duc Van, Hoang Anh Hung and Luu Kim Thai—went on trial at the Hai Phong People's Court on charges of using their powers to allocate land to 33 individuals or families not authorised to receive the land. On 28 August, their trial ended with the issuance of a warning (*canh cao*) and a fine of 50,000 *dong* each (about US$3.25). The fourth defendant, the former head of the Hai Phong environment bureau, had not been brought to trial because the procuracy had decided that the evidence did not support the charge against him; he was only punished internally and administratively.

Public and media fury now reached a new crescendo in the wake of this shambles of a trial. One newspaper noted that:

> the views of the people of Hai Phong were expressed strongly against the overly light treatment meted out by the court against these defendants.

Another newspaper noted sarcastically, 'they've let them "eat the land"!' And a third national newspaper issued a blistering attack on the proceedings, pointedly asked whether the trial had been conducted in a 'strict and clear' manner.

Two days later, as protests among the public and in the media continued to grow rapidly and loudly on the trial process in Hai Phong, Prime Minister Nguyen Tan Dung suggested in a formal official letter (*cong van*) to the Procurator-General of the Supreme People's Procuracy and the President of the Supreme People's Court that they lead an investigation to clarify collective and individual responsibility for the public prosecution and the trial in the Do Son case. He also announced that the government would investigate whether the Hai Phong party and state authorities had 'interfered excessively (*can thiep qua sau*) in the case'.

The Prime Minister said that 'at a time when the Party, state, and people are resolutely implementing' laws and policies against corruption, 'if this case has not been handled strictly and clearly it will reflect poorly on the struggle against corruption'. He suggested that the Procurator-General and Chief Justice provide guidance for a formal review of the proceedings carried out the by Hai Phong People's Court, with a view toward formally protesting against and opposing the results of that trial. Once again, Deputy Prime Minister Truong Vinh Trong was assigned to re-investigate the case, now together with the local court's process and verdict, and to report back in a month.

The intervention from Hanoi further emboldened local activists who were protesting against the warning and fine issued by the Hai Phong court. Colonel Dinh Dinh Phu, who had led the original protests against the land grab and demanded indictments of the key officials, told the press that:

> if a citizen of Do Son takes a couple of plants from the house of Party Secretary Vu Duc Van he'll be sentenced to six months imprisonment. But if some of us give ourselves more than 100 pieces of land with a value of billions of *dong* he is given a warning.

Local residents told the press that the court in Hai Phong had been 'influenced' to reduce the punishments against the defendants by Hai Phong party authorities.

Almost immediately, central investigators and national reporters learned that the local Hai Phong party leaders, working through the Hai Phong People's Committee, had on two occasions 'suggested' that the Supreme People's Procuracy 'waive prosecution' of some of the officials implicated in the Do Son land scandal. Those two requests came in October 2005 and March 2006, also in the form of official letters (*cong van*). The reasons given were variously that the officials had good accomplishments in their work, that their health was precarious, that waiving prosecution would not cause economic damage and that the officials in question had already been punished administratively in a timely manner. The requests were signed by one of Hai Phong's most powerful officials, the Vice Chair of the city's People's Committee.

However, the involvement of high officials went even beyond that level. Newspapers revealed that these requests for exemption from prosecution had been sent to and approved by the Hai Phong

Communist Party Committee, the most powerful body in the city. Furthermore, the Party Secretary of Hai Phong, the powerful Nguyen Van Thuan, who was also a member of the Central Committee of the Communist Party, admitted that he had 'proposed waiving prosecution under the jurisdiction of the municipal People's Committee'.

The press further reported that in early May 2006 the Supreme People's Procuracy in Hanoi had agreed to Hai Phong's request to waive prosecution against one of the accused officials, Chu Minh Tuan, the former Director of the municipal Environment Bureau. It did so because the Hai Phong People's Committee had cancelled the land allocations and 'corrected all of the consequences of this matter', because the evidence was not fully clear against Tuan, and because he had contributed greatly to the local area. The Supreme People's Procuracy sent out a mid-level official supposedly responsible for the decision on the prosecution to tell the press that he had been influenced by the official letters (*cong van*) sent by the Hai Phong authorities in his decision to waive prosecution and end the case against Tuan. At the time Tuan's prosecution was waived, he was the only municipal-level Hai Phong official formally charged in the case; the others were officials in Do Son township, not in the central Hai Phong administration.

For its part, the Supreme People's Court came to the media placing blame solely on the local court for the mere warning and small fine issued to the other three accused officials. The presiding judge of the Supreme People's Court's criminal tribunal told the press that the original charges that could have been brought against the original three local officials—misusing official powers in the exercise of public duties under article 281(1) of the Criminal Code—would have carried a punishment range of reform through labour of up to three years or imprisonment of one to five years. This was considered a 'serious crime', he told the press, and 'a warning could not be applied in these circumstances even where the circumstances were relatively light'.

In the midst of this chaos, the central political and legal institutions acted quickly, convening a meeting four days after the Prime Minister's official letter (*cong van*) to announce that they had completed a full-scale review of the Hai Phong case and had decided to overrule the original judgment issued by the Hai Phong local court and to re-investigate and re-prosecute the officials whose prosecution had been waived. The meeting explicitly decided that the sentences given to the three charged defendants were too lenient, and that the court had incorrectly applied the substance of the crimes of which they were accused. At least one newspaper reported that some of the officials might now be tried under the more serious provisions of article 281 of the Criminal Code, which called for five to 10 years' imprisonment upon conviction.

For the first time, central officials formally announced that the Hai Phong party and state authorities had sent official documents to the municipal people's court 'in order to interfere in the trial; they did not act in accordance with regulations'. As central legal institutions scrambled to protect themselves, Procurator-General Ha Manh Tri said that the documents issued by the Hai Phong People's Committee to the local court:

> [to] interfere with the court proceedings were not in accordance with regula-
> tions, and violated the principle that in administering justice the courts act
> independently and obey only the law.

Another official attending the joint meeting of central-level legal institutions told *VnExpress* that:

> the participants in the meeting stated that the institutions responsible for
> defending the law must work independently, and must not be subservient
> to local authorities.

The President of Vietnam stepped into this affair in early September 2006, calling the Hai Phong court's verdict an 'incorrect and unjust case', a strong term in Vietnamese. Once again, a senior official called for extra-judicial order to be used to force the judiciary to handle the matter correctly; the President told the Supreme People's Court that 'the leaders of the judiciary must directly issue guidance on this matter, not shielding this case'. The leaders of the Supreme Court chimed in to lambast the Hai Phong court's verdict, decrying the damage caused to the party and state.

SIDESTEPPING A CONSTITUTIONAL GUARANTEE THROUGH POLICY AND OFFICIAL LETTERS (*CONG VAN*)

The issue of interference with the judiciary—or 'over-interference' (*can thiep qua sau*), an assumption that some interference was justified—was regarded as a major problem not because judicial autonomy was tram-pled, but because the party and state were suffering severe criticism. Furthermore, the entire process was carried out extra-judicially, with the courts as mere pawns of duelling official letters (*cong van*) issued by national and local party and state officials.

Because the courts were compromised and subservient, officials both seeking to escape from justice and those wanting justice to be done could not rely on the courts: they worked through *cong van* and verbal instructions, all seeking to force the courts to do their bidding. Official letters were the mechanism both for illegality and for extra-judicial attempts to order the courts to set that illegality right. Central party officials demanded that the Supreme Court and procuracy reopen the case through *cong van*. Hai Phong authorities sought to escape their own prosecution by forcing the local courts and the national procuracy to waive prosecution of local officials, also through *cong van*. One of the defendants had written several *cong van* to the Hai Phong authorities attesting to the legality of the land allocations.

The political stakes continued to be raised in September 2006 when the national press revealed a report by the Hai Phong local court to the Supreme Court in Hanoi, documenting direct communications by the powerful Party Secretary of Hai Phong, Nguyen Van Thuan, urging the local prosecutors and judges to respect the decision of the Supreme People's Procuracy to exempt the Director of his Environment Bureau from prosecution, or to issue a light punishment if that was needed. After the fact—having complied earlier—the local court directly termed this 'interference' with the court.

However, they also revealed the fundamental difficulty in naming and overcoming judicial interference in Vietnam: under local party regulations, since the officials charged were cadres under the Hai Phong Party Committee, the local people's court and procuracy had reported as required to the Standing Board of the Party Committee on the case. Because the courts were required to seek guidance from local party authorities in cases in which party officials were charged, interference with the judiciary was actually institutionalised—at the same time as it was officially barred by the constitution. In the case of charged party members, in effect, interference is built into the system. The Hai Phong Party Secretary even directly cited precedents of other cases in which local courts sought guidance from party authorities in dealing with cases in which party officials were implicated—a cynical resort to extra-judicial precedential authority in a country where elements of the common law are still being resisted. The courts are not allowed to use precedent in their daily work, but party secretaries have a form of *carte blanche* to cite it in defence of corruption and judicial interference.

The Party Secretary's instructions to the local court were direct and specific: 'If there are ameliorating factors', he noted that the defendants could be punished under a specific section of article 281 of the Criminal Code that brought far lighter punishment—namely a warning and a small fine. Having interfered with the national procuracy to obtain exemption from prosecution for one Hai Phong party official, Chu Minh Tuan, the Party Secretary then told the local court that it must obey the national procuracy's decision not to prosecute him. All proceeded as the Party Secretary instructed. *VnExpress* noted dryly that on 28 August, the Hai Phong court issued a verdict that 'coincided relatively closely' with the 'views' of the Hai Phong Party Committee, including both the light sentence (the warning and the 50,000 *dong* fine) and letting Chu Minh Tuan escape prosecution.

Under these circumstances, the Deputy Prime Minister criticised the 'over-interference' in the trial process in Hai Phong and called for a full investigation and report to the Prime Minister—despite the fact that the interference that occurred was actually built directly into the system of trying party officials. In turn, the Supreme People's Court announced that it would supervise a retrial of the case in Hai Phong.

Beginning in early December, the powerful Party Secretary of Hai Phong mounted a strong defence of his actions. He argued that he and the Standing Board of the Hai Phong Party Committee 'must provide their views' on cases 'to implement regulations when trial bodies ask for their views'.

> Although the municipal Party Committee has views, this never means detailed guidance, but falls within the realm of a general line and resolving [issues]. And the conclusions put forward are collective, certainly not the personal views of the Secretary of the municipal Party Committee.

He also cited a decision issued by the Political Bureau of the party (Decision No 52) requiring party committees such as his own to reply to questions asked by courts about party cadres, in effect wrapping himself in the mantle of institutionalised judicial interference under party regulations.

The central legal institutions re-examined the case of Chu Minh Tuan and proposed that the police charge and investigate under article 285 of the Vietnamese Criminal Code, which criminalises 'derogation of responsibility resulting in serious consequences', or under article 165, for 'intentional violation of state regulations on economic management with serious consequences'.

As various forces splintered to protect themselves, the local Hai Phong court now spoke up for the first time in direct contradiction to the Party Secretary's defences, providing a frank description of the mechanism of judicial interference in Vietnam. 'I felt quite lonely in trying this case', said Duong Van Thanh, Deputy Chief Judge of the Hai

Phong People's Court and the chief judge at the first Do Son trial, in a newspaper interview.

> Of course no one told me that I had to try this case this way or that way. But there were 'hints' (*goi y*) and 'directions' (*dinh huong*) for the trial, and I had to consult those. If the upper levels have proposals, then it's difficult for me to do things differently … If the upper levels set a direction for trial, I must follow.

All of those investigated were 'cadres under the administration of the Hai Phong municipal Party Committee', making the situation very difficult, according to a report that Judge Thanh wrote to the Supreme People's Court in Hanoi.

JUDICIAL INTERFERENCE UNRESOLVED

By the autumn of 2006, the discussion of judicial interference in the Do Son case began to fade from the newspapers. By that time there was no significant sanction, either judicial or party-based, against the actions taken by the Hai Phong party and state officials to interfere with and mould the judgment of the local court. The Deputy Prime Minister forced Hai Phong Party Secretary Nguyen Van Thuan to attend a meeting to describe and explain the Hai Phong authorities' interference in the case, but there appears to have been little other punishment.

Eventually, an expanded pool of defendants was put on trial for the criminal aspects of their corrupt misallocation of land in Do Son; they were convicted this time around and were sentenced to jail terms. By 2007, the case had faded from the headlines, but public anger in Do Son and Hai Phong and demands for accountability by higher officials forced the authorities to revisit the possibilities of charges against more senior officials. In mid-2008, prosecutors were considering additional charges in the Do Son land case against municipal-level party and state officials, including a leader at the Deputy Party Secretary level in Hai Phong, and in late 2008 some new charges were brought.

THE LONG AND TORTUOUS ROAD AHEAD FOR JUDICIAL INDEPENDENCE IN VIETNAM

The Do Son land grab case was one of the few occasions in recent times in Vietnam where the press, party, government and judiciary have openly raised the failure by party and state officials to comply with constitutional guarantees of judicial independence. Therefore, in one sense, that public discussion of some judicial independence issues was itself a step forward.

However, while Hai Phong party and government officials were criticised for interfering with the judiciary, the critique of that interference was ambivalent, and the party's and government's methods for resolving that interference relied entirely on their own interference with and direct instructions to the courts and prosecutors (seeking to trump the original Hai Phong interference with the local courts). The Vietnamese courts themselves have virtually no means of ensuring their own autonomy without political direction, and the consequences of Do Son show little promise for enhanced protection of judicial independence and the constitutional guarantee that embodies it.

DEMANDING RESULTS FROM THE COURTS, NOT SEEKING THEIR AUTONOMY

Several aspects of the Do Son case illustrate these continuing problems. First, how can the judiciary secure substantive implementation of the 1992 Constitution's guarantee that '[i]n administering justice, judges and assessors are independent and shall only obey the law' when it is surrounded by political authorities giving them contradictory orders—all of which need to be obeyed? The Do Son case shows that the courts have no means to exercise autonomy in such high profile cases that attract political direction, without recourse to political support from a higher level than the political officials interfering in judicial processes. That support from above—in this case the Party Central Committee and the government in Hanoi, acting through the Prime Minister and Deputy Prime Minister—does not, in fact, take steps to ensure judicial autonomy. Rather they merely represented a higher level of interference in judicial decision making, a results-oriented attempt to assuage public anger by interfering once again in judicial processes to get the 'right' result.

The Do Son case indicates this problem clearly through the tortured history of the proceedings. When the laughable verdict of the local Hai Phong court is released and publicised by an angry press, higher level political officials ask the Supreme People's Court and Supreme People's Procuracy to retry the case and those political officials declare, in advance, that the primary defendants in the case have committed significant crimes, should be found guilty and should be punished far more severely than in the original action. The higher level party and government officials also trump both local legal institutions and the guarantee of judicial independence by declaring, in effect, that the Hai Phong official exempted from prosecution was exempted in violation of law, that he indeed committed crimes and should be tried.

The language used indicates the party's own understanding of judicial interference—and the need for it. On a number of occasions, party and state officials refer to Hai Phong's 'over-interference in the judiciary' (*can thiep qua sau*). The term strongly indicates that a certain amount of 'interference' (*can thiep*) is acceptable, but that when it goes too far (*qua sau*), that is unacceptable. Never in this process did party and government authorities in Hanoi state the principle that *no* interference with the judiciary is acceptable.

In addition, the harms done by judicial interference are almost never stated in terms of the effects on judicial performance, harm to the process of doing justice, violations of fairness or other rationales for judicial independence. Rather, the Hai Phong authorities are criticised for their interference because of the political damage done to the party, government and their policies. So, for example, the President of Vietnam tells the Supreme Court that 'prestige of the Party and state has been damaged' by the local court's handling of the case under instructions from Hai Phong party authorities. The Prime Minister also focused on the political fall-out, not the implications for the courts: '[A]t a time when the Party, state, and people are resolutely implementing' laws and policies against corruption, he said, 'if this case has not been handled strictly and clearly that reflects poorly on the struggle against corruption'.

In the specific context of this case and the weaknesses of judicial independence in Vietnam, political authorities stepping in to criticise local party and government officials' domination of lower courts is, in one sense, a positive development. However, the means used leave much to be desired—in effect, a re-interference with the judiciary, treating the judiciary as an object for instructions rather than a deciding institution in its own right. Higher level interference with the judiciary has substituted for lower level interference, as a result of popular dissatisfaction, the failures of local political leaders and the local court, and the weakness of that court. It may be that this instrumentalisation of the judiciary in the longer-term interest of strengthening judicial independence is the only step forward possible in the Vietnamese polity at this time, but it is primarily a means to guarantee that the courts follow Hanoi's will, rather than bow to local interests, and it does not substantially strengthen judicial independence.

OFFICIAL LETTERS AND THE PERVERSION
OF JUDICIAL AUTONOMY

A second problem arises from the methods used to correct the local errors and, supposedly, strengthen judicial autonomy. At each level of the Do Son case, each political and administrative actor employs 'official letters' (*cong van*) and other official documents to drive government officials, the courts, procuracy and police toward the results they want, in a parallel system of government documents that carries the force of law. As indicated above, official letters were the mechanism both for illegality and extra-judicial attempts to order the courts to set that illegality right.

A few examples will suffice on the use of these 'official letters' which, in this case and others, carry the force of political authority and thus law. The Director of the Hai Phong Environment Bureau uses official letters to assure the Do Son authorities that their land allocation plan is lawful. The Government Inspectorate in Hanoi uses an official letter to ask the government to force the Hai Phong authorities to redress the land problems. The Hai Phong authorities use official letters to request the procuracy to exempt high-ranking local officials from prosecution. The Hai Phong authorities use an official letter to instruct the local court to find the defendants not guilty or, if necessary, to mete out a very light punishment. Central party officials use an official letter to instruct the procuracy, courts and police to re-open their investigations and to refuse to accept the verdict of the Hai Phong court.

This is justice by 'official letter', where the judiciary is expected to function almost entirely as the administrative arm of the party and state in implementing the instructions contained in the letters. The use of official letters as a parallel system of legal authority in Vietnam backed up by political strength has been criticised by legal reformers and scholars in Vietnam, as well as by foreign donors, and attempts have been made to rein in the use of these very flexible, and often secret, forms of decision making and adjudication.

However, '*cong van* justice' remains deeply rooted in Vietnam, a method by which powerful and flexible political authorities assert their will separate from and over the formal legal institutions whose power remains weak and dependent. Rooting out '*cong van*' political culture and methods will be exceptionally difficult—especially because, in administrative matters, there certainly is a role for administrative documents in managing the state—and delineating the appropriate role for such documents and preventing interference with the courts and other legal institutions is a long and difficult process of legal development.

PARTY REGULATION VERSUS THE CONSTITUTIONAL
GUARANTEE OF JUDICIAL AUTONOMY

Hidden in the corners of the Vietnamese coverage of the Do Son case are tantalising references to specific party rules and policies that appear to require local prosecutors and courts to seek guidance from local party organisations when party officials within their jurisdiction are investigated or charged with crimes, and that give party organisations the prerogative to give 'guidance' to the local courts. These features of legal and administrative life are well known in Vietnam, but they are rarely referred to in the public press or in party or judicial documents.

It is, however, reasonably clear that party documents and practice seem to require local prosecutors and courts to seek guidance from local party organisations when their officials are investigated, charged or tried, and give party organisations the right to provide 'guidance' to the courts in other cases as well. In one sense, this is in direct contradiction with the constitutional principle that: 'In administering justice, judges and assessors are independent and shall only obey the law.' In another sense, however, more conservative party official and legal scholars argue that the role of the party in cases can be made consistent with article 130 of the Constitution. They say that judicial autonomy in Vietnam is largely limited to the trial stage, that the courts are obligated to come to their own conclusions and 'only obey the law' at trial, but that pre-trial guidance in the form of official letters, oral communications and other 'guidance' does not eviscerate that constitutional guarantee of autonomy at trial. Other Vietnamese scholars and judges scoff at that attempt to bridge clear party interference with the constitutional guarantee of autonomy, noting that judicial autonomy at trial is a formalism signifying nothing when party and state officials have, in effect, determined the result through guidance to the court before a proceeding begins.

THE RESULTS OF DO SON

Despite the strong reaction in the media and in Hai Phong to the party's interference in the trial of the local Do Son officials, there was little punishment for the officials involved in that interference. The central party apparatus in Hanoi and the Hai Phong Party Committee treated the judicial interference as an internal party matter. The Hai Phong Party Committee wrote a self-criticism that was given some publicity in the newspapers. However, no public disciplinary action, either within the party or outside, was taken by mid-2008 or at least none can be found.

Nor were new rules announced—either within the party or outside—to control and channel such interference in judicial affairs. Any new such rules or guidelines would have been difficult to draft in any case, for the party's leadership role over the courts falls within the role for the party defined in article 4 of the 1992 Constitution, and a party role in judicial affairs is a fact of life at central, provincial and local levels throughout Vietnam. The party's role is well known. It occurs in many contexts, but among the most common is for party or state officials to provide 'guidance' (*chi dao*) to local courts in handling sensitive matters, a process that is allowed by the party, but is conceptually indistinguishable from judicial interference.

The only potentially difficult question for the party was when interference went too far—the 'excessive interference' in the Do Son case, as Hanoi party and state officials called it. The party was not prepared to address that difficult problem in 2006 and 2007, because the party's right to give 'guidance' as the constitutionally appointed dominant political authority in Vietnam clearly conflicted with any prohibition on judicial interference—a contradiction that could not be resolved on a clear and long-term basis without rethinking the party's relationship to the courts. And so the party officials' interference in the Do Son land case faded from view even as a reinvigorated police and prosecutorial net retried the original defendants and then gradually, over the next several years, charged other officials—including a very high-ranking Deputy Party Secretary of Hai Phong—in connection with the Do Son land grab.

LIFTING THE VEIL ON INTERFERENCE WITH THE JUDICIARY AND LEGAL PROCESS

However, echoes of the judicial interference lasted. At the National Assembly session in November 2005, deputies severely criticised the Do Son judicial interference incident in terms that implicitly recognised the contradiction of party rule and an independent judiciary. One senior deputy told the Assembly:

> We do not have the separation of powers [in Vietnam], but the courts must be independent, obeying only the law in judicial work. Now we have situations in which phone calls and letters are sent to chief judges before trials. That is not appropriate, and it provides external influences which are a source of incorrect verdicts.

In late 2006, the Secretary of the Ho Chi Minh City Party Committee, Le Thanh Hai, told the popular Saigon daily newspaper *Tuoi Tre* that:

> in Ho Chi Minh City, we affirm that the Party Committee never interferes in the process of investigating and trying cases, especially cases involving corruption because those generally relate to officials, and it is very easy to be understood as shielding one's own. The viewpoint of the Party Committee requires that investigation and trial must proceed in accordance with law … The Party Committee affirms one point, that it does not shield anyone.

However, very gradually, additional cases of official interference in judicial decision making began to appear in the Vietnamese media, sparking additional controversy and discussion. In March 2007, the Secretary of the Party Committee of the large city of Vinh in central Vietnam was criticised in the national media and in the party for interfering in the investigation and disposition of several cases in which lower-level officials had taken land for their use or arranged for its assignment to others. In May 2007, the police general and a senior party official in the Ministry of Public Security responsible for a major drug trafficking case in Ho Chi Minh City were forced to deny that there had been any party interference in the disposition of that case.

In the absence of effective party action to limit interference in judicial cases, it was inevitable that other cases would occur, and eventually that another egregious case involving official interference with a high profile case would be discussed in the Vietnamese national media. In late 2006 and early 2007, Vietnamese newspapers exposed significant interference by the Party Secretary of Ca Mau Province in far southern Vietnam into a large corruption case underway in his province. In that case, a senior corporate official in the Ca Mau Fisheries Processing and Import and Export Corporation (Camimex) had been charged with fraud and corruption-related charges. According to the Vietnamese press, the Party Secretary of Ca Mau, a former military official named Vo Thanh Binh, directly interfered in that case by instructing the director of the Ca Mau provincial procuracy, in writing, to waive criminal charges.

The case caused great public dissatisfaction in Ca Mau, especially because one of the officials in question had earlier been accused of profiting from land taken from a woman who was the widow and mother of martyred Vietnamese soldiers from the war, building housing on the land, and selling it at cheap prices to high-ranking provincial officials, pocketing the profits and distributing them to other officials.

The interference case languished until April 2008, when allegations surfaced in national newspapers that the provincial Party Secretary had taken substantial amounts to arrange for promotions and transfers of provincial officials, both benefiting from and accelerating a culture of corruption throughout the province, and spurring calls in the National Assembly in Hanoi for reforms in cadre appointments throughout the country. Hanoi sent a high-level investigation group from the party's Central Inspection Commission to Ca Mau. They recommended suspending the process of appointing and promoting senior officials in the province.

In that new context, the Party Secretary's earlier intervention in the Camimex case came under new scrutiny. The Ministry of Interior in Hanoi came under criticism for failing to stop the widespread practice of officials' paying for appointments and promotions particularly after promising to crack down on the practice under earlier questioning at the National Assembly. In mid-2008, the case was unresolved, but had emerged as another example of interference with the judicial process.[10]

There were, of course, important differences from the Do Son land case. In Ca Mau, the interference was with the procuracy (state prosecutors), an institution that has never been guaranteed autonomy or independence by the constitution or in other forms of law. But the fact remains that, increasingly, cases of party and state interference with legal process (and occasionally, the courts themselves) are making their way into the Vietnamese press. In addition, Vietnamese legal officials and scholars are beginning to discuss ways of giving more force to guarantees of judicial autonomy in a complex environment where the Communist Party is still, as the 1992 Constitution makes clear in article 4, 'the force leading the state and society'. Those discussions are likely to accelerate in the years ahead, particularly as Vietnam approaches another possible revision of the constitution and as consideration of 'constitutional protection' and the establishment of a constitutional court or other adjudicative mechanism heats up again in Hanoi.

---

[10] This discussion of the Ca Mau case is drawn from contemporaneous newspaper and news service reports in *VnExpress*, *Vietbao*, the BBC Vietnamese Service, *Lao Dong*, *Vietnamnet* and other outlets.

FURTHER READING

Nicholson, P (1999) 'Vietnamese Legal Institutions in Comparative Perspective: Constitutions and Courts Considered' in Jayasuriya, K (ed) *Law, Capitalism and Power in Asia: The Rule of Law and Legal Institutions* (London, Routledge) 300.

—— (2001) 'Judicial Independence and the Rule of Law: The Vietnam Court Experience' 3 *Australian Journal of Asian Law* 37.

—— (2007) *Borrowing Court Systems: The Experience of Socialist Vietnam* (Leiden, Martinus Nijhoff).

—— (2007) 'Vietnamese Courts: Contemporary Interactions Between Party-State and Law' in Balme, S and Sidel, M (eds) *Vietnam's New Order: International Perspectives on the State and Reform in Vietnam* (New York, Palgrave Macmillan) 178.

Nicholson, P and Quang, NH (2005) 'The Vietnamese Judiciary: The Politics of Appointment and Promotion' 14 *Pacific Rim Law and Policy Journal* 1.

To Van-Hoa (2006) *Judicial Independence* (Lund, Jurisförlaget i Lund) (particularly Pt V, chs XVI–XIX).

9

Enforcing the Constitution: The Debate over 'Constitutional Protection' and a Constitutional Court

══━◆━══

I
T MAY BE surprising to some that in Vietnam, where party control of judicial and constitutional processes remains exceptionally robust, a vigorous debate has now developed over 'constitutional protection' (*bao hien*) and the role of judicial, executive and legislative institutions in interpreting the constitution and redressing constitutional violations. Yet observers of constitutional developments in China would show less surprise, for a parallel debate has long been underway in China on the primacy of the constitution and the means of enforcing and reviewing it.[1] In this chapter, I discuss the contours of the politically sensitive debate in Vietnam on constitutional review and enforcement, the stages of discussion and the institutional and other forces taking sides on this issue, and the solutions proposed.[2]

The four Vietnamese constitutions adopted in Hanoi (1946, 1959, 1980 and 1992, revised in 2001) are a source of pride and a subject of political struggle in Vietnam. It is axiomatic that Vietnam, still dominated by the Communist Party in the reform (*doi moi*) era, has a party-controlled constitution. However, recognising the dominant role of the party only begins the discussion. Within that framework,

---

[1] On the important developments in China, see KJ Hand, 'Citizens Engage the Constitution: The Sun Zhigang Incident and Constitutional Proposals in the People's Republic of China' in Balme and Dowdle (eds), *Constitutionalism and Judicial Power in China* (London, Palgrave, 2008); T Kellogg, 'NPCSC: The Vanguard of China's Constitution?' 8:2 *China Brief* (February 2008); and KJ Hand, 'Using Law For a Righteous Purpose: The Sun Zhigang Incident and Evolving Forms of Citizen Action in the People's Republic of China' 45 *Columbia Journal of Transnational Law* 114 (2006).

[2] This chapter is based on and updated from chs 2 and 3 of M Sidel, *Law and Society in Vietnam* (Cambridge, Cambridge University Press, 2008).

debate has developed over constitutional principles and structure, particularly at three key recent points: 1991 to 1992, when Vietnam adopted a constitution for the reform era; 2000 to 2001, when that 1992 Constitution was redrafted to re-emphasise the role of private business and other reform-era policies; and 2003 and after, when Vietnamese policymakers and a few academics engaged in a wide-ranging debate about the enforcement, review and 'protection' of the constitution, and a high profile dispute in Hanoi fuelled public interest in constitutional protections.

It is not surprising that the constitutional review and enforcement had only a minor role in a party-dominated constitutional schema. The Vietnamese Constitution has been defined as the 'fundamental law' of the nation since 1946, and yet it remains largely unused to rescind inconsistent legislation, to establish the hierarchy of legislation or as a standard to judge acts that violate its terms or those who commit such acts. In China, filling this important but symbolic constitutional vessel with substantive enforcement became a significant issue over the last two decades. In Vietnam, there were early signs of these questions—discussed largely behind closed doors—during the drafting of the 1992 Constitution.

These debates sprang into the open in 2000 and 2001, when the 1992 Constitution was redrafted in a process that encouraged and drew strong views and discussions. For the first time, in 2000 and 2001, some Vietnamese policymakers (including party officials), legislators and academics began to call publicly for a structure of constitutional review and a means to enforce constitutional guarantees against both legislation and acts that violate the constitution.[3] Those debates picked up steam from 2003 to 2005 before being temporarily quieted in 2006 and 2007, as Vietnam prepared for and held a major Party Congress, hosted a full Asia-Pacific Economic Cooperation (APEC) meeting and undertook National Assembly elections in May 2007.

---

[3] For among the stronger statements, see the work of the scholar Nguyen Van Thao, 'Soan thao, sua doi hien phap va thuc hien bao ve Hien phap' ('Revising and amending the Constitution and mechanisms for Constitutional protection'), *Tap chi Cong san* (*Communist Review*) (October 2001), <http://www.tapchicongsan.org.vn> accessed 26 February 2008; and 'Ve kiem tra tinh hop hien, hop phap cua van ban phap luat va cac co quan tu phap' ('On the inspection of the constitutionality and legality of legal documents and judicial agencies'), *Bao Khoa hoc va Phat trien* (*Science and Development News*) (3 October 2001), reprinted at <http://www.na.gov.vn> accessed 26 February 2009.

By 2007 and 2008, there were strong signs that explorations of constitutional review, enforcement and protection were once again accelerating as Vietnam prepared to revise the constitution again over the next several years. Going back to the 1990s and continuing to this day, waves of domestic dissenters as well as Vietnamese in the diaspora who are critical of the regime have called for an independent mechanism for constitutional enforcement and interpretation. In particular, as I discuss in Chapter 2, the voices of Vietnamese dissenters and critics going back to the 1950s have been important in maintaining a vision of constitutionalism beyond party domination.

What do the Vietnamese mean by constitutional 'protection' or enforcement? In Vietnam, as in China, these terms have primarily implicated three problems: (i) how to handle statutes or other actions by the national legislature that may violate the constitution; (ii) how to handle national statutes, local laws or other national or local regulatory documents that violate higher law; and (iii) how to treat acts by state or party officials that may violate the constitution.

EARLY DISCUSSION OF CONSTITUTIONAL REVIEW,
ENFORCEMENT AND PROTECTION IN VIETNAM (1946–57)

Today, Vietnam's first DRV Constitution of 1946 is hailed as a relatively democratic document, but it contained little protection for constitutional rights or means of enforcing the constitution. Article 4 required Vietnamese citizens to 'respect the Constitution' and article 21 gave citizens a 'right to referendum on the Constitution', but, as discussed in Chapter 2, the National Assembly, government and judiciary were not given any powers to undertake constitutional interpretation, enforcement or review.

As dissent gathered steam in Hanoi in the mid-1950s, fuelled by a rapid land reform policy that left many dead and increased pressure on urban intellectuals, fidelity to constitutional promises was among the demands of those who pressed for democratic legal reforms in the mid-1950s during the *Nhan van Giai pham* movement. Two key figures in this early call for putting teeth in constitutional guarantees and backing them up by more independent institutions were the northern intellectuals Nguyen Huu Dang and Nguyen Manh Tuong. In their writings and speeches, discussed in Chapter 2, we have the first modern echoes in the north of calls for some form of judicial review and constitutional enforcement.

CONSTITUTIONAL SUPERVISION AND
ENFORCEMENT (1959–92)

The 1959 Constitution made no significant progress on the idea of constitutional protection and enforcement. It formally invested the National Assembly with the role of 'supervision' (*giam sat*) of the 'enforcement of the Constitution'.[4] The 1980 Constitution expanded the formulation, giving the National Assembly the power 'to exercise supreme supervision over the Constitution and the law', with the Standing Committee assisting the National Assembly in the exercise of such supervisory powers. The 1980 Constitution also gave the Council of State (roughly equivalent to the presidency) power 'to interpret the Constitution, laws and decrees' and delegated to the Council of Ministers (executive and administrative authority) power 'to ensure observance of the Constitution and the law'.[5]

However, as Vietnamese scholars such as Nguyen Dang Dung, Nguyen Van Thao and Bui Ngoc Son have now assertively pointed out, neither the National Assembly nor the government undertook any review or enforcement whatsoever of constitutional norms in 1960s, 1970s and 1980s Vietnam.[6] The constitutional commentary of the era rarely focuses on constitutional enforcement or review, reciting the supposed role of the National Assembly. Criticism of the weaknesses of the constitutional framework and party control grew in the 1980s, particularly in the diaspora community, but diaspora criticism of abuses involving re-education camps and other rights violations took a higher priority.

THE 1992 CONSTITUTIONAL FRAMEWORK AND BEYOND:
CONSTITUTIONAL ENFORCEMENT AND REVIEW IN THE
VIETNAMESE CONSTITUTIONAL SCHEME

As discussed in Chapter 5, the 1992 Constitution brought significant changes to the Vietnamese constitutional scheme, particularly with regard to the role of the state, private business, intellectuals and

---

[4] 1959 Constitution, art 50.

[5] 1980 Constitution, arts 83, 92, 100 and 107.

[6] Nguyen Dang Dung, *Y tuong ve mot Nha nuoc chiu trach nhiem* (*Thoughts on the responsible state*) (Da Nang, Da Nang Publishing House, 2007); Bui Ngoc Son, *Bao Hien o Viet Nam* (*Constitutional Protection in Vietnam*) (Hanoi, Judicial Publishing House, 2006); Nguyen Van Thao, 'Soan thao, sua doi hien phap va thuc hien bao ve Hien phap' ('Revising and amending the Constitution and mechanisms for Constitutional protection'), *Tap chi Cong san* (*Communist Review*) (October 2001).

other groups in society. However, while it addressed questions of constitutional interpretation and enforcement in more textual detail than earlier constitutions—primarily by expanding responsibility for enforcement and observance of the constitution in the National Assembly and to additional branches of government—no mechanisms were established to ensure interpretation and enforcement.

The 1992 Constitution, which remains in effect after a 2001 revision, stipulates that constitutional issues are the province of the National Assembly, through article 83's provision that '[t]he National Assembly is the only organ with constitutional and legislative powers' and article 84, stipulating that the National Assembly has 'obligations and powers' that include the 'exercise [of] supreme control over conformity to the Constitution, [and] the law and the resolutions of the National Assembly'. Article 84 also provides that the National Assembly shall:

> abrogate all formal written documents issued by the country's President, the Standing Committee of the National Assembly, the Government, the Prime Minister, the Supreme People's Court, and the [Procuracy] that run counter to the Constitution.

More specifically directed toward constitutional enforcement, the 1992 Constitution also provided that the Standing Committee of the National Assembly holds the power to 'interpret the Constitution, the law, and decree-laws' and:

> to exercise supervision and control over the implementation of the Constitution, the law, the resolutions of the National Assembly, decree-laws, the resolutions of the Standing Committee of the National Assembly; over the activities of the Government, the Supreme People's Court, the Supreme People's [Procuracy]; to suspend the execution of the formal written orders of the Government, the Prime Minister, the Supreme People's Court, the Supreme People's [Procuracy], that contravene the Constitution, the law, the resolutions of the National Assembly; [and] to report the matter to the National Assembly for it to decide the abrogation of such orders.[7]

However, the Assembly and its Standing Committee have never undertaken, nor have they been permitted to undertake, those constitutional tasks. Furthermore, the frequent mentions of constitutional duties by the government, Prime Minister, state agencies and others result in a lack of responsibility and activity rather than in multiple, effective caretakers of

---

[7] 1992 Constitution, art 91.

the constitution.[8] None of this was accidental, of course: party officials took charge of the traditionally infrequent discussions of consistency between local and national laws and regulations and the constitution, and of the infrequent allegation (other than by harassed dissidents) that governmental and party acts violated constitutional norms. The result was clear: no effective constitutional review, enforcement or protection under the 1992 Constitution despite its formal terms.

These limitations drew the attention of domestic academics and reform-minded officials in the 1990s. Domestic dissidents also raised their voices for constitutional reform in the 1990s. In 1997, for example, three prominent domestic dissidents petitioned the National Assembly to establish a constitutional court 'to have an institution with jurisdiction to review petitions and to adjudicate (*xet xu*) cases of Constitutional violations'. In addition, diaspora voices began to grow once again for constitutional reform, especially to revisit the leading role of the Communist Party enshrined in article 4 of the 1992 Constitution.

THE CONSTITUTIONAL REVISION OF 2000–01 AND THE DEBATE ON CONSTITUTIONAL REVIEW AND ENFORCEMENT

These issues came to public light in 2000 and 2001, when the party launched a revision of the 1992 Constitution to attempt to keep it up to date with the significant economic and social reforms underway in Vietnam. This vigorous debate, discussed in Chapter 6, included calls by legal scholars, citizens and overseas Vietnamese as well as some policymakers for the establishment of a viable mechanism for constitutional review and enforcement to replace the responsibility of the

---

[8] The 1992 Constitution also mandates that: 'all Party organisations operate within the framework of the Constitution and the law' (art 4); the government 'shall ensure respect for and implementation of the Constitution and the law' (art 109) and 'ensure the implementation of the Constitution and the law in State organs, economic bodies, social organisations, units of the armed forces, and among the citizens, the Prime Minister, and state ministries and other agencies' (art 112); 'all State organs, economic and social bodies, units of the people's armed forces, and all citizens must seriously observe the Constitution and the law' (art 12); the Prime Minister 'suspend or annul' decisions, directives, circulars, resolutions and other legal documents issued by ministries, other national government agencies and local government bodies 'that contravene the Constitution, the law, and other formal written documents of superior State organs' (art 114); local People's Committees must 'implement the Constitution' (art 123); and even the Vietnam Fatherland Front 'ensures the strict observance of the Constitution and the law, strive to prevent and oppose all criminal behaviour and all violations of the Constitution and the law' (art 9).

Standing Committee for constitutional interpretation—a mechanism that has never been utilised—and the unused provision of constitutional enforcement duties to a wide range of other bodies as well. The constitutional revision process of 2000 and 2001 marked the 'mainstreaming' of calls for a constitutional review and enforcement mechanism. These appeals reflected a changed vision of the role of the constitution, as well as a more activist perspective that viewed the party and government as at least partly subject to law, rather than law being subject to policy. This accelerating Vietnamese discussion also took as reference points the development of constitutional courts in Thailand, Korea and other Asian states, and the eruption of major debates on constitutional review and enforcement in China. However, it was also a highly sensitive discussion, for it implied that the constitution itself might really become the nation's primary authority, and that a body outside the party or the party-controlled National Assembly might interpret and enforce it.

As discussed in Chapter 6, the party, National Assembly and the Constitutional Revision Commission worked diligently to narrow the debate on constitutional amendment and to defer sensitive issues like constitutional review. However, officials, academics and others continued to raise these issues throughout the process, often in official fora that reflect official support for some form of constitutional review, even if the timing were not perceived to be correct. Speaking in September 2001 in Ho Chi Minh City, for example, Fatherland Front officials called for:

> the establishment of a Constitutional Defense Commission (*uy ban bao ve Hien phap*), or constitutional courts (*toa an Hien phap*), or adding to the functions of the National Assembly's Law Committee

to handle issues of constitutional review and enforcement. In October 2001, a wide-ranging call for strengthened constitutional protection was raised in the main theoretical journal of the Communist Party, *Tap chi Cong san* (*Communist Review*)—about as official a platform as could be imagined, and an early indication that stronger measures to enforce the constitution had some resonance in some quarters of the party and state.

In that October 2001 article, legal scholar Nguyen Van Thao mooted the two key options of a constitutional court (*toa an hien phap*) or constitutional commission (*uy ban hien phap*) to 'adjudicate unconstitutional documents'. He also raised the possibility of allowing the new administrative courts, established in the mid-1990s, broader authority to judge whether 'the activities of administrative institutions are based upon the

Constitution and the laws'.[9] In another article, this time for a domestic development policy journal, Thao again addressed the difficult problems of 'constitutionality' and 'legality' of government acts and texts in another autumn 2001 article. 'In nearly ten years of Constitutional implementation', he wrote:

> we have never once seen the National Assembly or its Standing Committee abrogate, cancel, or suspend the implementation of a single document issued by the President, the Government or the Prime Minister. The system of monitoring is almost never exercised by the Government or the Prime Minister with respect to the ministries or local authorities, despite the fact that some legal documents issued by ministries and local authorities evidently violate the Constitution or laws.

For Thao, the fundamental reason for this failure was clear: 'The 1992 Constitution did not delegate to any institution judgment on the constitutionality of laws', and it was vague on the National Assembly's abrogation and cancellation powers.[10] For Thao and others, the question of adjudicating constitutionality should now be on the agenda for debate, but the party and the Constitutional Amendment Commission did not agree.

In a view echoed by Party General Secretary Nong Duc Manh at a party meeting discussing the scope and wording of the constitutional amendments, National Assembly and Constitutional Amendment Commission chair Nguyen Van An reaffirmed the party's and government's intent that the constitutional amendment process only:

> concentrate on issues that are truly urgent, that are ripe for adoption and practical testing, and must ensure a high spirit of unity.

The difficult and controversial issues of constitutional review and enforcement did not fit in those categories. Official focus remained on the amendments that would clarify and improve the functioning of the state machinery, rather than broader issues of constitutionalism.

When the constitutional amendments reached the National Assembly for debate in November 2001, delegates again raised issues of constitutionalism beyond the bounds of the party's efforts to channel and narrow

---

[9] Nguyen Van Thao, 'Soan thao, sua doi hien phap va thuc hien bao ve Hien phap' ('Revising and amending the Constitution and mechanisms for Constitutional protection'), *Tap chi Cong san* (*Communist Review*) (October 2001), <http://www.tapchicongsan.org.vn> accessed 26 February 2009.
[10] Nguyen Van Thao, 'Ve kiem tra tinh hop hien, hop phap cua van ban phap luat va cac co quan tu phap' ('On the inspection of the constitutionality and legality of legal documents and judicial agencies'), *Bao Khoa hoc va Phat trien* (*Science and Development News*) (3 October 2001), reprinted at <http://www.na.gov.vn>.

the discussions. For example, an Assembly delegate and senior legal official in Ho Chi Minh City again called for establishment of a constitutional court to 'defend the Constitution … against the many forms of constitutional violation that at present cannot be investigated or adjudicated'.[11]

THE RENEWED DISCUSSION OF CONSTITUTIONAL REVIEW AFTER THE 2001 CONSTITUTIONAL REVISIONS

The discussion of constitutional review and enforcement was deferred in 2001, but it has re-emerged prominently in recent years, encouraged by party and legal theorists. In addition, the Vietnamese debate on constitutional enforcement and review has been spurred by increasing reports of provincial and local laws that violate national laws or constitutional norms, and expanding complaints against the acts of government and party officials, including a prominent case in Hanoi discussed further below.

In the wake of the 2001 revision to the constitution, domestic dissidents and diaspora critics were again emboldened to call for significant constitutional reform, including a mechanism for constitutional review and enforcement. They included 21 domestic critics who again petitioned the National Assembly in 2002 to 'establish a Constitutional Court to adjudicate violations of the Constitution' because, according to the petitioners, this is an institution 'any state ruled by law must have'.[12] In mid-2002, domestic political dissidents protested:

> the arrest and harassment of fellow dissidents and call[ed] for democratic reforms, establishment of an anti-corruption body, creation of a constitutional

---

[11] This clear call for formation of a constitutional court was accompanied by a strong tactical sense for potentially acceptable arguments in its favour. The rhetorical case for the court centered not on unconstitutional acts by party and government officials (although those would be covered), but on 'the many legal documents in effect that constantly violate the Constitution and the laws … and cause harm to the people'. The institutions responsible for investigating and acting on such documents are 'unable to do much', mentioning the public prosecutors together with the Assembly and the government. 'A Constitutional Court could adjudicate unconstitutional acts. Any person against whom an unconstitutional document has been applied could appear before the Constitutional Court. In this way millions of people would have the power of supervision, and the system would be more democratic and more objective.' 'Quoc hoi tiep tuc thao luan ve noi dung sua doi, bo sung Hien phap nam 1992', *Bao Lao Dong* (27 June 2001), <http://www.laodong.com.vn> accessed 26 February 2009.

[12] Petition to the National Assembly 2002 (<http://www.ykien.net/vd20cutri.html> accessed 26 February 2009). For another such call, see 'Quyen va loi thu chinh dang trong hien phap nhan ban' (5 February 2004), <http://www.lenduong.net> accessed 26 February 2009.

court to examine violations in constitutional law, and publication of Vietnam's border treaties with China,

among other demands.[13]

The 2002 petitioners raised considerably more detailed arguments to bear than the 1997 group. They cited specific laws that, in their opinion, violated the constitution and were appropriate for constitutional review. In their view, for example, article 69 of the 1992 Constitution, which guarantees 'freedom of speech and of the press, and the right to receive information', was violated by the later-enacted Law on Newspapers, which 'does not recognize newspapers organized by the people or private newspapers'. In addition, in their view, article 71 of the 1992 Constitution, which prohibits imprisonment without a judicial verdict, was violated by the oft-criticised Decree 31/CP that has provided the state and security forces with a broad basis for administrative detention and punishments (Decree 31/CP was annulled in 2007). The 2002 petitioners' rationale for a constitutional court relied on the concept of the constitution as the nation's 'mother law'. Citing the 1992 Constitution's concept of the constitution as the 'fundamental law of the state', the petitioners wrote:

> the Constitution is the mother law. Every other law must comply with the mother law, be consistent with the mother law, and may not violate the mother law.
>
> But who can the people appeal to? Who can resolve [such violations]? Who can try them? Because these 'offspring laws' do violate the Constitution!

In these early days of debate, official documents did not immediately confirm the need for a structure of constitutional review and enforcement. Thus, the Party Political Bureau's Resolution 8 of 2002 on important legal reform tasks did not directly address these basic problems of constitutionalism.[14] Furthermore, a major effort undertaken by the Ministry of Justice, the government and foreign donors to systematise priorities in development of the Vietnamese legal system discussed detailed legislative and other work, but unfortunately did not address important issues of constitutionality and constitutional

---

[13] Human Rights Watch, World Report 2003: Vietnam, <http://www.hrw.org/wr2k3/asia9.html> accessed 26 February 2009.

[14] Communist Party of Vietnam, Political Bureau Resolution 8 (2002) on Some Crucial Tasks in Legal Work in the Forthcoming Period (*Nghi quyet 08 (2002) cua Bo Chinh tri ve mot so nhiem vu trong tam cong tac tu phap trong thoi gian toi*), summarised at <http://www.cpv.org.vn> accessed 26 February 2009.

review, a failing of both timid donors and their domestic institutional partners.[15]

THE CURRENT DEBATE: DELINEATING OPTIONS AND DEBATING STRUCTURES FOR CONSTITUTIONAL 'PROTECTION', ENFORCEMENT AND REVIEW

In the years after the constitutional revision process of 2000 and 2001, discussion of the options for 'constitutional protection' has accelerated, both through party and state initiative and increasingly forceful calls by academics and others. The dialogue continued to expand, particularly in 2003, 2004 and 2005, and included reformist figures arguing for a constitutional court or constitutional commission as well as indications of official support in the party and state. Much of that dialogue was carried out in relative privacy, in party, National Assembly or academic fora far from the mass media. But enough appeared in the press and in volumes published by legal officials and scholars to give an increasingly detailed sense for the discussions.

In April 2004, for example, one of the most popular newspapers in southern Vietnam carried a commentary about the roles of constitutional courts by Pham Duy Nghia, a law professor at Hanoi National University. Nghia reviewed the difficulties in establishing supervision by citizens over officials and official acts in societies that have 'long been sunk in Confucian ideology', citing China, Japan, Korea and Vietnam, and noted the difficulties in adjudicating 'acts by public institutions that violate the Constitution and the laws'. He emphasised that the dominant model in Asia involves 'constitutional courts, or as they may be called constitutional protection courts, constitutional protection commissions, or other similar names', explaining that in the United States constitutional review is carried out by the US Supreme Court without establishing a separate institution. Nghia also pointed out that a council for constitutional protection and oversight over administrative agencies was established in French Indochina in the 1920s.

Professor Nghia then turned to a particularly difficult problem in the Vietnamese discussions of constitutional review—the role of the

---

[15] 'Legal System Needs Assessment 2002: Report on Comprehensive Needs Assessment for the Development of Vietnam's Legal System to the Year 2010', <http://www.jus.umu.se/Vietnam/pdf/LNA_FINAL.pdf; <http://www.vnforum.org/docs/gov/law/en/Exsum_5_8_English.doc>.

National Assembly. He reaffirmed the constitutional provision that the National Assembly holds supreme constitutional power, and that:

> the oversight of acts that violate the Constitution or the laws by administrative institutions in Vietnam is fundamentally within the jurisdiction of the National Assembly.

However, Nghia continues:

> Of course, undertaking that supreme supervisory power cannot be easy. With 498 delegates, of whom only one quarter are full-time deputies, and meeting but two times each year, the Vietnamese National Assembly certainly has difficulties in supervising central authorities as well as dozens of ministries and agencies and 64 provincial authorities from the North to the South. For those reasons, studying the experience of neighboring countries in order to move step by step toward mechanisms for appropriate constitutional protection, may also be highly necessary.

Nghia pointed out that numerous 'neighbouring countries' have 'imported the mechanisms of societies ruled by law' that also reflect their 'Asian values'. He pointedly noted that:

> the peoples of Japan, Korea, Thailand, Malaysia, Indonesia and the Philippines have all established constitutional courts, a mechanism for protecting the constitution, resisting illegal actions and unconstitutional actions by the government and legislature. The people of Campuchia have also established a constitutional protection commission along the French model.[16]

Later in 2004, summarising several years of party and academic discussions, President Tran Duc Luong, chair of the Party Judicial Reform Committee responsible for drafting a national Judicial Reform Strategy, announced that the Committee was prepared to recommend 'study of the establishment of a Constitutional Court'. This news sparked increased public discussion, at least on web dialogue sites, including detailed references to French, American, Russian and other models of judicial review, and differing views on the utility of establishing a constitutional court, commission or other form of constitutional review in Vietnam.

However, a number of issues and opposing views have also been raised in a difficult and sensitive discussion, particularly with regard to the role of the Communist Party and the potential problems with

---

[16] Pham Duy Nghia, 'Mot phuong cach giam sat day to nhan dan' ('A supervisory mechanism for the servants of the people'), *Tuoi Tre* (5 April 2004), <http://www.tuoitre.com.vn> accessed 26 February 2009.

varying forms of constitutional review. Early in 2005, in a speech to the party's Theoretical Council, President Luong noted that the party's understanding of the rule of law in capitalist democracies included the division of power into legislative, judicial and executive power, and the party's understanding that 'for resolving conflicts between the three branches of power [in the west], there is the Constitutional Court'. President Luong continued, echoing some still powerful critics of a constitutional review system for Vietnam:

> But in our state system, we do not advocate such a division of power ... Isn't the task of harmonizing and coordinating among the areas of Party leadership?[17]

CONSTITUTIONALITY AND THE HIERARCHY OF LAW: THE PROBLEM OF OVER-REACHING LOCAL AND MINISTRY LEGISLATION AND LEGAL DOCUMENTS

At the same time as legal and party leaders were debating the need for a mechanism for constitutional review and enforcement, the contours of such a structure and the dominant role of the party, the party and government began dealing with a pressing issue on which all sides could generally agree: the increasing tendency of provincial and local officials to legislate on all manner of matters, particularly administrative violations by citizens, often in conflict with higher law and, arguably, in violation of constitutional norms. Concern for this conflict between local law, national law and the constitution sprang into the open in 2001 and 2002, although the problem had quietly existed for a long time.

By 2003, managing these conflicts was a frequent and serious enough issue that the government formed a General Department for Inspection of Legal Documents within the Ministry of Justice and gave it the primary task of ferreting out local laws that conflicted with national law (and, conceivably, the constitution itself), and seeking to force local authorities to annul them. That department worked under the authorisation of a new set of regulations intended

---

[17] Tran Duc Luong, 'Tiep tuc day manh nghien cuu ly luan, tong ket thuc tien, nham lam sang to hon nhan thuc ve chu nghia xa hoi va con duong di len chu nghia xa hoi o nuoc ta' ('Continue strengthening theoretical research, summarize experience, aim at creating stronger consciousness of socialism and the road toward socialism in Vietnam') *Tap chi Cong san* (*Communist Review*) no 75 (2005) <http://tapchicongsan.org.vn>.

to help the government and Ministry of Justice harmonise local and national law.[18]

The new department got to work quickly, surveying provincial and local laws and actively seeking to force local governments to withdraw conflicting legislation. In early 2004, for example, the department sent documents to the Saigon city leadership 'informing' Saigon that it should annul a local regulation on the treatment of property owned by overseas Vietnamese and confiscated by local authorities because of conflict with national law.[19] In early 2006, the department 'suggested' to Ho Chi Minh City that it annul another eight legal documents that conflicted with national laws.[20] The problem was not limited to local authorities: in a report compiled for the National Assembly in the summer of 2005, the department identified more than 400 legal documents promulgated by national ministries as well as by local authorities that conflicted with higher national law, a result the Minister of Justice called 'startling'.

By itself, resolving the conflicts between local and national law need not detain us as we discuss constitutional review and enforcement. However, the department's tasks included examining the constitutionality of local and ministry law-making, and in 2005 the National Assembly increased the pressure by declaring that some of the legal documents identified by the Ministry of Justice also violated the constitution. Among them the Assembly included an infamous 2003 circular from the Ministry of Public Security limiting motorbike registration to one per person. It called the ministry's motorbike regulation a restriction on citizens' right to own property guaranteed in article 58 of the constitution and article 221 of the Civil Code.[21]

The department continued to press local authorities to comply with national law. In early 2006, it released another list of nearly 90 legal documents from 33 provinces and municipalities that violated the law specifically in the area of administrative punishments of citizens, a

---

[18] Decision 135/2003/ND-CP of the Government on the Inspection and Handling of Legal Documents (14 November 2003), <http://www.na.gov.vn> accessed 26 February 2009.

[19] Cuc Kiem tra van ban quy pham phap luat—Bo Tu phap cam on Bao Thanh Nien, *Bao Thanh Nien* (18 March 2004), <http://www.thanhnien.com.vn> accessed 26 February 2009.

[20] 'De nghi UBND TPHCM huy bo 8 van ban trai luat' ('Proposing that the People's Committee of Ho Chi Minh City annul eight documents that violate the law'), *Nguoi Lao Dong* (12 January 2006), <http://www.nld.com.vn> accessed 26 February 2009.

[21] '42 tinh, thanh pho ban hanh van ban "xe rao"' ('42 provinces and municipalities promulgate "fence breaking" documents'), *Vietnamnet* (28 August 2005), <http://www.vnn.vn/xahoi> accessed 26 February 2009.

newly popular area for local regulation.[22] In January 2006, the department took on the powerful Hanoi People's Committee, announcing that three Hanoi legal documents—among them an unpopular rule allowing city authorities to seize motorcycles and other vehicles for legal violations and hold them for 15 to 60 days—conflicted with national law.

MOTORCYCLE RIGHTS: CONSTITUTIONALISM HITS THE STREETS IN HANOI AND THE IMPLICATIONS FOR CONSTITUTIONAL REVIEW AND ENFORCEMENT

Until 2005, these discussions occurred largely within reasonably narrow circles of domestic party, government, legislative and judicial officials, legal scholars, and some domestic and overseas dissidents. However, a consciousness of constitutional rights also appears to be increasing in the general population, and nothing illustrates that better than the great motorcycle registration debate of 2005.

Chaotic and unsafe traffic conditions have long plagued Hanoi and other major Vietnamese cities, a deadly legacy of economic prosperity, the use of motorcycles as an outlet for social relaxation as well as work and family transport, insufficient road infrastructure, unsafe driver training, exceptionally lax driver licensing and a host of related issues. In Hanoi, where the problem is particularly difficult because of highly concentrated prosperity and a road infrastructure largely unimproved since the colonial era, the city's police authorities have attempted many methods to exert some control over the increasingly chaotic traffic scene.

In one of many such measures, the Hanoi police began limiting motorcycle registration to Hanoi residents with drivers' licences in early 2003, while debating whether to limit motorcycle registrations to one vehicle per resident. Pressure increased during 2003, with the city police calling for a moratorium on all motorcycle registrations in Hanoi, and residents—including delegates in Hanoi's People's Council—expressing firm opposition.

In response, the police announced a pilot programme to temporarily cease registration in the 'saturated' four inner-city oldest districts of Hanoi and began implementing this in September 2003. The Hanoi police sought to extend that moratorium to three more districts in 2004

---

[22] '33 tinh, thanh pho ra van ban xu phat trai luat' ('33 provinces and municipalities issue punishment documents that violate the law'), *Nhan Dan* (13 January 2006), <http://www.nhandan.org.vn>.

and another two in 2005, but public criticism delayed that timetable; in April 2004, Hanoi announced that three more districts would be added to the registration moratorium in 2005, and another two in 2008. In addition, Hanoi police began enforcing lower speed limits mandated by the national Ministry of Transportation.

However, the real trouble began in 2005, when Hanoi and other local police departments began enforcing a legal provision in the national police force's regulations on the registration of vehicles that had originally been released in 2003. Under those regulations, implemented by local rules, 'each person may register only one motorcycle or moped'. The attempts to enforce this provision in Hanoi and Saigon in 2005 met with substantial resistance—arguments with registration personnel, angry letters to officials and the newspapers, and growing complaints to government offices and local and national legislators.

In August 2005, the Ministry of Justice entered the fray, arguing that the police regulations violate national regulations on administrative sanctions and on transport safety. Other critics—including members of the Law Committee of the National Assembly—took the fight further, arguing vociferously throughout the autumn of 2005 that the local rule-making and implementation of restrictions on motorcycle and moped registration to one per person violated the right to property enshrined in the 1992 Constitution and the Vietnamese Civil Code.[23]

This was arguably among the first mass claims to constitutional rights in recent Vietnamese history, and it had enormous public appeal. It centered on two areas of life close to the hearts of many Hanoians and other Vietnamese—encounters with the police and the motorcycle culture that has enveloped Vietnam. The enforcement of the restriction was part of a broader attempt to limit the growth in motorcycle ridership that was already being resisted by many citizens. Furthermore, it was a constitutional claim that may have infuriated the national police and the Ministry of Public Security, but posed no major political threat to the party—in short, it was a relatively 'safe' constitutional claim in Vietnam's broader politics.

For several weeks, claims of constitutional rights and violations echoed in discussions in Hanoi and also in the Vietnamese press. In late November, one day before the Minister of Justice was scheduled

---

[23] The constitutional claim was based on art 58 of the 1992 Constitution: 'The citizen enjoys the right of ownership with regard to his lawful income, savings, housing, goods and chattels, means of production, funds and other possessions in enterprises or other economic organizations'.

to report formally to the National Assembly on violations of law by national ministries, the Ministry of Public Security issued a directive annulling the provision in its earlier regulations that limited registration of motorcycles and motorbikes to one per person.

However, the fight was not yet over, for Hanoi, Ho Chi Minh City and other municipalities had promulgated similar one-person-one-motorcycle rules based on the national regulations, and those were not automatically ineffective merely because their original policy and legal basis in a public security ordinance had been removed. Hanoi and Saigon retained rights to regulate on such matters within their borders, and they were not committed to removing those restrictions, since these rapidly growing cities suffered from the worst glut of motorcycles, traffic accidents, traffic jams and motorcycle pollution in Vietnam's history. However, elite and public pressure began to grow again, particularly on the Hanoi authorities to annul their local rule. Again, the claim of constitutional rights was in the forefront of the calls to annul the local regulations limiting motorcycle registration to one bike per resident.

Faced with the retreat by the powerful national Ministry of Public Security on its one motorcycle/one citizen rule, the Hanoi authorities had little choice on that matter, and announced in early December that its own one-motorcycle rule was being abrogated. However, once again, citizens, the press and legislators upped the stakes, setting their sights on the Hanoi regulation that had temporarily barred registration of motorcycles in four urban city districts in early 2004 and another three districts in 2005. Having emerged victorious using the argument that the one-motorcycle rule violated the constitutional protection of the right to property and provisions of the Civil Code, opponents of the seven-district registration ban now widened their target, arguing that the registration moratorium also violated the constitution. City police and transport authorities now tried to stand firm, arguing that public safety and transport gridlock justified this temporary, lawful limitation on the exercise of 'rights' to register motorcycles that passed constitutional muster.

However, they were swept away by public sentiment that was both reflected and fanned by Hanoi local legislators and the local press. At the end of December 2005, the 'constitutionalist' forces were victorious again: the Hanoi People's Council and the local government decided to annul the temporary moratorium on motorcycle registration in seven Hanoi districts, sending police and transport authorities back to search for other methods of controlling traffic growth and accidents in Hanoi.

This episode was striking in the use of the constitution as a means of argument and a political bludgeon against opponents. The conflict was fuelled by multiple forces: the Ministry of Justice, in assertively and publicly comparing local regulations to national law, partly to bolster its own institutional standing; an increasingly active press; local legislators eager to satisfy constituents and become part of a gradually broadening political process; and citizens who had a heady sense of their 'constitutional' rights and a down-to-earth sense of the differing value of their motorcycle investments with or without Hanoi registration.

They combined in a lethal mix of citizens' anger at the perceived constitutional wrongs. Nor was this a politically dangerous form of constitutional argumentation to be suppressed: motorcycles are not multi-party democracy, opposition to police torture or other topics on which constitutionalist arguments can be made in Vietnam that could well be far more risky to the speaker.

MOVING FORWARD ON CONSTITUTIONAL DEBATE

Beyond the issues of 'motorbike constitutionalism', the Vietnamese discussion on constitutional review and enforcement focused on three key questions in recent years: the role of the party, the role of the National Assembly and the role of potentially new institutions, such as a court or commission. Theoreticians continued to raise the two key problems of the 1992 Constitution for constitutional review and enforcement: the constitution gives the Standing Committee of the National Assembly the key role in constitutional interpretation and the Assembly a broad constitutional supervision role as well, while also requiring supervision of fidelity to the constitution by a number of other state agencies.

Sorting out this basic text and the political and ideological problems it embodies has proven a very difficult task, for it is enveloped by the politics of the party's role. As calls for some form of constitutional 'protection' mounted, two important meetings were convened in 2005 to study the issue. One was a conference on constitutional protection convened by a Hanoi law faculty. The other and more important conference, on 'the system of constitutional protection in Vietnam', was held in the coastal city of Vinh—far from southern or northern dissidents or politically aware students—in March 2005, under the auspices of the Standing Committee of the National Assembly and the party's Internal Affairs Commission.

This meeting reviewed the discussions over 'supervision and protection of the Constitution', comparisons from other countries and suggestions for further research, with the goal of producing 'an effective system of constitutional protection in the process of constructing a socialist state ruled by law in Vietnam'. At the opening of the meeting, National Assembly Vice Chair and Central Committee member Nguyen Van Yeu—a leading actor in the constitutional discussions—reviewed the obligatory political claim that Vietnam has a 'relatively comprehensive' system for constitutional review. However, for the first time, he also provided in clear, public terms a definition of the three types of constitutional review under official discussion:

> supervising the constitutionality and legality of legal documents; supervising the constitutionality of the execution, accession to and enforcement of international treaties; and supervising the resolution of petitions and accusations by citizens with respect to actions that violate the Constitution or the laws.

The discussants quickly reached the nub of the problem:

> Supervising the protection of the Constitution in Vietnam is different than many other countries around the world because Vietnam has not delegated to a specialized body the role of supervising the defense of the constitution (such as a Constitutional Court or Constitutional Protection Commission ...) but has delegated this to a number of state bodies which have jurisdiction.

The delegates' view, carefully articulated in the party statement, was that 'the most important issue is the supervision and guarantee of the constitutionality and legality of legal documents', and that the problem of supervising the activities and statutes adopted by the National Assembly is particularly problematic—given that the National Assembly is also given primary responsibility for constitutional review under the 1992 Constitution.

Finding a workable system to suspend or annul legal documents issued by state bodies that fail to pass constitutional muster was also a significant issue. After beginning with the obligatory refrain that Vietnam has a 'relatively comprehensive' system for constitutional review, the statement concluded that:

> the researchers as well as many officials ... felt that research on ... effective solutions in continuing to perfect the system for supervision and defense of the Constitution in Vietnam was an urgent necessity.

A 'majority' of the delegates to the meeting believed that the 'effectiveness was not high' in the current system of declining to assign constitutional

review to a specialised body, but relying on state bodies to carry out protection of the constitution as part of their regular tasks, and that the current system 'does not effectively heighten responsibility for Constitutional
protection in the state and society'.

The current structure of vesting supreme supervisory powers in the
National Assembly 'causes confusion between lawmaking powers and
review powers (judicial powers)'. Furthermore, the practice of vesting
these issues in subordinate offices of the National Assembly 'makes it
impossible to avoid dependency and passivity in the work of constitutional protection'. The problem was clear:

> The National Assembly is the important body for (structuring) State bodies
> and should itself abide by the Constitution and the laws, but has no body
> whatsoever to undertake supervision of Constitutional fidelity (*tuan thu*) with
> respect to the Assembly [itself] and individuals acting in the jurisdiction of
> the Assembly; especially whether laws and ordinances that are being promul-
> gated are constitutional or not?

Based on these 'shortcomings', the meeting agreed that it was 'necessary
to study the establishment of a mechanism for constitutional protection in Vietnam that will be more effective' under current Vietnamese
conditions.[24]

As the discussion continued, an important article in Vietnam's main
law newspaper, *Phap luat Viet Nam* (*Vietnam Law*), reviewed the terms
of the debate for the widened audience of policymakers and legal
professionals.[25] The article noted the continuing debate over the need
for a constitutional review and enforcement structure: 'there remain
some views', the article noted diplomatically, that constitutional review
should not be delegated to a specialised body because of the difficulties in defining that body's jurisdiction and the potential that resulting
weaknesses in that body (a court or commission) would then weaken
rather than strengthen constitutional review. However, the remainder

---

[24]   Vietnamese Communist Party, 'Ban Cong tac lap phap cua Uy ban thuong vu Quoc
hoi to chuc hoi thao khoa hoc ve "Co che bao hien o Viet Nam"' ('The legal drafting
work group of the Standing Committee of the National Assembly organizes a research
meeting on "the system of constitutional protection in Vietnam"') (22 March 2005),
<http://www.cpv.org.vn> accessed 26 February 2009. The volume resulting from this
meeting is Dang Van Chien (ed), *Co che bao Hien* (*Systems of Constitutional Protection*) (Hanoi,
Judicial Publishing House, 2006).

[25]   'Co che bao hien o Viet Nam: Co thanh lap toa an hien phap?' ('Mechanisms for
constitutional protection in Vietnam: Should a constitutional court be established?'),
Phap Luat Viet Nam, reprinted 27 April 2005 at <http://www.vnlawfind.com.vn>
accessed 26 February 2009.

of the article seemed generally to assume that the primary question was not whether to form a structure of constitutional review, but which structure it would be. In addition, the article usefully outlined the 'three different viewpoints' on the appropriate mechanism for constitutional review.

The first option and view expressed by some participants in the debate is to 'establish a Constitutional Court under the Supreme People's Court'. The second option:

> agrees with establishing a Constitutional Court but as an independent structure, not as a specialized court within the Supreme People's Court.

The third viewpoint holds that 'a Constitutional Court is a model that does not suit the current realities of Vietnam'. To this might be added two other options expressed by officials and legal scholars: that a constitutional commission or other body should be established under the National Assembly; and that nothing significant should be done—that the current system was fine for the time being.

Most of the commentators interviewed for that article—and most of the other legal officials and scholars commenting on the matter in 2005 and 2006—agreed that some kind of constitutional review mechanism was necessary. Most of those also seemed to lean toward a constitutional court, probably separate from the existing Supreme People's Court, and with some autonomy from the National Assembly and the party as well, difficult though that might be to achieve.

As mentioned earlier, in 2004, the party's Judicial Reform Committee chaired by President Tran Duc Luong had announced that the Committee was prepared to recommend 'study of the establishment of a Constitutional Court'. In June 2005, the party's Political Bureau adopted two important policy documents guiding development of the legal system over the next 15 years. One of those, Resolution 48 on Strategy for Development and Improvement of Vietnam's Legal System to 2010, was largely drafted by the Ministry of Justice and other government agencies and focused on specific legislative and other challenges.[26] The other, Resolution 49 on Judicial Reform Strategy to 2020, was drafted primarily by the Party Judicial Reform Committee and the Party Internal Affairs Commission, and

---

[26] Resolution 48 on the *Strategy for Development and Improvement of Vietnam's Legal System to 2010, and Directions to 2020* (*Chien luoc xay dung va hoan thien he thong phap luat Viet Nam den nam 2010, dinh huong den nam 2020*) (Legal System Development Strategy 2005), Political Bureau of the Communist Party of Vietnam, June 2005.

dealt largely with the role of courts and some other broader judicial reform issues.[27]

The Legal System Development Strategy did not deal in depth with constitutional review and enforcement, calling only generally for a mechanism 'to protect the laws and the Constitution' and for a strengthening of the capacity of the National Assembly to undertake constitutionality review of legislation. The Judicial Reform Strategy, drafted by the party, also did not deal directly with constitutional review. Notably, it did not contain any mention of a mechanism for constitutional review, such as a constitutional court or commission, although the Party Judicial Reform Committee had discussed those issues and President Luong had specifically endorsed the 'study of the establishment of a Constitutional Court'. The lack of specific discussion of a mechanism of constitutional review in the 2005 judicial review strategy reflected continuing differences over the need, scope and form of constitutional review, according to Hanoi lawyers and academics.

The Judicial Reform Strategy did propose the establishment of a 'Judicial Committee' (*Uy ban Tu phap*) in the National Assembly charged with 'assisting the National Assembly in exercising its oversight of judicial activities, with a focus on arrest, detention, prosecution, and adjudication'. This is certainly not constitutional review or enforcement, but it may be a way of gradually establishing a group within the National Assembly that could begin focusing more intently on constitutional issues than the general 'supervision' exercised by the Standing Committee has ever been able to do, consistent with the model initially developed in China.

Within months after the reporting on the important meeting at Vinh and the two party legal and judicial reform strategies, an article in the official party theoretical journal *Tap chi Cong san* (*Communist Review*), reprinted in the main party daily newspaper *Nhan Dan* in November 2005, set the tone for further discussions. National Assembly Vice Chairman and Party Central Committee member Nguyen Van Yeu, who had also chaired the Vinh meeting, called for:

> building an effective structure for constitutional protection. We should study whether we can establish a Constitutional Court (or Constitutional Protection Commission) with the responsibility for protecting the Constitution through

---

[27] Resolution 49 on the *Strategy for Judicial Reform to 2020* (*Chien luoc Cai cach Tu phap den nam 2020*) (Judicial Reform Strategy 2005), Political Bureau of the Communist Party of Vietnam, June 2005.

jurisdiction to adjudicate and issue judgments on Constitutional violations in legal documents, to adjudicate unconstitutional decisions and acts of agencies and individuals holding authority in state institutions and carry out the task of interpreting the Constitution and the laws (and ordinances where implementing ordinances have been issued.[28]

Yeu's article was notable for its broad definition of constitutional review to include not only the hierarchy and constitutionality of legislation, but also 'unconstitutional decisions and acts of agencies and individuals holding authority in state institutions'. It did not recommend a specific constitutional protection or review option, nor did it imply that the party itself would be subject to the jurisdiction of any such mechanism, but it was important nonetheless for indicating clearly that the debate was still open.[29]

As 2006 dawned, the issues of constitutional protection, enforcement and review faded temporarily from Vietnamese political discourse. Many fewer articles appeared in the press, and Vietnamese officials and legal scholars began to regularly say that the issues would take a number of years to work out.[30] The slowing of debate certainly reflected

---

[28] Nguyen Van Yeu, 'Xay dung Nha nuoc phap quyen XHCN Viet Nam cua nhan dan, do nhan dan va vi nhan dan' ('Constructing a state ruled by socialist law in Vietnam of the people, for the people, and by the people'), *Nhan Dan* (9 November 2005), published in *Tap chi Cong san* (*Communist Review*), October 2005, <http://www.tapchicongsan.org.vn> accessed 26 February 2009.

[29] A number of academic articles also appeared. See, eg Le Minh Tam, 'Bao hien, co che bao hien va co che bao hien Vietnam' ('Constitutional protection, constitutional protection systems, and systems of constitutional protection in Vietnam') (August 2005) *Tap chi Luat hoc* (*Law Journal*) 32–7; Nguyen Van Manh and Tao Thi Quyen, 'Co che bao dam tinh toi cao cua Hien phap o Viet Nam' ('Mechanisms for ensuring the supremacy of the Constitution in Vietnam') (January 2006) *Ly luan Chinh tri* (*Political Theory*) 26–31; Ho Duc Anh, 'Bao ve Hien phap va chu the bao ve Hien phap o Viet Nam' ('Constitutional protection and the subjects of constitutional protection in Vietnam') (June 2006) *Dan chu va Phap luat* (*Democracy and Law*) 30–35; and Nguyen Hoai Nam, 'Co nen xay dung co che bao Hien moi' ('Should we establish a new system of Constitutional protection?') (November 2006) *Nha nuoc va Phap luat* (*State and Law*) 3–5.

[30] However, a key exception was the publication of two important Vietnamese volumes on constitutional protection, which occurred in 2006: Bui Ngoc Son, *Bao Hien o Viet Nam* (*Constitutional Protection in Vietnam*) (Hanoi, Judicial Publishing House, 2006); and Dang Van Chien (ed), *Co che bao Hien* (*Systems of Constitutional Protection*) (Hanoi, Judicial Publishing House, 2006, published for internal use). But these important volumes were prepared earlier and now serve as source materials for later debate. The publication of articles did not, however, disappear. See, eg the hard-hitting statements by senior National Assembly official Vu Mao, 'Ai "huyt coi" khi hien phap bi xam pham' ('Who "blows the whistle" when the Constitution is violated?'), *Tuoi Tre* (25 March 2006), <http://www.tuoitre.com.vn> accessed 26 February 2009; and 'Can co co quan bao ve hien phap' ('We must have an institution for constitutional protection'), *VnExpress* (26 March 2006), <http://vnexpress.net> accessed 26 February 2009.

political timing and a tightening political climate in Vietnam in late 2005 and into early 2007: by early 2006, the Vietnamese leadership and officials around the country were immersed in preparations for the Tenth Party Congress (April 2006), the APEC Economic Leaders meeting in Hanoi (November 2006) and forthcoming National Assembly elections (May 2007).

Difficult issues like constitutional review began to leave the immediate policy agenda, at least temporarily, as the party and government focused on the Party Congress, the APEC leaders forum and the National Assembly elections. At the Tenth Party Congress in April 2006, the party's Political Report mentioned constitutional protection as an issue, but without undue focus. By 2007 and 2008, after several years of relative quiet during a party congress, an APEC meeting and other events, the question of constitutional enforcement and judicial review was back on the agenda. By now, views seemed to be moving toward agreement on the need for a separate constitutional court, with some clear autonomy from the Supreme People's Court, the National Assembly and the party.

Although locating a constitutional court within the Supreme Court was still a real possibility, most knowledgeable Vietnamese observers dismissed the capacity of the Supreme Court—both its substantive capacity on legal issues and political capacity to resist control and interference—as quite weak. Therefore, they generally agreed that the Supreme Court was not the appropriate location for a constitutional court. For the same reasons, they generally dismissed the notion that the Supreme People's Court, or the court system as a whole, could be vested with a general power of judicial review to include constitutional issues—the view in Hanoi was that the Supreme Court and the judicial system were simply substantively and politically incapable of carrying out such a task. Some officials, however, continued to argue for judicial review through the Supreme Court, both on substantive grounds and to bolster the weak judiciary.

Locating a constitutional commission within or closely allied to the National Assembly was another clear alternative, and one made easier because the constitution already provides the Assembly with supervisory and interpretive authority over the constitution. China's initial decision to establish a constitutional review unit within the Legal Affairs Commission of the National People's Congress has been observed in Vietnam and might also influence developments there. However, many legal officials and scholars believe that locating a constitutional commission within the National Assembly may be politically unworkable as well, and that locating constitutional review and interpretation within at least the existing structures of the National

Assembly (before the formation of a Judicial Committee in 2007) was unworkable as well. Furthermore, many of them agreed that the broader functions of judicial review—including review of legislation at the central and provincial level, and review of government acts—could not be carried out by a constitutional commission located within or affiliated closely to the National Assembly, and that some kind of court was necessary.

In these discussions, the role of constitutional or judicial review of the party's actions (as opposed to the state's legislation and actions) has only rarely ever been broached. This remains a key problem as central level political and legal officials and scholars give careful consideration to establishing a constitutional court or another mechanism when the constitution is next revised, perhaps in 2011 or 2012.

THE FUTURE OF CONSTITUTIONAL
REVIEW AND ENFORCEMENT
IN VIETNAM

Constitutional review and enforcement, at least of laws and other legal documents, and potentially also of official acts, fulfils several important roles that would help to buttress the developing Vietnamese state system: it would give some force to constitutional provisions, including some force to the constitutional idea that the constitution is the 'fundamental law' of Vietnam superior to all others. A system of constitutional review and enforcement would begin to deal with the rapidly growing problem of contradictory legal documents, an issue exacerbated by the willy-nilly release of thousands of legal documents at national, provincial, metropolitan and local levels since the early 1990s. Furthermore, if extended to the review of official acts, it could begin to treat growing problems in state–society relations caused by the dictatorial practices of some officials, primarily at the local level.

Therefore, two interlocking sets of issues remain to be resolved. How far should the scope of constitutional review and enforcement extend in Vietnam: only to the problem of legal texts or to actions as well? If to official acts, to acts by the party as well as the state? Secondly, what form should constitutional review take and should that form be a constitutional court? If so, where should that court lie—as an independent court or within the Supreme People's Court? Or should the National Assembly continue to perform this function, but at a higher level of intensity, attention and competence?

The second question—the form of constitutional enforcement and review—is a fundamentally political issue in Vietnam. Once the need and demand for such a structure is generally agreed to by the party and other elites, the construction of such a body becomes a complex question that will take at least several years to work out. At the time of this writing, a somewhat autonomous constitutional court appears to be the alternative most often mooted in Hanoi, but that very tentative and early consensus could certainly change, and what emerges could become a specialised constitutional court within the Supreme People's Court in Hanoi, a constitutional commission affiliated with the National Assembly or even conceivably another form. Vietnam could also move in steps, like China, first establishing a constitutional review group tied to one the National Assembly's committees, such as the new 'judicial committee', while exploring future institutional options. Alternatively, Vietnam could recognise the growing need for these functions, but decide (probably for political and institutional reasons) to leave the system largely as it is with some additional administrative capacity to deal with pressing issues. This 'status quo plus' option would leave the National Assembly formally responsible for 'constitutional protection' and the government (delegating the Ministry of Justice) responsible for examining the immediate problem of over-reaching by provincial and municipal authorities beyond national law.

In Vietnam, there appears to be a growing acceptance both of the need for an institutional arrangement to sort out statutory conflicts with the constitution and other laws, and of the demand for some sort of 'constitutional protection' by business groups, academics and others. In addition, somewhat more particular to the Vietnam case, acceding to that demand and need also enables the party and state to wrest away a constitutional initiative from both domestic and overseas dissidents. However, the key issues of scope and form remain, they are fundamentally political and they are closely related to whether the party will be subject to the constitutional review and enforcement that emerges.

This crucial question of whether constitutional review and enforcement would apply to the Communist Party at national and local levels

remains almost completely unaddressed, at least publicly. The party
has played a leading role in discussions of 'constitutional protection'
and new potential mechanisms, primarily through the Judicial Reform
Steering Committee originally chaired by former President Tran Duc
Luong and now by President Nguyen Minh Triet, other party groups,
and a research group under the party's Organisation Commission.[31]
The application of constitutional review and enforcement to the party
itself is almost never raised in the public discussions of these issues,
and it remains unclear whether any constitutional protection structure
would have any capacity to evaluate and adjudicate the constitutionality of party documents, whether those documents conflict with current
law, and the constitutionality or legality acts committed by the party
or party officials.

This limitation helps to enable political support for a 'constitutional
protection' structure to begin to emerge—the party may well be allowing, even encouraging discussions and planning of constitutional review
and enforcement mechanisms to go forward on the understanding that
the new structure will not include the party within its jurisdiction. In
other words, any new constitutional court or other structure would, like
the remainder of the judiciary and the legal system, remain subordinate
to the party.

As in virtually all debates on law reform in Vietnam, solutions abroad
are significant reference markers for domestic debate. The Chinese
solution to the problem of constitutional review and enforcement is of
some particular interest for Vietnamese policymakers and academics. In
China, party concern for the potential independence of a constitutional
court, the power that constitutional review could give the regular judiciary and the political tradition (since 1949) of leaving an entirely formal constitutional supervision to the national legislature (the National
People's Congress) led to a political decision to delegate constitutional
review and enforcement to a strengthened unit of the Legal Affairs
Commission of the National People's Congress, at least in the short
term, rather than to a constitutional court, a constitutional commission
or the Supreme People's Court.

It may be that what results from the Vietnamese debate may, at
least initially, approximate the Chinese formation of a unit within the

---

[31] Institute of Organizational Research, Party Organization Commission, 'Cac
phuong an thanh lap co quan bao hien' ('Options for establishing a constitutional protection mechanism') (28 April 2007), http://www.hongphuclaw.com. Report in possession
of the author.

National People's Congress to investigate allegations of constitutional violations, to provide both the perception and reality of addressing these important issues and perhaps to forestall broader calls for a constitutional court or other review mechanism. Alternatively, that may not be the direction in which Vietnamese decisions go—for example, the discussion of '[institutional] models of constitutional protection' in the authoritative 2006 volumes on constitutional protection issued by the National Assembly as a result of the party and National Assembly conclave in 2005 reviews structures in France, Germany, Austria, Slovakia, the United States, Japan, South Korea, Thailand, Cambodia, Portugal, Spain, Russia, Turkey, Bulgaria and Slovenia, but does not even mention China.[32]

Whatever the foreign reference points, the calls in Vietnam for a constitutional court, commission or other institutional form for constitutional enforcement and review are likely to continue to grow in the years ahead, and may well be at least initially resolved when the next planned revision of the constitution takes place in 2011 or 2012.

FURTHER READING

Bui Ngoc Son (2006) *Bao Hien o Viet Nam* (*Constitutional Protection in Vietnam*) (Hanoi, Judicial Publishing House).

Dang Van Chien (ed) (2006) *Co che bao Hien* (*Systems of Constitutional Protection*) (Hanoi, Judicial Publishing House, published for internal use).

Nguyen Van Thao (2001) 'Soan thao, sua doi hien phap va thuc hien bao ve Hien phap' ('Revising and amending the Constitution and mechanisms for Constitutional protection') *Tap chi Cong san* (*Communist Review*) (October 2001), <http://www.tapchicongsan.org.vn> accessed 26 February 2009.

Nguyen Dang Dung (2007) *Y tuong ve mot Nha nuoc chiu trach nhiem* (*Thoughts on the Responsible State*) (Da Nang, Da Nang Publishing House).

To Van-Hoa (2006) *Judicial Independence* (Lund, Jurisförlaget i Lund) (particularly Pt V, chs XVI–XIX).

---

[32] Dang Van Chien (ed), *Co che bao Hien* (*Systems of Constitutional Protection*) (Hanoi, Judicial Publishing House, 2006, published for internal use) 209–74.

Afterword: The Future of the Vietnamese Constitution

This volume has sought to outline the development of the Vietnamese Constitution in the Democratic Republic of Vietnam and the Socialist Republic of Vietnam since the mid-1940s. As this volume goes to press in 2009, Vietnam continues to face significant constitutional issues— the role of the party, the structure and role of the National Assembly, local government, the judiciary, the procuracy and other institutions, the implementation of citizens' rights and duties, and other important matters. Three important trends are likely to help shape the continuing adaptation of the Vietnamese Constitution, long after this volume is published. They are: (i) the increasingly rich debates in Vietnamese academic, political, legal and dissident circles on key elements of constitutionalism, including those issues mentioned above; (ii) the decisions to be made on revising the Vietnamese Constitution once again in several years, when all of the issues identified above will be on the agenda for discussion; and (iii) the resolution of the discussion of constitutional review, constitutional protection and the potential role of a constitutional court or commission.

Debates on the key elements of constitutionalism and constitutional revision are growing in intensity and volume by the year in Hanoi, Ho Chi Minh City and other Vietnamese academic and policy centres. Vietnam's constitutional law scholars have turned from description to analysis of the key debates on constitutionalism in Vietnam, a shift that has taken place in the last 10 years and is still continuing to evolve. The works of senior scholars such as Nguyen Dang Dung and younger scholars such as Bui Ngoc Son referred to in the bibliography attest to this growing vibrancy of research, analysis and debate. They have joined older scholars and lawyers, some now gone and some still active—figures like Pham Van Bach, Vu Dinh Hoe, Nguyen Van Thao and others—in their committed pursuit of issues of constitutionalism in Vietnam. Many others in each such generation could also be named.

At times in modern Vietnamese history—in the mid-1950s, for example, and in certain episodes thereafter—these debates on constitutionalism and constitutional enforcement have been joined by highly critical or dissident intellectuals and lawyers within Vietnam.[1] In earlier years, this group included intellectuals and lawyers such as Nguyen Huu Dang and Nguyen Manh Tuong. In the 1970s, and 80s, others argued for a new understanding of constitutional rights in Vietnam. Today, younger lawyers and intellectuals such as Nguyen Van Dai, Le Thi Cong Nhan, Le Cong Dinh, Ha Si Phu, Le Quoc Quan, Pham Hong Son and others are exploring these issues as well, sometimes from freedom and sometimes from behind bars, as a new generation of critical and dissident intellectuals and lawyers explores constitutionalism and the Vietnamese Constitution of 1992 to call for more rapid reform and transition to democracy. All of these figures—from mainstream scholars to dissidents—will have roles to play in the Vietnamese constitutional debates that are to come.

Vietnam plans to revise its constitution again in several years, and the role of the party, the structure and role of the National Assembly, local government, the judiciary, the procuracy and other institutions, the implementation of citizens' rights and duties, and other important matters will be under direct debate as that revision process unfolds. Vietnamese constitutional scholars and officials have already indicated that issues for discussion in the next revision to the constitution include the applicability of the constitution to the Communist Party and the future of article 4 of the 1992 Constitution; the structure of the courts and the level of autonomy to be accorded to the judiciary; the prospects for a system of judicial and constitutional review; the changing role of the National Assembly and local legislative and executive bodies; revising the fundamental rights and duties of citizens; and other complex issues.

The party, working with the National Assembly and a constitutional Revision Commission, will determine how far those debates are permitted to go. However, there is little doubt that they will rival and likely surpass the vitality of the discussions in 2001 on amending the 1992 Constitution, which was the liveliest and most vibrant debate on issues of constitutionalism in Vietnam since the *Nhan van–Giai pham* era of the mid-1950s. Vietnam's constitutions have proven highly adaptable to changing political, economic and social conditions, and no doubt will do so again. The story of constitutionalism and constitutions in Vietnam is thus an ongoing story, and one that readers of this volume may wish to follow in the years ahead.

---

[1] See, eg Human Rights Watch, 'Vietnam: Eight Vietnamese Writers Receive Prestigious Human Rights Prize' (22 July 2008), <http://www.hrw.org/english/docs/2008/07/22/vietna19419.htm> accessed 26 February 2009.

Bibliography

The 1946 Constitution of the Socialist Republic of Vietnam (adopted by the National Assembly of the Socialist Republic of Vietnam, 9 November 1946).

The 1959 Constitution of the Socialist Republic of Vietnam (adopted by the National Assembly of the Socialist Republic of Vietnam, 31 December 1959).

The 1980 Constitution of the Socialist Republic of Vietnam (adopted by the National Assembly of the Socialist Republic of Vietnam, 18 December 1980).

The 1992 Constitution of the Socialist Republic of Vietnam (adopted by the National Assembly of the Socialist Republic of Vietnam, 15 April 1982) (as revised by Resolution No 51/2001/QH 10 of 25 December 2001 Amending and Supplementing a Number of Articles of the 1992 Constitution of the Socialist Republic of Vietnam).

Bui Ngoc Son (2004) *Tu tuong lap Hien cua Ho Chi Minh* (*The Constitutional Thought of Ho Chi Minh*) (Hanoi, Political Theory Publishing House).

—— (2006) *Bao Hien o Viet Nam* (*Constitutional Protection in Vietnam*) (Hanoi, Judicial Publishing House, 2006).

Civicus and Vietnam Institute of Development Studies (2005) *The Emerging Civil Society: An Assessment of Civil Society in Viet Nam* (Civicus), <http://www.undp.org.vn> accessed 26 February 2009 and <http://www.civicus.org> accessed 26 February 2009.

Dang Van Chien (ed) (2006) *Co che bao Hien* (*Systems of Constitutional Protection*) (Hanoi, Judicial Publishing House, published for internal use).

Dao Tri Uc (2005) *Xay dung Nha nuoc phap quyen xa hoi chu nghia Viet Nam* (*Building a Socialist State Ruled by Law in Viet Nam*) (Hanoi: National Political Publishing House).

Do Ngoc Hai (2006) *Hien phap 1946 ban Hien phap dat nen mong chon en lap hien Nha nuoc Viet Nam* (*The 1946 Constitution: Setting a Foundation for Constitution Making in Viet Nam*) (Hanoi, National Political Publishing House).

Fall, B (1954) *The Viet-Minh Regime: Government and Administration in the Democratic Republic of Vietnam* (New York, Institute of Pacific Relations).

—— (1959) 'North Viet-Nam's New Draft Constitution' 32:2 *Pacific Affairs* 178.

—— (1960) 'North Viet-Nam's Constitution and Government' 33:3 *Pacific Affairs* 282.

—— (1960) 'Constitution-Writing in a Communist State—The New Constitution of North Vietnam' 6 *Howard Law Journal* 157.

—— (1960) 'Notes and Comment: The President in the Constitution of the Republic of North Vietnam' 34 *Pacific Affairs* 165.

—— (1966) *Viet-Nam Witness, 1953–66* (New York, Praeger).

Gillespie, J (2004) 'Concepts of Law in Vietnam: Transforming Statist Socialism' in Peerenboom, R (ed) *Asian Discourses of Rule of Law* (London, Routledge).

—— (2006) 'Concepts of Human Rights in Vietnam' in R Peerenboom (ed) *Asian Discourses of Human Rights* (London, Routledge).

—— (2006) *Transplanting Commercial Law Reform: Developing the Rule of Law in Vietnam* (Aldershot, UK, Ashgate).

—— (2007) 'Rethinking the Role of Judicial Independence in Socialist Transforming East Asia' 56 *International & Comparative Law Quarterly* 4, 837–70.

—— (2007) 'Understanding Legality in Vietnam' in Balme, S and Sidel, M (eds) *Vietnam's New Order* (London, Palgrave-Macmillan).

Gillespie, J and Nicholson, P (2005) *The Diversity of Legal Change in Socialist China and Vietnam* (Canberra, Asia Pacific Press).

Ha Mai Hien et al (1987) *Cac nganh luat trong he thong phap luat Viet Nam (The Branches of Law in the Vietnamese Legal System)* (Hanoi, Law Publishing House).

Hannah, J (2007) *Local Non-Governmental Organizations in Vietnam: Development, Civil Society, and State-Society Relations* (PhD dissertation, University of Washington).

Hanoi Law University (1994) *Giao trinh Luat Hien phap Viet Nam (Text on Vietnamese Constitutional Law)* (Hanoi, Hanoi Law University).

Ho Chi Minh National Political Academy, Department of State and Law (2004) *Mot so nganh luat trong he thong phap luat Viet Nam (Branches of Law in the Vietnamese Legal System)* (Hanoi, Political Theory Publishing House, 2 vols).

Heng, RHK (2002) 'The 1992 Revised Constitution of Vietnam: Background and Scope of Changes' 4:3 *Contemporary Southeast Asia* 221.

Kerkvliet, B (2005) *The Power of Everyday Politics: How Vietnamese Peasants Transformed National Policy* (Ithaca, Cornell University Press).

Kerkvliet, B, Heng, R and Koh, D (eds) (2003) *Getting Organised in Vietnam: Moving In and Around the Socialist State* (Institute of Southeast Asian Studies).

Kim, C (1981) 'Recent Developments in the Constitutions of Asian Marxist-Socialist States' 13 *Case Western Reserve Journal of International Law* 483.

Le Huy Bao (2003) *Dieu le Dang tu Dai hoi den Dai hoi (Ly luan va thuc tien) (Party Constitutions from Congress to Congress (Theory and Practice))* (Hanoi, National Political Publishing House).

Moise, E (1983) *Land Reform in China and Vietnam: Consolidating the Revolution at the Village Level* (Chapel Hill, University of North Carolina).

Ngo Ba Thanh (1993) 'The Constitution and the Rule of Law' in Thayer, C and Marr, D (eds), *Vietnam and the Rule of Law* (Canberra, Australian National University Political and Social Change Monograph).

Ngo Huy Cuong (2006) *Dan chu va phap luat dan chu (Democracy and Democratic Law)* (Hanoi, Judicial Publishing House).

—— (2006) *Gop phan ban ve cai cach phap luat o Viet Nam hien nay (Contributions to the Discussion of Legal Reform in Contemporary Viet Nam)* (Hanoi, Judicial Publishing House).

Nguyen Dang Dung (2001) *Mot so van de ve hien phap va bo may nha nuoc* (*Some Issues of the Constitution and the State Apparatus*) (Hanoi, Transport and Materials Publishing House).

—— (ed) (2006) *Nha nuoc va nha nuoc trach nhiem* (*The State and the Responsible State*) (Hanoi, National Political Publishing House).

—— (ed) (2007) *Quoc hoi Viet Nam trong Nha nuoc phap quyen* (*The National Assembly of Vietnam in a State Ruled by Law*) (Hanoi, Hanoi National University Press).

—— (2007) *Y tuong ve mot Nha nuoc chiu trach nhiem* (*Thoughts on the Responsible State*) (Da Nang, Da Nang Publishing House).

Nguyen Dang Dung and Ngo Duc Tuan (approx. 1998) *Luat Hien phap Viet Nam* (*Vietnamese Constitutional Law*) (Ho Chi Minh City, Ho Chi Minh City University Law Department).

Nguyen Huu Dang (20 November 1956) 'How are Democratic Freedoms Guaranteed by the Vietnamese Constitution of 1946?', *Nhan van* no 5.

Nguyen Manh Tuong (1958) 'Qua nhung sai lam trong Cai cach Ruong dat—Xay dung quan diem lanh dao' ('The errors of Land Reform: Constructing leadership viewpoints'), <http://www.talawas.org> accessed 26 February 2009.

Nguyen Phuong-Khanh (1981) 'Introduction to the 1980 Constitution of the Socialist Republic of Vietnam' 7(3) *Review of Socialist Law* 347 (including the text of the 1980 Constitution).

Nguyen Tran Bat (2005) *Suy Tuong (Meditations)* (Hanoi, Writers Publishing House).

Nguyen Van Thao (October 2001) 'Soan thao, sua doi hien phap va thuc hien bao ve Hien phap' ('Revising and amending the Constitution and mechanisms for Constitutional protection'), *Tap chi Cong san* (*Communist Review*), <http://www.tapchicongsan.org.vn> accessed 26 February 2009.

—— (3 October 2001) 'Ve kiem tra tinh hop hien, hop phap cua van ban phap luat va cac co quan tu phap' ('On the inspection of the constitutionality and legality of legal documents and judicial agencies'), *Bao Khoa hoc va Phat trien* (*Science and Development News*), reprinted at <http://www.na.gov.vn> accessed 26 February 2009.

—— (2006) *Xay dung Nha nuoc phap quyen duoi su lanh dao cua Dang* (*Building a State Ruled by Law under the Leadership of the Party*) (Hanoi, Judicial Publishing House).

Nicholson, P (1999) 'Vietnamese Legal Institutions in Comparative Perspective: Constitutions and Courts Considered' in Jayasuriya, K (ed) *Law, Capitalism and Power in Asia: The Rule of Law and Legal Institutions* (London, Routledge).

—— (2001) 'Judicial Independence and the Rule of Law: The Vietnam Court Experience' 3 *Australian Journal of Asian Law* 37.

—— (2007) *Borrowing Court Systems: The Experience of Socialist Vietnam* (Leiden, Martinus Nijhoff).

—— (2007) 'Vietnamese Courts: Contemporary Interactions between Party-State and Law' in Balme, S and Sidel, M (eds) *Vietnam's New Order: International*

Perspectives on the State and Reform in Vietnam (New York, Palgrave Macmillan) 178.

Nicholson, P and Quang, NH (2005) 'The Vietnamese Judiciary: The Politics of Appointment and Promotion' 14 *Pacific Rim Law and Policy Journal* 1.

Ninh, K (2002) *A World Transformed: The Politics of Culture in Revolutionary Vietnam, 1945–1965* (Ann Arbor, University of Michigan Press).

Pham Ngoc Ky (1996) *Ve quyen giam sat toi cao cua Quoc hoi* (*On the Supreme Supervisory Power of the National Assembly*) (Hanoi, National Political Publishing House).

Pham Van Bach and Vu Dinh Hoe (1984) 'The Three Successive Constitutions of Vietnam' 1 *International Review of Contemporary Law* 105.

Quinn, BJM (2002) 'Legal Reform and Its Context in Vietnam' 15 *Columbia Journal of Asian Law* 219.

Resolution 48 on the Strategy for Development and Improvement of Vietnam's Legal System to 2010, and Directions to 2020 (*Chien luoc xay dung va hoan thien he thong phap luat Viet Nam den nam 2010, dinh huong den nam 2020*) (Legal System Development Strategy 2005), Political Bureau of the Communist Party of Vietnam, June 2005.

Resolution 49 on the Strategy for Judicial Reform to 2020 (*Chien luoc cai cach tu phap den nam 2020*) (Judicial Reform Strategy 2005), Political Bureau of the Communist Party of Vietnam, June 2005.

Sidel, M (1997) 'The Emergence of a Voluntary Sector and Philanthropy in Vietnam: Functions, Legal Regulation and Prospects for the Future' 8 *Voluntas: International Journal of Nonprofit and Voluntary Organizations* 283.

—— (1997) 'Vietnam: The Ambiguities of State-Directed Legal Reform' in Tan (ed) *Asian Legal Systems: Law, Society and Pluralism in East Asia* (Sydney, Butterworths).

—— (2002) 'Analytical Models for Understanding Constitutions and Constitutional Dialogue in Socialist Transitional States: Re-interpreting Constitutional Dialogue in Vietnam' 6 *Singapore Journal of International and Comparative Law* 42.

—— (2008) *Law and Society in Vietnam* (Cambridge, Cambridge University Press).

Tim hieu Hien phap Nuoc Viet-Nam Dan Chu Cong Hoa (*Understanding the Constitution of the Democratic Republic of Viet Nam*) (Hanoi, Truth Publishing House, 1976).

To Van-Hoa (2006) *Judicial Independence* (Lund, Jurisförlaget i Lund).

Index